ENTER S　　　　　　　**WORLD
OF ASTROLOGY, LOVE, SEX, AND YOU.**

With expert information from the world's astrological
authority, this fascinating guide will help you understand the twelve signs of the zodiac. You will learn
how to use sun sign astrology as a guide through
the tangles of love, sex, and romance in the twenty-
first century.

Inside, you'll find:

- An in-depth description of each sign for men
  and women

- Myths and symbols associated with each sign

- An introduction to each sign's shadow

- A fantastic section on romantic dinners for two

- An insightful exploration of the seventy-eight
  possible romantic combinations

- And much more!

Let Sydney Omarr guide you through a lifetime of
romantic possibilities!

♈ ♉ ♊ ♋ ♌ ♍

Sydney Omarr's

♎ ♏ ♐ ♑ ♒ ♓

Astrology, Love, Sex, and You

Ⓢ
A SIGNET BOOK

SIGNET
Published by New American Library, a division of
Penguin Putnam Inc., 375 Hudson Street,
New York, New York 10014, U.S.A.
Penguin Books Ltd, 80 Strand,
London WC2R 0RL, England
Penguin Books Australia Ltd, Ringwood,
Victoria, Australia
Penguin Books Canada Ltd, 10 Alcorn Avenue,
Toronto, Ontario, Canada M4V 3B2
Penguin Books (N.Z.) Ltd, 182–190 Wairau Road,
Auckland 10, New Zealand

Penguin Books Ltd, Registered Offices:
Harmondsworth, Middlesex, England

First published by Signet, an imprint of New American Library,
a division of Penguin Putnam Inc.

First Printing, September 2002
10 9 8 7 6 5 4 3 2 1

love is the voice under all silences,
the hope which has no opposite in fear:
the strength so strong mere force is feebleness:
the truth more first than sun more last than star

—e.e. cummings

being to timelessness as it's to time, 95 Poems

Contents

Introduction

Because thou hast the power and own'st the grace
To look through and behind this mask of me,
. . . and behold my soul's true face . . .

—Elizabeth Barrett Browning
Sonnets from the Portuguese

Are you searching for your soul mate?

Longing for companionship?

Hoping to find a partner who is caring, tender, and understanding?

Yearning for a passionate romantic encounter?

Attempting to put the zing back into your marriage?

Trying to save a deteriorating love affair?

Looking for a way to end a bad relationship?

Astrology, Love, Sex, and You is an up-to-date guide to finding, exploring, and enjoying intimate relationships. It is for everyone who is in love, has ever been in love, or ever hopes to be loved. This book is written in a lively down-to-earth style that will provide you with amazing new insights into yourself and others, even if you have absolutely no prior knowledge of astrology. It will show you how to use sun

1

sign astrology as a guide through the many pitfalls of love, sex, and romance in the twenty-first century.

The majority of people who consult an astrologer are looking for answers regarding matters of the heart. No matter what your age or circumstances, young or old, rich or poor, married or single, straight or gay, the presence or absence of love in your life is likely to be a primary concern. *Astrology, Love, Sex, and You* will help you find answers to many of your questions about relationships. The in-depth analysis of each of the signs will provide you with a clear understanding of why the people in your life act as they do. The knowledge you gain will help you to pinpoint negative life patterns that have been holding you back, and will illuminate the path that leads to more meaningful relationships, and romantic and sexual fulfillment.

Part One of this book deals with the twelve sun signs in general terms and specifically with regard to love, sex, and romance. The description of each sign is broken down into six main sections.

The section on how to identify the sun sign includes a general description of the character and personality traits associated with the sign, and the mental and emotional characteristics of its members. Answers the question: Who is this person?

The section on the myths and symbols associated with the sun sign includes the ruling planet and astrological symbol for the sign, its color, metal, gemstone, and some of the myths and legends commonly identified with the sign.

The section on the man of the sun sign includes

an in-depth analysis of the male native of the particular sign. Answers the question: What is this man like?

The section on the woman of the sun sign includes an in-depth analysis of the female native of the particular sign. Answers the question: What is this woman like?

The section on the shadow side of the sun sign includes a description of the sign's shadow, which is the dark underside that lurks just beneath the surface of the personality. The shadow usually manifests when the natural inclinations of the sign are blocked or thwarted. Answers the question: When, how, and why does the shadow side of the particular sign manifest?

The section on a romantic dinner for two for the sun sign explains how a native of the particular sign acts and reacts as a cook and as a dinner guest. It describes the foods and flavors traditionally associated with the particular sign. It also includes a complete menu for each sign with easy-to-prepare kitchen-tested recipes for a delicious romantic dinner for two. Answers the questions: How should I act when this person invites me to dinner? What should I serve when I invite this person to dinner?

Part Two of this book offers an insightful exploration into each of the seventy-eight romantic combinations. Answers the questions: Who is the ideal partner for you? What signs are most, and least, compatible with your own?

In his classic book, *The Astrological Guide to Marriage and Family Relations*, the esteemed astrologer and author Carroll Righter says, "Because of the basic characteristics of each sign their members generally have more in common and get along better with some signs than with others." What he says is absolutely true. Some astrological combinations are inherently easier or more difficult than others. However, no combination should be written off as impossible. Armed with a little knowledge and understanding, the native of any sign can get along with the native of any other sign. Armed with the knowledge and understanding provided by this book, *you* will be able to initiate, sustain, and delight in a romantic relationship with virtually any member of any sign in the zodiac.

Sun Sign Overview

The Sun sign is the most important single factor in interpreting the horoscope. It indicates the way a person expresses his basic energy potential and his creative drive to grow and develop as an individual.

—Frances Sakoian & Louis Acker
The Astrologer's Handbook

Why are the sun signs so important?

Sun sign traits define your character and provide you with an authentic picture of your true nature. When someone asks, "What's your sign?" he is really asking you what section of the zodiac the sun was in at the moment of your birth. In the natal chart, the sun is considered the most powerful body because without its presence our physical world would cease to exist. If the sun were removed from your horoscope, your very essence would be missing. In the absence of a comprehensive horoscope analysis, knowledge of the characteristics of each of the sun signs can provide you with a quick and reliable method for understanding yourself and others.

Born on a cusp?

The dates given in the Sun Sign Chart below are only an approximation. The sun does not enter each of the signs on the same day, or time, each year. If you or the person you are interested in happened to be born on a cusp—the point between one sign and another—you need to find out which sun sign is the correct one.

Assuming that you know the exact time and place of birth, you have several options available to you. For the computer-literate, there are software programs that don't cost very much money. With one of these programs you can compute anyone's natal chart in a minute or two. If you don't want to try your hand at making charts, check with your local astrologer or a New Age bookstore. For a nominal fee, most will happily provide you with a computerized copy of your natal chart. Or you may order the charts you need from the consummate professionals at Astro Communications Services in San Diego, California, 1-800-888-9983 or http://www.astrocom.com.

If you were born on a day when the sun changed signs, and you don't know the exact time of birth, you may never know for sure which sun sign is the correct one. If this applies to you, or the person you are inquiring about, read the interpretations given for both signs.

Traditional groupings of the signs

The signs of the zodiac are divided up in several different ways. The principal divisions are into the three qualities (the triplicities), which represent types of activities, and the four elements (the quadruplicities), which represent tendencies of temperament. The qualities are cardinal, fixed, and mutable. The elements are fire, earth, air, and water. The signs are also divided into polarities. The polarities may be called masculine and feminine, positive and negative, direct and indirect, yang and yin, or external and internal.

SUN SIGN CHART

♈ **Aries:** *March 21–April 19*
(Cardinal, Fire, Masculine)

♉ **Taurus:** *April 20–May 20*
(Fixed, Earth, Feminine)

♊ **Gemini:** *May 21–June 20*
(Mutable, Air, Masculine)

♋ **Cancer:** *June 21–July 22*
(Cardinal, Water, Feminine)

♌ **Leo:** *July 23–August 22*
(Fixed, Fire, Masculine)

♍ **Virgo:** *August 23–September 22*
(Mutable, Earth, Feminine)

♎ **Libra:** *September 23–October 22*
(Cardinal, Air, Masculine)

♏ **Scorpio:** *October 23–November 21*
(Fixed, Water, Feminine)

♐ **Sagittarius:** *November 22–December 21*
(Mutable, Fire, Masculine)

♑ **Capricorn:** *December 22–January 19*
(Cardinal, Earth, Feminine)

♒ **Aquarius:** *January 20–February 18*
(Fixed, Air, Masculine)

♓ **Pisces:** *February 19–March 20*
(Mutable, Water, Feminine)

QUALITIES

Cardinal: Aries, Cancer, Libra, Capricorn

The cardinal signs are the first signs in each season: Aries, spring; Cancer, summer; Libra, autumn; Capricorn, winter. Cardinal signs initiate action, then often lose interest. They tend to be active, independent, social, and outgoing.

Fixed: Taurus, Leo, Scorpio, Aquarius

The fixed signs fall in the middle of each season: Taurus, spring; Leo, summer; Scorpio, autumn; Aquarius, winter. Fixed signs stabilize and preserve what has been started. They tend to be constant, reliable, and determined, but also stubborn, inflexible, and resistant to change.

Mutable: Gemini, Virgo, Sagittarius, Pisces

The mutable signs fall at the end of each season: Gemini, spring; Virgo, summer; Sagittarius, autumn; Pisces, winter. Mutable signs diffuse and pass on what has been started and stabilized. They tend to be flexible, resourceful, adaptable, and quick to learn, but also changeable and easily swayed away from their purpose.

ELEMENTS

Fire: Aries, Leo, Sagittarius

The fire signs are active, energetic, courageous, idealistic, self-sufficient, and dynamic. Their initiative, vision, and need to always be first pushes them toward positions of leadership.

Earth: Taurus, Virgo, Capricorn

The earth signs are practical, definite, cautious,

pragmatic, and good at managing people and things. Their need for stability and security keeps them down to earth and focused in the material world.

Air: Gemini, Libra, Aquarius

The air signs are intellectual, communicative, social, and articulate. Their need to acquire, understand, communicate, and compare information prompts them to use, share, and apply what they know.

Water: Cancer, Scorpio, Pisces

The water signs are sensitive, emotional, intuitive, romantic, and fruitful. Their need to feel rather than think makes them psychic, creative, fluid, and changeable.

Blending of the Elements: In astrological tradition there are compatibilities between the elements. Fire gets along best with fire and air. Air gets along best with air and fire. Earth gets along best with earth and water. Water gets along best with water and earth. Conversely, the blending of fire with earth, fire with water, air with earth, and air with water may be considerably more difficult.

POLARITIES CHART

Masculine: Aries, Gemini, Leo, Libra, Sagittarius, Aquarius

The air and fire signs are referred to as masculine, positive, direct, yang, or external energies because they tend to take aggressive action rather than waiting for things to come to them.

Feminine: Taurus, Cancer, Virgo, Scorpio, Capricorn, Pisces

The earth and water signs are referred to as feminine, negative, indirect, yin, or internal energies because they tend to be passive and receptive, and prefer to wait for things to come to them.

♈ ♉ ♊ ♋ ♌ ♍

Part One

The Twelve Signs of the Zodiac

♎ ♏ ♐ ♑ ♒ ♓

Aries ♈

March 21–April 19

Symbol: The Ram   Element: Fire
Quality: Cardinal   Planetary Ruler: Mars
Polarity: Masculine

Conquering, holding, daring,
venturing as we go the unknown ways,
Pioneers! O pioneers!

—Walt Whitman
Leaves of Grass

How to Identify Aries

As the first sign of the spring, Aries represents beginnings. Its members are the infants of the zodiac, and they usually retain their youthful enthusiasm throughout their lives. No matter what their age, all Aries natives are children, who, like the Toys Я Us kid, refuse to grow up. Extremely competitive in every aspect of life, the Aries child will burst into tears if her big sister gets a better report card, or bests her in a game of Monopoly. Similar to the newborn baby that this sign represents, the ram views the world as revolving around him or herself. When they want something, they want it *now*. Impatience and self-absorption are part and parcel of their basic nature, and should not be confused with deliberate

15

selfishness. Suggest to an Arien that he is being thoughtless or self-centered, and he'll react with surprise. After a moment he will readily acknowledge his fault and apologize—then turn right around and do the same thing again.

Ruled by Mars, the god of war, Aries natives tend to be bigger than life. Heroic, bold, and energetic, they love nothing more than a challenge or a good fight. Possessed of the true pioneering spirit, their innate courage, quick wit, and restless impulsiveness come from the combination of the cardinal quality with the element of fire. Their driving need is to always be *first*, which makes them aggressive, assertive, and enterprising natural leaders. Once these rams make up their minds to do something, look out and stand aside—nothing and no one can stop them.

Rams are instigators who can't abide inactivity. Erratic by nature, the Arien mind will bounce from idea to idea, and thought to thought, rather than follow any system of logical progression. Their perceptions are razor-sharp, and they're inclined to follow impulse and intuition. When called upon to make a snap decision, they invariably make the right one.

Like the knights of yore, today's Aries is chivalrous, idealistic, and concerned with slaying dragons and rescuing those in distress. As champion of the underdog the ram readily answers the call to adventure. Never one to look before he leaps, he rushes headlong to the defense of those who can't defend themselves. His tendency to dramatize allows him to see himself as a mythological hero, and he uses his ideals as justification for his aggressive actions.

Generous to a fault, Aries is loyal to friends and honorable and just with adversaries. The ram may be quick to anger, but he is even quicker to forgive and forget. As one who holds no grudges, and takes no prisoners, he rarely stoops to revenge or petty behavior toward his enemies. Jealousy is not an Arien trait, although the bold, brash, and usually triumphant ram often inspires envy and jealousy in others.

Nothing is hidden in the Arien personality. What you see is what you get. Words like sneaky, secret, clandestine, covert, and surreptitious have no place in his vocabulary. Innocent as a baby, the ram trusts everyone until given a good reason to do otherwise. When hurt or burned by someone, he reacts by pitching a fit. However, when the screaming and hollering is done, he will usually shrug off the betrayal, deem it an aberration, and return to his naive ways.

Members of this sign have a hard time understanding the need for cooperation and compromise. Living with them, while never dull or boring, can be difficult. In their single-minded pursuit of a goal, idea, or ideal, rams are often totally unaware of the feelings of others. When the adrenaline starts pumping, his inclination is to rush full speed ahead, and anyone who gets in his way is likely to be run over. The Arien's insensitivity is not intentional. He simply doesn't notice or concern himself with emotions and opinions that conflict with his own.

No Aries can ever be accused of laziness. Hardworking rams are generally prized in the workplace because when they agree to do something it is as good as done. However, Aries natives have little sense of corporate hierarchy and protocol. Outspoken, direct, and honest to a fault, they rarely censor their true thoughts or feelings. Discipline bores them, and their natural inclination to take the lead prompts them to forget who's in charge. Generally unable or unwilling to delegate responsibility, or ask for help, they truly believe that no one else can do the job as well. Never one to suffer fools gladly, the Aries employee who doesn't respect the boss may get into trouble repeatedly for not following orders.

Most Mars-ruled people are a mixture of tremendous mental and physical energy, a resolute attitude, and a positive outlook. However, their emotional nature is extremely volatile. Of all the signs, Aries is the most audacious and will rush in where everyone else fears to tread. Impatient, smart, and ambitious, members of this sign tend to race through life. They can't stand it, or understand it, when others are slow, cautious, or unable to keep up with or match their frenetic pace.

Myths and Symbols Associated with Aries

The astrological ruler of Aries is the planet Mars. The parts of the body ruled by Aries are the head and face. Its symbol, ♈ , is thought to denote the eyebrows and nose. The sign is classified as cardinal, fire, and masculine (positive, direct, yang, external). Represented by the ram, Aries' color is red, its metal is iron, and its gemstone is the diamond.

The legend most often associated with Aries is the Greek myth of The Golden Fleece. In this complex story Poseidon (Neptune), god of the sea, falls in love with Theophane who rejects him. Undaunted, he changes her into a ewe and himself into a ram. The product of their union is a magical ram with a beautiful golden fleece.

In the land of Thessaly dwells the heroic Phirixus and his sister Helle. They are the children of King Athamas of Boeotia and his first wife Nephele. When the royal children become the target of a death plot initiated by their jealous stepmother Ino, their real mother takes steps to send them far away. Hermes (Mercury) assists her by giving her the magical ram with the golden fleece. Nephele takes the ram to her children and tells them to ride him to the kingdom of Colchis on the eastern shore of the Black Sea. The ram vaults into the air with Phirixus and Helle on his back. As they make their escape, the girl Helle falls from the ram's back into a narrow strip of sea. The place where she drowns is thereafter known as Hellespont.

Upon his safe arrival in Colchis, Phirixus, following his mother's instructions, sacrifices the ram to Jupiter, and gives the golden fleece to Aeetes, king of the country. Aeetes places it in a consecrated grove under the care of a dragon that never sleeps.

In another kingdom in Thessaly nearby that of Athamas, Jason is told by his usurping uncle Pelias that he can have his share of the kingdom only if he brings back the golden fleece, which he falsely claims is the rightful property of their family. Jason builds a ship, the *Argo*, gathers a band of heroes, the Argonauts, and sets out on his quest.

After a series of adventures, Jason arrives at the kingdom of Colchis. King Aeetes promises to give him the golden fleece if he can yoke two fire-breathing bulls with hooves of bronze to a plow, and use them to plant a field with dragon's teeth. Jason enlists the help of the king's daughter, the sorceress Medea, whom he agrees to marry. After the wedding Medea gives Jason a charm that allows him to safely encounter the breath of the fire-breathing bulls and succeed in his task. When the king goes back on his word, Medea also helps Jason subdue the dragon that guards the golden fleece. Jason seizes the fleece, and accompanied by Medea and the Argonauts escapes aboard the *Argo*.

Other scenarios identified with this sign are those astrologer Liz Greene has dubbed tales of "The Knight in Shining Armor syndrome." One example she gives is Robin Hood who fights for the return of Good King Richard to the throne of England. When Richard returns he's not a very good king, but to an Arien personality such as Robin Hood the actual outcome matters less than the battle for a cause.

The Aries Man

Like the Knight of Wands, his counterpart in the tarot deck, the Aries male is the embodiment of high spirits, enthusiasm, and passion. As the original macho man, he often feels obliged to live up to his tough guy image. He'll rush in to rescue the damsel in distress, even if she in reality is in no need of his protection. When it comes to love, he plunges headlong into a new relationship without a thought to where it might lead. If spurned, this Romeo's pride will be hurt. But in all likelihood he'll pick himself up, dust himself off, get back up on his horse, and ride off in search of a new Juliet.

The ram views his life as a quest for romance and adventure, and he can sweep you off your feet and carry you off to a magical place where too much reality is a definite no-no. As long as he believes you are his soul mate, he'll shower you with attention, affection, and gifts. Your days will be filled with fun, your nights with pleasure. For as long as it lasts your relationship will be idyllic. But when it's over, your Aries knight will end the affair as quickly and impulsively as he began it.

For all that, the Aries man is definitely not a loner. Most rams prefer being half of a couple to being on their own. However, in spite of their sociability, many Aries men do seem to live alone, perhaps because they resent too much restriction placed on their personal freedom. Although he likes being married and part of a family, responsibility and fidelity are not among his strongest points. When the thrill begins to fade, Aries' inclination is to leave, or at least to start looking elsewhere for excitement. The partner of an Aries man who wants their love to last needs to find ways to constantly reignite the Arien fire.

There is virtually no subtlety in the Aries nature. If you're not ready for straight talk, you had better look elsewhere because he tells it like it is. The Mars-ruled male refuses to play romantic games. Ask him a question, and he'll tell you the truth as he sees it. He refuses to mince words, and you won't get flattery or empty compliments from this boy. If he does compliment you, it will be because he genuinely admires you, your appearance, or your talents and abilities.

When the Aries male is finished with a relationship, his natural fire turns to ice. He'll tell his unfortunate partner, in no uncertain terms, that the affair is over. His anger, on the other hand, generally means very little. During a heated argument he may sometimes say things he doesn't mean, but then he'll apologize quickly. The Aries man is usually the first to say he is sorry after a quarrel. Once his temper cools, he does everything he can to make up, and he expects his partner to forgive and forget as readily and completely as he does ("Fight? What fight? I don't remember any fight!").

If you are looking for a man who is intellectually and emotionally mature, you may need to look elsewhere. The typical ram is intelligent and witty, but no one ever called him sensitive. The uncomplicated Aries male is generally too busy living to get involved in long-winded discussions about thoughts and feelings. He knows *what* he feels, and he really doesn't care *why* he feels it.

The Aries man wants to be the aggressor, and he doesn't appreciate being chased by potential lovers. Because of his compulsion to lead, he needs to be the one who makes the first move, and is usually not flattered by regard he does not seek. However, once committed he expects his significant other to lavish attention upon him and him alone.

The ego of the average Arien is quite fragile and in need of constant reassurance. If you want to hold onto the ram, you must learn to walk a narrow line between indifference and independence on the one hand, and attention and devotion on the other.

The combination of the Arien's need to excel with his inclination to seek the romantic *ideal* usually means that he is attracted to only the best-looking potential partners. Youthful or immature rams can be quite shallow when it comes to choosing a lover. Strongly sexed and passionate by nature, when he spots someone he wants he makes his move without hesitation. Many an Aries man will refuse to be deterred even if the object of his affection is involved with someone else.

Rams are energetic and aggressive. They love the challenge, chase, and conquest of a new romance. Highly sexed, they exude a caveman type of masculine appeal, and no sign in the zodiac is more ardent or exciting. Impatient and impulsive, he wants what he wants—and he wants it now. He takes great pride in his sexual prowess, and once you have given him the go-ahead there is no turning back.

Your Aries lover can be domineering and selfish, but he can also be charming, affectionate, and extremely generous. His sexual partners rarely complain about either the quality or quantity of his lovemaking. If he loves you, and you can succeed in keeping him interested, you may have many happy, exciting years together.

The Aries Woman

Like the Queen of Wands, her mirror image in the tarot deck, the Aries female is a modern superwoman who is capable of having it all. Filled with energy and exuberance, she lives her life at an unbelievably hectic pace yet somehow manages to find time for everything she considers important. Although she is one of the most independent females in the zodiac, and totally capable of making it on her own, the Arien woman is usually not alone for long. Her wit, intelligence, and warm heart attract friends and lovers like flies to honey.

Aries is no shrinking violet, and patience is definitely not one of her virtues. When this gal is in a hurry to get something done, which is most of the time, better stand aside or she'll run you down. Given her headstrong, competitive, aggressive nature, and her ability to make quick decisions, the twenty-first-century Aries female is often found in executive positions of great authority. Although her forthright manner and need to take charge are thought by some to be unfeminine characteristics, the Aries woman is only following her natural inclination to lead. Above all else she requires a challenge or cause to inspire and stimulate her restless soul, and she won't find it at home playing the role of the compliant little woman.

Arien women are usually career oriented. They are not afraid of hard work, love a challenge, and they are virtually assured of success in any job they undertake. Ariens are often the first ones to break through the glass ceiling to previously male-dominated positions of prominence. Once there she won't hesitate to give her superiors advice on how to run the company. While they appreciate her energy and ability to get the job done (the first time . . . and without mistakes), they don't always take kindly to her lack of understanding as to exactly what her place is in their grand scheme. As a boss she's demanding, but generally fair, and she won't ask her employees to do anything she wouldn't do herself. Of course there is little that she can't do, and those who can't keep up with her fast-paced agenda may not always appreciate her energy and dedication.

Although Arien females are not particularly maternal, most make excellent mothers. The Aries mom devotes herself to her children's interest with the same energy she puts into everything. She's usually the first one to volunteer to make costumes for the school play, drive the little league team to the ballpark, or sell cookies with the Girl Scouts. She may become impatient when the kids are too slow to keep up with her, but she is never in too much of a hurry to sit down with them and help them with homework or a school project. Aries women invariably have careers, hobbies, or causes of their own, and they don't need to fulfill themselves by living through their kids. As their children get older, Aries mothers easily make the transition from loving parent to trusted friend and companion.

Totally devoted to her ideals, the Aries female will defend them against all comers. If you want to stay friends with her, do not criticize her lover, husband, kids, family members, friends, pets, or crusades. She often puts her people and causes on a pedestal, and she is the only one allowed to knock them off.

All Aries natives are exceptionally romantic and sentimental. Like her male counterpart, the female Arien is in love with love. She's the unlikely believer in fairy tales, who dreams that a romantic knight will come along someday and carry her off to some idealistic never-never land. In her dream he is always a strong heroic type who runs the show. In real life, however, this Mars-ruled lady won't stand for anyone telling her what to do. When she does link up with a strong-minded man, they are sure to butt heads. If you are the one in love with a fiery Aries woman, you'll need to gain her respect by matching her strength for strength without trying to dominate.

Sexually the Aries woman is a fireball. Once aroused, she can be more passionate than any sign except perhaps Scorpio. Her ego, however, is quite fragile, so the easiest way to woo her is with a little flattery. Be careful what you say because she's a stickler for sincerity. If your compliments don't ring true, they may have the opposite effect from what you intended. Seek to build up her confidence and self-esteem, be especially careful not to hurt her feelings either in the bedroom or out of it. Although she is always open to straight talk, you need to choose your words carefully when discussing her lacks. When it comes to criticism, Ariens are a lot more comfortable dishing it out than receiving it.

Although she can be difficult to live with, when Aries is met halfway her noble spirit becomes evident. She demands freedom, but with the right partner will remain devoted and faithful for a lifetime. She can be impulsive and domineering, but when she calms down after one of her temper tantrums she can be as reasonable as any sign in the zodiac. She definitely has issues with completion. Aries often loses interest in projects or relationships that have become dull or boring. However, once she makes a genuine commitment, if you can hold her interest, she'll stick with you till the end.

The Shadow Side of Aries

Your car breaks down, leaving you stuck out on the highway in the middle of the night. You're experiencing chest pains and need someone to phone for an ambulance or drive you to the nearest hospital. You've lost your job and your bank account balance dips to an all-time low. After a fight with your significant other you're looking for a place to crash for the night. When these things happen to you, who do you call? Not Ghostbusters, that's for sure, unless the Ghostbusters are Aries natives. In times of crisis your Arien friends are the ones to call on because they are at their best in an emergency. Before most members of the other zodiac signs can even respond to your plea for help, the Aries native already has the situation well in hand. He or she will fix your car, drive you to the hospital, lend you money, help you find another job, put you up for the night, and then proceed to convince you that everything happens for the best.

The shadow side of Aries manifests most often when there is no crisis to overcome or problem to solve. Rams *need* a battle, cause, quest, or crusade. When their inclination to fight for something larger than themselves is thwarted or blocked, they become restless and bored. Then, like the soldier in peacetime or the knight without a dragon to slay, Aries is left without a place to direct that aggressive energy.

If the Mars-ruled native has no legitimate outlet for aggression, stress builds and he becomes irritable and temperamental. Although the quieter Aries native may turn his anger and frustration in on himself, most take it out on those around them. Spoiling for a battle, he will fight with anyone who rubs him the wrong way. This combative mood usually surfaces when his life has become routine, humdrum, or tedious.

When General Douglas MacArthur said, "Old soldiers never die, they just fade away," he obviously wasn't talking about Aries soldiers. Aged Arien warriors don't ever fade away—they retire. And when they retire, they better have something challenging to engage their minds and occupy their time. If they don't, they will wage war on everyone they meet ("I told that supermarket checkout clerk a thing or two. Next time she'll think twice before overcharging me a quarter!").

Aries continually needs variety and change, and is capable of walking away from a relatively good job or relationship because it no longer stimulates him or is exciting enough to hold his interest. At the very point where the natives of most of the other zodiac signs are starting to feel relaxed and comfortable, Ariens begin to get antsy. With their thoughts turned toward new horizons, these addicted risk takers will often throw caution to the winds and plunge head-first into uncharted waters.

The advice most often given to restless Ariens is to relax. Unfortunately this is easy for others to suggest, but difficult for Aries to do. Aries is rarely a couch potato, and is probably better off working out at the gym than consciously trying to unbend in front of the TV. Suggesting that an Aries needs to develop patience, tolerance, and understanding is tantamount to asking the sun not to rise. If you are intimately involved with an Aries native, you may be the one who is forced to practice patience, tolerance, and understanding.

Aries Romantic Dinner for Two

Aries the cook

Aries natives love to cook, but they don't relish spending a lot of time at it. Pots and pans seem to fly in every direction as the Mars-ruled chef whizzes around the kitchen. Speed and innovation are key to the ram's cooking style. Their unique combination of quick-witted efficiency with the desire to impress helps them to devise excellent meals in record breaking time.

Members of this sign cook spontaneously and love to improvise. Most Ariens excel at creating shortcuts

and time-savers and in using convenience and prepared foods in new and different ways. His attention
span is short, and he's usually too impatient to follow
the specific steps and carefully measured amounts
found in traditional recipes, but when the mood hits,
he will tackle the most complex recipe with enthusiasm. Since everything Aries does reflects a passionate, creative nature, the meals are sure to be
delicious, as appealing to the eyes and nose as they
are to the mouth.

When invited to dinner by an Aries, expect to be
treated to the best money can buy. Rams tend to be
warmhearted and generous, and they rarely skimp
at the grocery store, or anywhere else. In all likelihood the foods and beverages served will be interesting and extravagant, the various dishes stimulating
and unusual. There certainly will be plenty of everything! The only thing you need to remember when
the ram cooks for you is to stay clear of the kitchen
and not offer any advice about what to prepare or
how to prepare it. Ariens actually prefer *not* to have
help of any kind because in their opinion well-
meaning assistants just get in the way—and slow
them down.

Aries the dinner guest

If you are cooking for an Aries, do not plan a meal
that keeps you tied to the kitchen. Soufflés or other
culinary creations that must be served immediately
are a definite no-no for your fiery, impulsive, Mars-
ruled lover. Your best choice is a dinner that will not

spoil if it is put on hold. Like as not, the ram will suggest that you begin with *dessert*, and he won't be referring to the Mocha Mousse.

Subtlety is wasted on Aries, so save your delicate specialties for someone who can appreciate them. Ariens usually have excellent appetites, and they like good hearty meals. They tend to favor protein-rich, colorful foods with pungent aromas and flavors. Most rams manage to burn enough energy to keep fit, so dieting is generally not a consideration. Their lives are so busy they often don't have time to eat. By the time they arrive for dinner, they are ravenous and ready to enjoy whatever you serve them.

Food is not the most important thing to an Aries native. They are equally interested in the company and the conversation. It's important to keep him amused and entertained. If he becomes bored and restless, he will not hesitate to invent an excuse that will allow him to make a quick getaway.

Always set a nice table when entertaining a ram. They do enjoy a touch of luxury and elegance. Above all, pay attention to your own appearance. Your companion prefers finding you looking good rather than sweating over a hot stove in the kitchen, even if it means a less elaborate meal.

Foods commonly associated with Aries

Meat: lamb
Fowl: chicken
Fish and Shellfish: shark, pike

Dairy Products: none

Vegetables and Beans: carrots, peppers, onions, leeks, tomatoes, chives, radishes, pimentos

Nuts and Grains: none

Fruits: pineapple, rhubarb, grapefruits, watermelons

Beverages: coffee

Herbs, Spices, and Miscellaneous: garlic, paprika, cayenne, chilies, ginger, horseradish, mustard, pepper, basil, curry

ARIES MENU

Gazpacho Andaluz

Lamb Chops with Balsamic Vinegar Sauce

Steamed Baby Carrots

Twice Baked Potatoes

Crusty French Bread

Red Wine

Mocha Mousse

Coffee

Aries Recipes

Gazpacho Andaluz

2 cloves garlic, peeled
3 large ripe tomatoes, cut in chunks

   1 small green pepper, cored, seeded, and cut
     in half
   3 ounces day-old bread (Spanish, Italian, or
     French)
   3 tablespoons olive oil
   1 tablespoon red wine vinegar
1½ teaspoons salt
  ¼ cup water
   1 small cucumber, peeled and diced
   1 small onion, diced

Place the garlic cloves, tomatoes, one half of the
green pepper, 2 ounces of the bread, olive oil, vinegar, salt, and water in a blender and blend until
smooth. Refrigerate for at least one hour, and serve
in chilled soup bowls. For the garnish: dice the remaining green pepper and cube the remaining bread.
Serve the diced cucumber, diced onion, diced green
pepper, and cubed bread in small dishes as an ac-
companiment to the Gazpacho.

*Lamb Chops with Balsamic Vinegar Sauce

   2 lamb shoulder chops cut ½ to ¾ inch thick
   1 cup good quality balsamic vinegar
   2 ounces cold butter or margarine cut into
     chunks

Trim fat from the chops. If desired, sprinkle with
salt and pepper. Place chops on the broiler or grill, and
cook to taste. While the chops are cooking, prepare the

sauce. Bring the balsamic vinegar to a simmer in a
small saucepan, and reduce by about two-thirds. Add
the butter, one chunk at a time, and combine until the
butter is completely melted and the sauce has a
smooth, velvety consistency. Pour the sauce over the
chops before serving.

Twice Baked Potatoes

2 medium baking potatoes
⅓ cup sour cream, plain yogurt, or milk
¼ teaspoon garlic salt
  salt and pepper to taste

Preheat the oven to 350 degrees. Bake the potatoes for
one hour, or until tender. Cut a lengthwise slice from the
top of each potato. Remove the skin from the slice, and
place the pulp in a bowl. Gently scoop out each potato,
leaving only the shells. Add the pulp to the bowl. Mash
or beat the potato pulp, add sour cream, yogurt, or
milk, garlic salt, and the salt and pepper. Mix well. Pile
the mixture into the potato shells. Bake at 425 degrees
for about 20 minutes, or until lightly browned.

Mocha Mousse

4 ounces semisweet chocolate chips
¼ cup strong coffee
1 cup heavy cream, chilled
2 tablespoons confectioners' sugar
½ teaspoon pure vanilla extract

Melt the chocolate chips in the coffee. Stir well and set aside to cool. In a chilled bowl, whip the heavy cream with the sugar and vanilla until it forms soft peaks. Carefully fold about one-quarter of whipped cream into the chocolate–coffee mixture. Fold in the remaining whipped cream in small amounts until the cream and chocolate are well blended. Spoon into dessert bowls and chill.

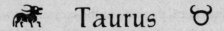

♉ Taurus ♉

April 20–May 20

Symbol: The Bull   Element: Earth
Quality: Fixed   Planetary Ruler: Venus
Polarity: Feminine

I like myself, but I won't say that I'm as handsome as the bull that kidnapped Europa.

—Cicero
De Natura Deorum

How to Identify Taurus

With its feminine polarity, fixed quality, and earth element, Taurus is generally considered the *earthiest* of the earth signs. More introverted than extroverted, the bull rarely makes the first move or initiates anything. The typical Taurean prefers to sit back and wait for opportunity to come knocking, which it invariably does. Bulls excel at getting things firmly established, and seeing that they stay that way. Their forte is preservation. They stubbornly and persistently resist all changes to the status quo.

Stable, sensible, and concerned with the practical necessities of life, the Taurean is arguably the most grounded of the twelve zodiac signs. Unswerving in their devotion to physical reality and the safety and security of the tangible world, the bull is rarely attracted to the realm of nebulous ideas. If he can't see it, feel it, hear it, smell it, or taste it, it just doesn't exist for him.

In spite of rumors to the contrary, the typical Taurean is not lazy—the tranquil bull simply refuses to waste energy. Bulls paw the ground, hem and haw, think and plan, and have an awful time taking that first step. But once a project is under way, they will stay with it until the bitter end. Although the Taurus native cannot be rushed, when left to his own devices and time schedule he'll do a great job, no matter what the task.

As one of the most reliable of the zodiac signs, the bull carefully guards that image of respectability. In spite of a good nature and amiable sense of humor, Taurus is afraid to appear silly or foolish, and rarely does anything that might make him or her the butt of other people's jokes. Down to earth and fixed in his ways, Taurus stays the course. Change of any kind usually has to be forced upon Taurus by outside forces. Lovers, friends, relatives, coworkers, partners, employers, or employees can rest assured that the dependable bull is not likely to abandon them, or let them down in any way.

No matter what career path he chooses, the Taurus native is primarily concerned with security. He usually steers clear of freelancing, preferring to follow a set routine and earn a regular paycheck. The average Taurean is hardworking, has infinite patience together with excellent business sense, and is a superior manager. Scrupulously honest, the bull protects an employer's or partner's interests as carefully as he does his own.

Taurus is the most sensuous of all the signs. Although sexuality is included among the bull's catalog of sensual pleasures, it is far from the only one on the list. Taurus actually enjoys anything that appeals to the senses, especially the sense of touch. Taureans have a real flair for color and texture. Many of them excel in design, photography, painting, and architecture. These Venus-ruled natives are also known for their love of music. A fair number of famous singers and musicians are Taureans. They have a great affinity for scents of various kinds, from flowers to luxurious perfumes and colognes. Bulls generally have an excellent eye for fashion and home furnishings, and they will buy the finest quality they can afford. Their taste leans toward the conventional rather than the shocking or absurd. Their wardrobes, homes, and offices are usually elegantly appointed and luxurious.

When it comes to food, the typical Taurus native loves to eat, and generally prefers classic meals served in elegant settings. Most members of this sign scrupulously avoid ultrafashionable, faddish restaurants or supercheap fast-food establishments. Taureans are often referred to as meat-and-potato people, but don't let that label fool you. Although they favor solid fare, fresh ingredients, and earthy tastes, they detest bland food of any kind. Meals should be relatively rich and highly seasoned in order to please their finely tuned palates. Often a talented cook, the bull is generally critical of any repast that is inexpertly prepared or embellished with unnecessary frills.

Sexually most Taureans are deeply passionate but somewhat shy and reserved. Fearful of rejection, they rely on the passive approach to romance. They prefer to attract love rather than pursue it. Since these Venus-ruled natives are personable, charming, and frequently good-looking, neither the males nor the females have much trouble attracting partners. Bulls are generally faithful, caring, and considerate lovers who treat their loved ones well, often showering them with gifts and attention. Once the bull has made up his mind about someone, he rarely changes his opinion. He will do everything he can to keep his mate happy and inter-ested. In a relationship the Taurus partner requires a great deal of emotional security. Problems can arise if he becomes overly needy or possessive.

You always know where you stand with a Taurus partner. You can count on them for help and support because they view relationships as ongoing commit-ments and take those obligations seriously. If you are looking for security and dependability, look no far-ther. Home and family come first, and the bull won't run off at the first sign of trouble. This is one person who really means "for better or worse."

Myths and Symbols Associated with Taurus

The astrological ruler of Taurus is the planet Venus. The parts of the body ruled by Taurus are the neck and throat. Its symbol, ♉, is thought to denote the bull's head with its horns in the shape of the crescent moon. The sign is classified as fixed, earth, and feminine (negative, indirect, yin, internal). Represented by the bull, Taurus' color is green, its metal is copper, and its gemstone is the emerald.

One legend associated with Taurus is the Greek myth of the Abduction of Europa. Zeus (Jupiter) spied Europa, daughter of Agenor the Phoenician king of Tyre, gathering flowers by the water's edge. Zeus, king of the gods, was seized with an uncontrollable desire for the beautiful princess, but she was constantly under the watchful eye of her father's servants.

Zeus transformed himself into a handsome bull with golden horns, and concealed himself among the herd that was grazing nearby. Struck by the bull's incredible beauty, Europa couldn't resist going up to him and draping a wreath of flowers around his neck. When he knelt at her feet, she sat upon his back and grasped his golden horns. The bull then sprang up and sped away with her across the ocean to the island of Crete. Once there, Zeus assumed his true form and made Europa his lover beneath a cypress tree. Europa bore Zeus three sons. Since he could not marry her himself, Zeus gave her in marriage to Asterius, king of Crete.

Another Greek myth associated with Taurus is the story of Theseus and the Minotaur. King Minos of Crete was one of the three sons of Zeus and Europa. He kept a herd of extraordinary bulls, which were dedicated to the sea god Poseidon (Neptune). Minos aspired to mastery of the seas, and he appealed to Poseidon for assistance. Poseidon sent a beautiful snow-white bull, which Minos was to sacrifice in return for the god's help. However, when Minos saw the wonderful bull, he wanted to keep it and add it to his stock. Prompted by greed, the king reneged on his deal with Poseidon and sacrificed a lesser bull in its place.

The angry god decided to teach Minos a lesson. He asked Aphrodite (Venus), goddess of love, to devise a suitable punishment. Aphrodite caused Minos' queen, Pasifae, to be filled with a great lust for the beautiful bull. Pasifae commissioned the palace's craftsman, Daedalus, to make a wooden bull in which she could disguise herself and mate with the white bull. Thus the queen copulated with the bull, was impregnated by it, and gave birth to the Minotaur, a monster with the head of a bull and the body of a man. The Minotaur's hunger could only be satisfied by human flesh.

When Minos found out about the monster, he ordered Daedalus to build an intricate labyrinth, wherein the Minotaur could be kept without the possibility of escape. The beast was confined in the labyrinth, and fed the youths and maidens that were sent as tribute by the king's vassals.

In Athens, Theseus, son of King Aegeus, voluntarily joined the sacrificial quota, vowing to deliver his countrymen from the horror of the Minotaur, or die trying. When the young Athenians arrived in Crete, they were exhibited before King Minos and his daughter Ariadne. Princess Ariadne took one look at

Theseus and fell deeply in love with him. She promised to help him slay the Minotaur and escape from the labyrinth. Ariadne provided Theseus with a sword and a ball of thread. He fastened the thread to the door of the maze and unwound it as he found his way into the labyrinth. He killed the Minotaur with the sword, and then found his way out again by following the skein of thread.

The Taurus Man

The Taurus man is earthy, practical, and conservative. He generally relates best in an atmosphere of peace and harmony. His customary demeanor is one of calm, good-natured patience. Most Taureans would rather suffer in silence than fight or leave, and will put up with a lot of negativity in order to avoid direct confrontation. However, on the rare occasion that his patience is pushed to the limit, his temper erupts dramatically.

Essentially what he's looking for in a romantic relationship is stability, emotional security, and good sex. To him good sex usually means a sensuous, passionate, but uncomplicated physical relationship. The sensible bull is romantic but never fanciful. His ideas of love are traditional, and he does not play mind games or make promises he can't keep.

Bulls are inclined to be overly conscious of status. They almost always care what other people think. The Taurus male perceives his social and financial status as one measure of his value as an individual. He will dress well, set a sumptuous table, take good care of his home and car, and place great emphasis on how his lover, spouse, or children appear to others. When choosing friends, he is easily influenced by rank and position. He collects celebrities as eagerly as material treasures. Name-dropping is definitely a favorite Taurean sport.

Of all the sun signs, Taurus is the one most likely to judge a book by its cover. Brains and good character impress this Venus-ruled native much less than beauty and charm, and he can be an absolute fool for a pretty face and attractive figure. He considers himself a good judge of quality, and believes that if a person is good-looking, nicely turned out, well behaved, and personable on the outside, he or she must be okay on the inside as well.

The typical male native of this sign is acutely aware of the value of things, and has a superior sense of appreciation for all that is beautiful and pleasurable. His persistence, intelligence, and well-grounded creativity tend to attract money and power, and he is often found at the top of his profession. However, on an emotional level he can be completely clueless. Remarkably ignorant of his own inner makeup, the bull has little understanding of what makes people tick, and virtually no interest in finding out. His comprehension of psychology is quite basic, and he rarely questions other people's feelings or probes too deeply into his own. Emotions tend to embarrass him, and Taurus hates to be embarrassed.

The naturally reticent bull is not given to introspection. He stubbornly resists emotional intimacy, preferring to keep his own counsel. Since he rarely shares his inner thoughts with anyone, his life partner can feel shut out. If you earn his trust, he may loosen up a little bit, but don't expect miracles. If you are looking for a soul mate to join you in an ongoing dialogue regarding the most intimate thoughts and feelings, you better look elsewhere.

Members of this sign are very good with their hands. Taureans like to build, preserve, and conserve things for future generations to enjoy. They are natural artists and artisans who particularly enjoy constructing things and making things grow. The second sign of the zodiac is about the search for value and meaning. There are bulls who put the same value on self-expression that their fellows affix to financial stability. They are generally the ones who are motivated more by the creative force than by the desire for money and power. However, there are other Taureans who spend their entire lives only dreaming of artistic success, while actually pursuing more secure lines of work. This type of bull will sometimes get so bogged down in minor details that he will lose sight of the forest and concentrate only on the trees. Still, no matter what they choose to do for a living, members of this sign are generally quite successful. Once they find their professional niche, they usually stay there.

When the bull makes up his mind that he wants something, or someone, he won't give up until he gets what he's after. Members of some other signs may be more imaginative or exciting, but few are as determined. In sex, as in all other things, he prefers to take his time, and may ingratiate himself as a good friend before attempting to become a lover. The typical Taurean is warm, tender, caring, and affectionate. His sensuality, generous nature, and legendary staying power make him an excellent lover. His partner is practically guaranteed a lovemaking experience that is joyful, pleasurable, and extremely satisfying.

Bulls do not like to spend too much time alone. The classic Taurean prefers to marry and settle into a routine of domestic bliss. Although his natural inclination is to be faithful and to stay put, the passionate Venus-ruled male is easily seduced. When tempted, he may carry on a sexual affair on the side, but only as long as it doesn't interfere with the stability of his marriage and family life. Taurus is a jealous and possessive sign, so he views his romantic partner as his property. Although *he* may choose to fool around from time to time, he expects absolute faithfulness and total devotion from his mate.

The Taurus Woman

With Venus as her ruling planet, the female Taurus is a quiet charmer who attracts romance the way honey draws flies. She is Gaia, the earth goddess, and her basic nature is composed of the eternally feminine virtues of loyalty, gentleness, and patience. Beneath her calm exterior she harbors strong desires and deep enduring passions. To her many admirers she appears to be the ideal woman. With her instinctive eye for beauty and love of luxury, the typical lady of this sign is usually beautifully dressed, carefully made up, and exquisitely coiffed and scented.

However, even those Taurean gals who choose to eschew perfumes, cosmetics, and fancy clothing for a more natural look somehow manage to exude an air of ultrafemininity.

The woman of this sign is domestic and creative. She usually doesn't mind spending time at home, whether alone or with family members. Actually she enjoys her own company, and can often be found reading, watching TV, cooking, gardening, sewing, or working at one of her many arts and crafts projects. Her rate of progress may seem slow, plodding to some, but she'll get the job done in her own good time. The excellent results make the wait worthwhile.

The urge to nest and nurture is strong in the women of this sign. Many young Taurus females are eager to marry and put down roots. Although she's happy spending time alone, the female bull feels the need to *complete* herself in a committed relationship. Married or single, every Taurus woman wants a home of her own, preferably one with some land around it with room for lots of trees, a garden, and sufficient space for her beloved pets. She's very good with money. No matter what her budget, she knows how to squeeze the most out of every dollar. While others are drowning in debt with little to show for it, the Taurean female is providing her family with luxury and comfort—and still managing to put something aside for a rainy day.

Bulls are herd animals who like to be surrounded by members of their own family. Taurean moms put the security of their children ahead of everything else, as they strive to provide a loving, well-regulated, stable environment for them to grow up in. No matter how successful she is in her chosen profession—and many Taurean women are *very* successful—she needs a sense of continuity and connection to her roots. She'll think long and hard before she agrees to uproot her husband, kids, and pets, and leave her carefully tended home and garden in exchange for a better job in a new place.

Unlike members of some of the more driven signs, Taurus knows how to unwind and enjoy life's material pleasures. When she is stressed or tired, the Taurean woman will stop what she's doing and take some time for herself. She'll kick back in the solitude of her garden, curl up in a comfortable chair to listen to her favorite CDs, luxuriate in a scented bath, or savor a cup of tea or coffee accompanied by a sinfully rich sweet. Although earth natives are the most physical of all the signs, exercise is not high on the sedentary bull's list of favorite things to do. Many Taurean females are couch potatoes who need to watch their diets. If they don't, too much food and too little physical activity can lead to obesity and associated health problems.

The female Taurus is a traditionalist. To some, her ideas of love and romance seem a tad old-fashioned. Her nature is not promiscuous. She usually needs to be in love, or believe she is in love, before engaging in a sexual relationship. Sensual and seductive, she knows how to set the stage for romance. When she overcomes her shyness and inhibitions, she is capable of depths of passion that can leave her lover gasping for breath and begging for more. Once her libido has been let loose, the lady bull can be a very demanding lover, but she is set in her ways and generally not given to radical sexual experimentation.

The Taurus woman is honest, candid, and very literal. She shies away from the type of tricks and feminine wiles that natives of other signs may choose to employ. Be careful what you say to her because she will believe whatever you tell her, and she'll hold you to it. Many misunderstandings occur when the fixed earth female comes up against someone who is given to frequent changes of mind. If you tell her you love her, you better mean it—she won't allow you to take it back. As far as Taurus is concerned, a promise is a promise. Once you've committed yourself, there is no acceptable excuse that will get you off the hook.

If you're the freedom-loving type, perhaps you should think twice before getting involved with a Taurean woman. True, she's sexy, affectionate, attentive, giving, and caring. But she can also be stubborn, dogmatic, possessive, and demanding. She will love you and take care of you no matter what happens. But she'll expect you to be as devoted to her and her needs as she is to you and yours. However, if you are willing to sacrifice at least some of your independence in order to live up to her expectations, you are virtually guaranteed an enduring union and a serene life together.

The Shadow Side of Taurus

If you are looking for a home-loving, protective, caring, and affectionate partner who will work hard to take care of you and yours, Taurus is your man or woman. The bull's finest quality is stability. Living with one, you almost always know exactly where you stand and what to expect next. When you are together, you will not suffer repeated disappointments due to unhappy surprises, fluctuating moods, or broken promises. The typical bull is as unchanging as the Rock of Gibraltar. Whatever he agrees to today, he will deliver tomorrow.

You can call on a Taurus when you're in trouble, and he'll never turn you down. Although it may take him a little longer than some to respond to your summons, especially if it is late at night or early in the morning, he will provide help and support no matter what the problem. Above all, you can count on this Venus-ruled native to remain calm in the midst of every type of storm.

The shadow side of Taurus manifests most often when his placid exterior serves as a cover for repressed rage. Bottled up animosity and displaced anger cannot be kept buried indefinitely. Inevitably the bad feelings will out, usually without any warning, and when they do the Taurean's fury can turn violent. On the rare occasion that Taurus snaps, his animosity and displeasure spew out all over the place, and you are face-to-face with the proverbial raging bull. When he is in this angry state, he will say and do things he is sure to regret. There is absolutely no chance of reasoning with him when he is upset and blinded by his own hostility. It is best to wait until the dust settles before attempting to defuse the situation.

Taureans tend to develop emotional blinders when

it comes to other people's feelings, yet they can become really resentful when their own feelings are hurt. Very touchy and sensitive to the smallest slights, the bull is constitutionally unable to laugh at himself. He'll nurse his wounds and hold onto grudges for a very long time. If you hurt or embarrass him, he's quite capable of cutting you out of his life forever.

Another side to Taurean darkness manifests when members of this sign become so set in their ways that they are unable or unwilling to adapt to change of any kind. When this happens, the bull's main virtues become his worst faults. In his ongoing search for security and stability, he can become so rigid and obstinate that he won't even consider altering his course or modifying his views. Taurus often remains in a bad situation until forced out because he can become so deeply involved in his effort to maintain the status quo that he willingly puts up with any negativity as long as it is familiar. Older Taureans often expect everyone close to them to share their values. Some bulls will pointedly ignore any opportunities or new ideas they view as radical or risky. This attitude can be infuriating to friends and family members. Those who get really annoyed may turn away from the intractable bull, leaving him alone with his regressive beliefs.

Taurus is often accused of selfishness. But it is his possessiveness that usually causes relationship problems, as those close to him resent his bossiness and outdated ideas of ownership. If you're the one involved with a Taurus, try to remember that he is truly insecure and fearful of losing what he has. Continue to assure him of your love and support, and eventually he may begin to relax and ease up on his impulse to try to control everything and everyone.

Taurus Romantic Dinner for Two

Taurus the cook

Go house hunting with a Taurus, and you will quickly discover that he or she generally regards the kitchen as the most important room in the house. This is really not surprising. Cooking, entertaining, and eating are very high on the Taurean's list of favorite activities. Many distinguished chefs, well-known hosts, and celebrated gourmets were born under the sign of the bull.

Down to earth and practical, most Taurus natives prefer to work in an area that is orderly and well organized, with a place for everything and everything in its place. Taurean culinary creations are generally substantial and nourishing, and although they may be quite rich, they are rarely frivolous or faddish.

When invited to dinner at the home of the Taurus native, you will surely dine in luxury. Many Taureans are collectors, so cooking utensils and tableware are among their favorite things to collect. The bull is proud of his possessions and likes to show them off. He invariably sets a beautiful table, and the proper presentation of a meal is very important to him. Even the most informal dinner is served with a special flair reserved for these Venus-ruled natives.

The individual born under this sign makes cooking look easy, but he actually takes great pains to see that everything is absolutely perfect. Although he is at his calm and collected best when cooking, he cannot be rushed or hurried. However, he does love having company while he prepares a meal, and he's usually willing to share a few of his culinary secrets with an interested bystander. So while you're waiting for your dinner, just pour yourself a glass of wine, then join him in the kitchen.

Taurus the dinner guest

When Taurus invites you to dine, expect to be kept waiting while he fusses, frets, and fine-tunes the repast. However, when you invite him, it's best not to wait too long before feeding him. Remember, a hungry bull is an unhappy bull. If you absolutely cannot serve at the appointed time, you can usually mollify him with some tasty before-dinner tidbits. Whatever you do, don't try to get by with stale nuts, pretzels, or potato chips left over from your last party. A nice cheese and fruit plate or a few special hors d'oeuvres should keep him happy until he's called to the table.

Bulls are very sensitive to their surroundings. If you want Taurus to really enjoy your dinner, it's important to create just the right atmosphere. Put flowers, candles, and your best linens, china, and silver on the table. Play soft music in the background. These elements will combine to make him feel relaxed and at ease. The bull does not demand a wide variety of foods. His main concern is satisfying his hunger and thirst with a solid meal. In short, while the setting may be quite decorative, the food you serve him should be hearty, rich, and well-seasoned but never frilly or fancy.

Of all the signs of the zodiac, Venus-ruled Taurus is the one most likely to be allied with the old saying, "The way to a man's heart is through his stomach." If you treat him with affection, kindness, and consideration and ply him with edible delicacies, chances are he'll soon be yours. Especially effective are those foods and drinks generally associated with love and romance such as ripe fruits, sparkling wines, and sinfully rich pastries or desserts made with chocolate or heavy cream.

Foods commonly associated with Taurus

Meat: beef

Fowl: chicken, partridge

Fish and Shellfish: scallops

Dairy Products: cream, milk, cheese, butter, ice cream, eggs

Vegetables and Beans: avocados, artichokes, potatoes, yams, spinach, lentils, chickpeas

Nuts and Grains: chestnuts, almonds, pecans, wheat

Fruits: apples, strawberries, raspberries, peaches, pears, grapes, persimmons, blackberries, cherries, kiwi, nectarines, plums, figs, gooseberries, dried fruits

Beverages: tea, wine
Herbs, Spices, and Miscellaneous: thyme, coriander,
mint, honey, sugar, bread, pastry

TAURUS MENU

Filet Mignon

Potato Fans

White Asparagus with Mayonnaise

French Baguette

Red Wine

Ricotta Pudding with Chocolate Sauce

Cappuccino

Taurus Recipes

Filet Mignon

1 teaspoon vegetable oil
2 strips bacon
2 filet mignon steaks, (6 to 8 ounces each) cut 1 to
   1¼ inches thick
   salt and pepper to taste

Brush the top with oil and wrap a bacon strip
around the edge of each steak. Fasten with toothpicks. Broil 4 to 6 minutes on each side, or until medium rare or medium (do not overcook). Remove the
toothpicks before serving.

*Potato Fans

¼ teaspoon minced garlic
1 tablespoon finely chopped parsley
2 medium baking potatoes
  salt and pepper to taste

Preheat the oven to 400 degrees. Melt the butter, and add the garlic and parsley. Scrub or peel the potatoes, and cut them crosswise into ¼ inch slices without slicing all the way through. Place in a small baking dish and drizzle with butter mixture. Sprinkle the salt and pepper on top of each potato. Bake for 70 minutes or until the potatoes are golden, crispy, and have fanned out

*White Asparagus with Mayonnaise

1 jar or can of good quality white asparagus, chilled
  mayonnaise

Drain the asparagus and place on a serving platter. Spoon some mayonnaise into a small bowl and serve with the asparagus.

*Ricotta Pudding with Chocolate Sauce

½ pound ricotta cheese
1 tablespoon heavy cream
2 tablespoons sugar

1 tablespoon orange-flavored or almond-flavored liqueur

2 tablespoons candied fruit, coarsely chopped

5 ounces semisweet chocolate chips

⅓ cup water

2 ounces cold unsalted butter, cut into small pieces

In a medium-size bowl, beat the ricotta until smooth. Add the cream, sugar, and liqueur. Continue beating until creamy. Fold in the candied fruit and 1 ounce of the chocolate chips. Chill for at least 1 hour. To make the chocolate sauce, combine the remaining chocolate chips with the water in a small saucepan and melt the chocolate by cooking over a low heat, stirring constantly. Remove the pan from the heat and beat in the butter, one piece at a time. Continue beating until sauce is smooth. Allow the sauce to cool. To serve, divide the ricotta mixture between two dessert bowls. Top each serving with 2 tablespoons of chocolate sauce. Pour the remaining sauce into a gravy boat and serve on the side.

♊ Gemini Ⅱ

May 21–June 20

Symbol: The Twins   Element: Air
Quality: Mutable   Planetary Ruler: Mercury
Polarity: Masculine

All who joy would win
Must share it,—
Happiness was born a twin.

—Lord Byron
Don Juan

How to Identify Gemini

Gemini is the first of the mutable signs—flexible, resourceful, changeable—and the first air sign—intellectual, social, articulate. Physically and mentally alert, Geminis are among the fastest moving members of the zodiac family. In their rush through life, these whirling dervishes are easy to recognize because they are perpetually in motion. Best known for their ability to communicate, these Mercury-ruled charmers really do love to talk. Ideas are their forte, and they will rarely pass up the chance to join in a spirited discussion. As Jacks-of-all-trades, masters of none, they are interested in everything, but not inclined to delve deeply into any one topic. There is just too much to do, to talk about, and, above all, to learn for them to take the time to plumb the depths of a single subject.

The quintessential Gemini story tells of the twin who goes to the corner for a loaf of bread and returns three days later. While this is an exaggeration, members of this sign are easily distracted and likely to go off on one tangent after another. Gemini's role is to gather and disseminate information, to stir things up and keep them moving. Nobody goes with the flow like a Gemini. Naturally curious and a master of non-linear thinking, his attention is quickly caught, and he tends to follow his mental processes wherever they lead. Although Gemini may never attain the type of specialized in-depth knowledge common to more detail-oriented signs, he does acquire a broad spectrum of useful information. Along the way he has many adventures, makes many friends, and generally enjoys himself to the fullest.

While it is true that Gemini is unpredictable and hard to pin down, this sign is neither undependable, shallow, or superficial. It's just that with so much to see and do, and so little time to do it, he is often distracted or late or a no-show for meetings and appointments. When Gemini makes promises he means to keep them, but his inclination to sample everything, stopping at every port along the way, inevitably slows him down.

The secret to Gemini's success, and failure, is his dual nature. Like the twins that symbolize this sign, there are two or more distinct sides to his character and personality. One twin is a happy-go-lucky, extro-

verted social butterfly, while the other is moody and
introspective. If you live with a Janus-faced Gemini,
you probably wake up each morning wondering
which twin you'll encounter at the breakfast table.
And, just when you believe you've got your Gemini
partner figured out, the other twin surfaces. If you
are a fixed sign native, these constant changes of
mind and mood can drive you a little batty, and it's
all you can do to try to keep up. It may surprise you
to know that your partner is more confused than you
are. When he's at odds with himself, it usually means
that his mind is telling him one thing, his heart
another.

Geminis are the ultimate multitaskers, and virtually everyone born under the sign of the twins seems
able to do two or more things at a time, usually in
less time than it takes others to do one. When it
comes to talking on the telephone, it's a rare twin
who isn't doing something else while chatting. One
Gemini writer continues tapping away at her computer keyboard while conversing with her many
friends and acquaintances on a portable phone
tucked under one ear. She never misses a beat in the
conversation. Judging from the quantity, quality, and
success of her work, she manages her writing without any breaks in her train of thought. Her secret is
Gemini's duality, which is so pronounced it often
seems as if one twin is writing the manuscript while
the other talks on the phone.

Gemini can talk you into or out of anything. One
recurring scenario in life with a twin happens something like this. He suggests that you go on a trip

together. If you say no, he sweet-talks you until you change your mind. Having reluctantly agreed, you begin to warm to the idea. The next day, while you are packing, he calls. Apologizing profusely, he tells you that something came up and he has to cancel. Before you get mad, try to understand that although he was enthusiasm itself yesterday, today is a new day, and something or someone else has caught his attention.

Gemini can't stand being boxed into a monotonous routine. Their mercurial nature is restless and demands constant change and stimulation, and they are easily sidetracked by anything or anyone new and interesting that happens to cross their path. Clock watching is definitely not their thing. When otherwise involved, they totally lose track of the time. Most twins are square pegs unlikely to fit into the round holes of conventional nine-to-five office jobs. They do best when self-employed or in situations where no one tells them what to do, or when to do it.

Gemini's problems, when he recognizes any, usually stem from boredom, an excess of nervous energy, or a tendency to overanalyze everything and everyone. Although the twin may enjoy life, he is rarely content. No matter where he is or who he is with, deep down he's convinced the grass is greener in another place. That restless mind is always somewhere else, seeking an ideal that probably can never be found.

Myths and Symbols Associated with Gemini

The astrological ruler of Gemini is the planet Mercury. The parts of the body ruled by Gemini are the lungs, hands, arms, shoulders, and nervous system. Its symbol, ♊, is thought to denote the principle of duality. The sign is classified as mutable, air, and masculine (positive, direct, yang, external). Represented by the twins, Gemini's color is yellow, its metal is mercury, and its gemstone is agate.

The story most often associated with Gemini is the Greek myth of Castor and Pollux. They were fraternal twins, offspring of Leda and the Swan, and brothers to Helen of Troy and Clytemnestra. Leda, wife of King Tyndareus of Sparta, was raped by Zeus (Jupiter) who had disguised himself as a swan. The boys were hatched from one of the eggs laid by Leda after the rape. Pollux was immortal because he was the son of Zeus, but Castor was the son of Leda's husband and therefore mortal. United by the warmest affection, the twins were inseparable friends and boon companions. Castor was a famous horseman, Pollux a champion boxer. Together they participated in many heroic adventures. They joined Jason and the Argonauts in the search for the Golden Fleece, and they led the rescue of their sister, Helen of Troy, from her abductor, Theseus.

Castor and Pollux fell in love with two sisters, Hilaeria and Phoebe, daughters of Leucippus. When Castor and Pollux found out that the women were already betrothed, they crashed their double wedding, kidnapped them, and then married them themselves. In the ensuing battle with Leucippus' nephews, Idas and Lynceus, Pollux killed Lynceus, but Castor was tragically slain by Idas. Zeus became so enraged at the death of Castor that he threw a thunderbolt at Idas, killing him instantly.

Inconsolable over the loss of his beloved brother, Pollux asked his father to take his life in exchange for Castor's. Zeus refused, but agreed to allow them to enjoy life alternately, each passing one day in the underworld and the next on earth. Eventually Zeus rewarded their brotherly love by honoring them as the Dioscuri (sons of Jove) and placing them side by side in the heavens as the constellation Gemini.

A number of the Greek myths associated with Gemini relate to Hermes (Mercury). Hermes, son of Zeus (Jupiter) and Maia, was messenger to the gods. Said to have been the smartest of Zeus' progeny, he was the only one who did not have a permanent home on Mount Olympus, probably because he was constantly in transit among the three worlds. Hermes wore winged sandals, a winged cap of invisibility, and was the patron of musicians, orators, travelers, merchants, thieves, liars, and confidence men.

Legend has it that Hermes once came across some cattle that belonged to his half brother Apollo. In the spirit of mischief, Hermes stole the cattle and attached some back-to-front hooves on the animals' feet, then herded them into an empty cave. Apollo, who was looking for his cattle, came upon the footprints coming out of the cave, not going in. He was not tricked by this childish ploy, and he demanded that Hermes be brought before Zeus' Tribunal to be judged. Curious to see if he could get away with what he had done, Hermes responded to the accusation with entertaining stories. Zeus and the other gods were so amused and impressed with his cleverness that they agreed to let him off scot-free.

The Gemini Man

The Mercury man is no couch potato. He is constantly on the move. It is unusual for Gemini to spend an entire day in one place. When he's at home, he is almost always busy doing something. You will find him in the hall talking on the phone, in the driveway washing or fixing the car, on the porch chatting with the neighbors, in the yard playing with the kids, in the bedroom getting ready to go out again.

Geminis are very well coordinated, and most enjoy competitive sports. Generally twins prefer participating to sitting on the sidelines watching others play. However, there are some Mercury-ruled men who are fanatic sports fans. This type of twin can spend a considerable amount of time with radio and TV following his favorite teams. More often than not he will set up two or more television sets and watch two or more games simultaneously—while talking on the phone, reading the paper, and channel surfing through the commercials.

No matter what their line of work, twins are essentially *idea* people. They study, they learn, they ponder, they brainstorm, they write, they talk, and they talk some more. As the major communicators in the zodiacal circle, networking is their forte. They can't wait to pass along the information they've gleaned. Although many twins choose careers connected to the media, they can be found in just about any type of job. Like chameleons, they fit in everywhere and adapt easily to new situations. However, most Geminis do not perform very well in conventional positions because it is extremely difficult for them to stay chained to a desk from nine to five. Twins usually choose a career path that offers them a lot of freedom and flexibility. The prototypical Gemini occupations are communications, sales, public relations, advertising, teaching, writing, computer programming, transportation, and travel.

As a dual sign, Gemini is seeking completion. He wants to be free, yet he does not want to be alone. He is generally willing to sacrifice some but not all of his freedom in exchange for true love. The trick is to keep him interested, and the only way to do that is by engaging his mind. Although love is important to Gemini, friendship and companionship are just as important or more important. While he thoroughly enjoys sex, in his mind it will never replace scintillating conversation. Once he commits to someone, the only thing a typical Gemini male wants to know is that he is cared about and appreciated—especially appreciated. As long as you are intelligent and amusing, you don't need to be sexy or beautiful in order to win and hold his heart.

If you are in love with a Gemini, don't expect a traditional moonlight-and-roses romantic experience.

A Taurean with marriage on his mind generally pulls out all the stops (candlelight, champagne, music, flowers, a carriage ride around the park), then gets down on one knee to pop the question. The typical Gemini, on the other hand, is casual and offhanded. Like as not, he will produce a ring from his pocket at the most unlikely moment, and casually say, "I saw this in the jeweler's window, and I figured it was time we got engaged. What do you think?" Or he may never actually propose at all. At some point in your relationship he'll begin saying, "*if* we should get married", then after awhile he'll change it to "*when* we get married." Although he's never really *asked* you, he'll assume you understand this is his way of making a commitment.

The average Mercury-ruled male is extremely social and loves to flirt. Although he may have an active sex life, he tends to be somewhat ambivalent about intimate relationships. He enjoys the physical act of lovemaking, and he loves being in love, but romance is rarely the most important thing in his life. While some Geminis do have reputations as notorious lotharios, they are motivated more by the novelty of new conquests and experiences than by emotional need or sexual desire. The *idea* of lovemaking often attracts them more than the act itself.

When Gemini sets his sights on a prospective lover, he knows exactly the right things to say to set the mood. Even the shy ones can be smooth operators. When the mood is upon him, the average Mercury man will make love just about anywhere, and he's glib enough to talk his way into virtually anyone's bed. Although the twin is often in too much of a hurry to bother with courting rituals, when he does take the time to sweet-talk you, he will tell you anything he thinks you want to hear. Moreover, he will be totally sincere in what he says—even if only for the moment.

Changeable, and often moody, the Gemini twins will constantly keep you on your toes. One moment your mercurial lover is totally solicitous and responsive to your needs and feelings, the next he is off on a tangent and couldn't care less. Fidelity is a scary word, foreign to the nature of the average Gemini. Many a Mercury-ruled male has a reputation for being fickle and inconstant. However, in spite of his belief that variety is the spice of life and his tendency to shy away from commitments, if he's involved with the right person Gemini can be as faithful as any sign in the zodiac.

The Gemini Woman

In her marvelous book, *Astrology for Lovers*, Liz Greene writes, "Air signs need air." Of the three air signs, the sign of the twins, which rules the lungs, is the one that requires the most air and space in which to breathe. As a result the Gemini woman often finds that her need for intellectual freedom, mental stimulation, and creative expression outweighs any desire she might have for comfort and security. Female twins tend to be restless, constantly in search of new ways to follow through their thoughts and ideas. They like to be surrounded by sophisticated, intelligent people with whom they can discuss the many subjects that interest them. For most twins personal satisfaction and intellectual stimulation go hand in hand. Many Mercury-ruled ladies don't feel fulfilled unless they have several irons in the fire. They actually thrive holding down two jobs while pursuing various hobbies and creative projects.

With so many demands on her attention, it's hard to believe that the Gemini woman can find the time to make a home or raise a family. However, female twins are experts at juggling their very full schedules. Lady Gemini does everything quickly. Watching her, you can see she accomplishes twice as much as her slower sisters, and usually with half the effort. She runs on sheer nervous energy, and she's the master when it comes to doing two things at once.

No matter what her age, the Gemini woman always seems young and vigorous. Her youthful quality, her innate sense of fun, and her playful, mischievous nature make her a great favorite with the younger set. The typical Gemini woman is like the Pied Piper—children flock to her side and follow her wherever she goes. Twins seem better able than most to remember exactly how it felt to be a child. As a little one, she probably got lots of advance practice for parenthood from a favorite aunt or cousin. The Gemini lady is not afraid to get down and dirty with the kids. She joins them in their games, and they love her for it.

The average Gemini female is an excellent parent though she appears to do her homemaking in a casual way. She's not the most demonstrative parent on the block, but she is the one most likely to keep the kids amused. Keen to see her youngsters receive a good education, she begins reading to them when they are very little. When they get older, she provides them with lots of books, puzzles, games, and creative projects designed to hold their interest and stimulate their minds.

Mercury-ruled moms can be counted among those modern superwomen who are determined to do it all, and they juggle career and home better than most. In spite of her enormous reserves of energy and stamina, the Gemini woman needs to be extremely careful not to fall victim to stress overload. Even when her body temporarily slows down, the twin's *mind* is always in motion. High-strung, nervous, and possibly plagued by insomnia, when she spreads herself too thin this gal can run into big trouble. She'll often lie awake at night, her thoughts racing from one thing to another. The wheels just keep turning. As they turn, the Mercury woman probes, studies, and analyzes every aspect of her life and relationships. Although it's difficult for her to sit still, let alone relax, Gemini really does need to take a time out once in a while.

Many individuals born under the air signs of Gemini and Aquarius are emotionally challenged. Libra's element is air as well, but Venus-ruled Libras seem better equipped to deal with their emotions. Gemini is extremely comfortable in the mental arena, but she just doesn't have a clue when it comes to bridging the gap she's created between her thoughts and her feelings. As the journalist of the zodiac, she interviews everyone she meets. She happily picks your brain and draws you out, while revealing very little about her own feelings. Born with a defense mechanism where her innermost thoughts are concerned, she allows herself only one real confidante—her Gemini twin-self.

The Gemini woman is almost always in control of her emotions. No amount of love, romance, passion, or idealism—and she *is* idealistic—will cause this lady to lose her head. When it comes to romance and relationships, the twin is afraid to trust her own feelings, or yours. It is unlikely she'll ever experience the emotional ecstasy of being totally swept away by love. Flirting comes easy to her, though. When the sexual banter becomes hot and heavy, she may surprise you with an impromptu invitation to join her in an evening of passion. However, when your relationship progresses to the nitty-gritty of serious commitment, Gemini's usual reaction is to hit the panic button. If you are the one with honorable intentions toward a cool-headed Mercury charmer, don't be surprised if she keeps you guessing for a long, long time before she actually says, "Yes!"

The Shadow Side of Gemini

One Gemini twin can be a hardheaded rational adult—while the other, contained within the same skin, can be the most naïve and gullible kid on the block. Intelligent, clever, intellectual, Gemini is generally careful to adhere to logic, scrupulously resisting opinions that are not based on hard facts. Gemini's role is that of the impartial journalist. He observes without getting emotionally involved, then passes on what he has learned. Like Sherlock Holmes, the fictional detective, the twin's mind is habitually cool, cunning, and calculating, and he uses pure reason to reach his conclusions. However, sometimes he gets so caught up in a story that he gets carried away. Pretty soon he is listening to, swallowing, and repeating all kinds of exaggerations. In such a woolly-headed, *mystical* mode, Gemini is predisposed to believe just about anything. It is interesting to note that the Gemini writer Sir Arthur Conan Doyle, creator of the superrational Holmes, had an overwhelming interest in the occult. He was one of the world's best-known advocates of Spiritualism, and was often characterized in the popular press of his time as "the man who believes in fairies."

Like The Magician, his counterpart in the tarot deck, the Mercury-ruled twin will sometimes cross the line from smooth-talking supersalesperson to slippery con artist. Gemini's power comes from an ability to connect with people and communicate with them in a way that they can accept and understand. However, sometimes the Gemini talker will let his proverbial gift of gab get out of hand. Then his conversation tends to escalate from playful exaggeration to outright lying. When in his *trickster* mode, the Gemini flimflam artist could sell phony coins to a collector who is talked into believing they are real.

Sometimes Gemini comes across as an emotional lightweight because he will bend over backwards in order to keep things light and bubbly. Most Gemini natives are incredibly witty, with a great sense of humor. It is not unusual for them to deliberately play the part of the clown or the court jester. The mercurial type loves to gossip and is a master at keeping friends amused with story after story about everyone and everything. Even if he tells all he knows about other people, he keeps his own secrets deeply buried. He dearly loves to pry and probe, but absolutely hates it when the tables are turned on him. The twin is afraid to have anyone know too much about his life, because he sees it as a way of giving up control.

Most twins do not like exposing the serious side of their own nature, nor do they examine it themselves on a regular basis. It is really important for Gemini to learn how to accept all the various facets of his makeup. On a psychological and spiritual level he needs to learn how to shut out the endless external chatter, then go deep within himself to explore his own psyche. Only then can he let go of the safety that comes from hiding behind a mask with a smile, and open up to a new dimension of self that is infinitely richer and more personally empowering.

The Gemini native longs for the safety and closeness of a committed relationship, but is afraid to surrender his freedom. He wants to be loved and cared for, but he doesn't want to be caged. Even mutual decisions hold little appeal for him because he prefers to remain one hundred percent in charge of his own destiny. He doesn't want to boss you around, and he absolutely refuses to be bossed by you.

Gemini Romantic Dinner for Two

Gemini the cook

It should come as no surprise that Gemini rules fast food. However, don't confuse *fast* with *bad*. The typical twin is always in a hurry, and is usually so busy that there is little time left over for cooking or eating elaborate meals. However, when the twin does cook or eat, he prefers a variety of interesting, flavorful, and exotic tastes. Don't be surprised if a Gemini invites you to dinner, and instead of cooking takes you out to a favorite Thai, Japanese, or Indian restaurant. Or he may decide to call and have dinner delivered. If you mistakenly think it's home-cooked, so much the better.

When left to his own devices, Gemini would rather grab a snack than eat a full meal. However, if the mood is upon him, the twin can spend an entire afternoon whipping up an incredible array of fantastic dishes. Nobody can prepare a feast quicker or more efficiently. The Mercury-ruled twin runs on nervous energy and absolutely thrives on the type of organized chaos that would cause members of most other signs to go to pieces. Gemini's kitchen is a virtual whirlwind of activity—pots bubbling, people talking, people snacking—and the Gemini cook racing around at warp speed seeing to everything and chatting with everyone.

Twins love gadgets, especially timesaving gadgets. Gemini cooks invariably stock their kitchens with a variety of unusual utensils and offbeat gourmet cookware. Gemini tends not to worry about the cost of things, especially fun things. If he feels like serving champagne and caviar, that's exactly what you'll get. When a twin invites you to dinner expect to be treated to good and unusual food made with the very best ingredients, scintillating conversation, and just a touch of his special brand of magic.

Gemini the dinner guest

When you invite a Gemini to dinner, do not prepare foods that must be served according to a strict time schedule. The elusive twin is often late, and may appear just as you are about to give up on him. Always have tasty snacks waiting because, late or not, Gemini usually arrives famished. Don't bother preparing his favorite dishes either—the snails in wine sauce with wild rice he was so hopped up about last week may have fallen from favor. Twins change preferences as easily as others change socks, and almost as often. Your best menu choices consist of a variety of interesting "make ahead" dishes, hot or cold, that will allow you to spend most of your time out of the kitchen, chatting with your guest.

Gemini would rather talk than eat. When the discussion becomes spirited, the food on your guest's plate may remain untouched. Do not take this as an aversion to your culinary skills. It is actually a positive response to your ability to make interesting conversation. Typically Gemini runs on nerves and burns so much energy that excess weight is rarely a problem. He adores cocktail parties because they offer some of his favorite things—hors d'oeuvres, nibbles, and snacks—invariably accompanied by delicious gossip and witty conversation.

Most Geminis don't like sitting down to formal dinners, preferring to choose their own fare from the variety of foods on a buffet table or salad bar. One Gemini gal, a prolific writer, always keeps an assortment of nuts, crackers, cheese, fruit, and breakfast cereals within easy reach. When she is busy, she doesn't bother to stop to eat. Instead, she quickly puts together a small plate of her favorite goodies and munches on them as she works.

Foods commonly associated with Gemini

Meat: hare

Fowl: chicken, capon

Fish and Shellfish: oysters, lobster

Dairy Products: cheese, yogurt

Vegetables and Beans: carrots, celery, avocados, artichokes, mushrooms, asparagus, beets, green beans, dried beans, broccoli, cauliflower

Nuts and Grains: almonds, hazelnuts, walnuts, brazil nuts, pecans, pistachios, oats

Fruits: apricots, strawberries, mulberries, lemons, oranges, pineapple

Beverages: white wine, coffee

Herbs, Spices, and Miscellaneous: fennel, sage, marjoram, cloves, caraway, parsley, aniseed, licorice, mace

GEMINI MENU

---

*Guacamole with Corn Chips

*Couscous with Chicken and Garbanzos

*Tomatoes Vinaigrette

Warm Pita Bread

White Wine

*Fresh Strawberry Parfait

Coffee

*Gemini Recipes

*Guacamole with Corn Chips

2 ripe avocados, peeled and pitted
1 teaspoon olive oil
1 tablespoon onion, finely chopped
1 chili serrano, finely chopped
1 sprig coriander, finely chopped
1 ripe tomato, finely chopped (optional)
  salt to taste

Mash the avocados with the olive oil. Add the onion, chili, coriander, tomato, and salt, and mix thoroughly. Serve in an earthenware dish with corn chips on the side.

*Couscous with Chicken and Garbanzos

    1 pound skinless chicken breasts
    1 can chicken broth (14.5 ounces)
    1 cup couscous, uncooked
    1 can (15.5 ounces) garbanzo beans, drained
    ½ cup raisins
    ½ cup blanched almonds
    ¼ cup scallions, chopped (optional)
      salt and pepper to taste

Poach chicken breasts in chicken broth until no longer pink. Remove chicken from broth, cut into bite-sized pieces and set aside. Add the couscous to the hot broth, stir, cover, and remove from the burner. Let stand five minutes and then fluff the couscous with a fork. Place the chicken in a large bowl and sprinkle with salt and pepper. Add the remaining ingredients and toss until well mixed. Add more pepper if desired. Serve warm or cold.

*Tomatoes Vinaigrette

    3 ripe tomatoes, thinly sliced
    1 small white onion, thinly sliced
    2 teaspoons salad oil
    1 teaspoon vinegar
    ½ teaspoon fresh dill, chopped
    ½ teaspoon sugar
      salt
      pepper

Slice the tomatoes and the onion, and arrange on a serving plate. Prepare the vinaigrette by mixing together the salad oil, vinegar, dill, sugar, salt, and pepper. Spoon the dressing over the tomato and onion slices.

Fresh Strawberry Parfait

    1 pint fresh, ripe strawberries
    ½ cup whipping cream, chilled
    1 tablespoon confectioners' sugar
    ¼ teaspoon pure vanilla extract

Rinse and hull strawberries; dry thoroughly. Whip the cream using a chilled bowl and chilled beaters until it forms soft peaks. Add confectioners' sugar and vanilla extract, and beat to form stiff peaks. Spoon whipped cream into two large parfait glasses, then layer with strawberries, ending with whipped cream and a single strawberry on top.

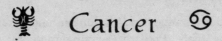

Cancer ♋

June 21–July 22

Symbol: The Crab   Element: Water
Quality: Cardinal   Planetary Ruler: Moon
Polarity: Feminine

Everyone is a moon and has a dark side which he
never shows to anybody.

—Mark Twain
Notebook

How to Identify Cancer

Moody is the keyword used most often to describe
Cancer natives. The constant shifting and changing
of the moon as it goes through its phases forms an
apt metaphor for the ebb and flow of Cancer's feelings, moods, and desires. Actually the moon does not
change at all, it only appears to change. So, too, the
crab, who *seems* different from one moment to the
next. However, it is only the *mood* of the Moon-ruled
that changes. Unlike Gemini, who truly possesses
two or more distinct personalities, deep down the
Cancer individual always remains essentially the
same person.

Cancer natives are generally peace loving, and they
heartily dislike becoming embroiled in noisy or vio-

lent arguments and disagreements. Secretive, self-protective Cancer prefers to work beneath the surface of a situation rather than confront it head-on. Cancers instinctively know the best way to manipulate circumstances and people, and like the crab, which moves sideways, will do everything possible to avoid a showdown. Normally gentle, kind, and caring, when angry, the crab undergoes a sea change and transforms into a sharp-tongued, vindictive, vengeful harpy. Cancer has one of the longest memories in the zodiac, and never gets over a slight. Crabs may forgive, but they don't forget.

As the sign of hearth and home, Cancer relates to family, domesticity, and security. The quintessential member of this sign is a confirmed homebody, and their own residence is the only place where they feel totally safe. However, the Moon as Cancer's ruler bestows both a predilection and a fondness for travel. Most crabs do seem to travel a great deal, especially for business. To truly understand the typical Cancer native, you need only to observe the hermit crab. Having no shell of its own, this creature takes up residence in a borrowed mollusk shell that it carries around for protection. When it outgrows one shell, it finds another into which it can fit. Like the hermit crab, the Cancer individual seems to carry his home around wherever he goes and can turn even the most impersonal hotel room into a snug, safe abode.

While Cancer is a water sign (imagination), it is also a cardinal sign (action). Tenacious, task oriented, and blessed with amazing powers of concentration, crabs are usually hardworking perfectionists, and their shrewdness with money is legendary. Cancer's unremitting search for security definitely extends to the workplace. Members of this sign are generally very successful in business, especially in those areas concerned with commerce, real estate, and industry. Often cited as one of the money signs, because so many of its natives number among the rich and powerful, Cancer also boasts a large number of creative individuals, including writers, artists, and musicians. However, artistic Cancerians are less likely to starve in a garret than their creative counterparts. Propelled by a combination of talent and ambition, Cancers often achieve fame and wealth.

Virtually obsessed with custom and tradition, most Cancers are conservative by nature. No sign is more focused on the past than that ruled by the Moon. Crabs are rarely attracted to the avant-garde or unconventional in art or in life. As self-appointed guardian of his or her personal, family, and country's history, the crab is concerned with preserving their heritage for future generations. Because they deplore waste, Cancer natives were reusing and recycling stuff long before it became the fashionable thing to do. They especially love to collect antiques and curios. Cancerians are fonts of information about the past history of the many aged treasures they own and love.

In spite of a hankering for the past, the average Cancer individual lives very much in the present, and can be as practical as any earth sign when it comes to paying bills and living on a budget. Security is everything to the crab, who is willing to sacrifice a great deal in return for an assured future. If the money and benefits are really good, the Moon-ruled native will hang on to the dullest job. The crab may complain about his lot, but his fears and insecurities generally outweigh any impulse he may have to follow his bliss. With his income on the line Cancer won't listen to his heart, especially when his head is urging shelter and protection from the vagaries of life.

Cancers of both sexes are very nurturing and maternal. Those who have no kids of their own tend to "mother" everyone they know. Typically Cancerians love to eat and feed others. They are constantly fretting over their children, and even their pets and plants are well loved and fussed over. Cancer parents may be tempted to use food, especially sweets, as a means of rewarding, and controlling, their children. Although the welfare and security of the kids are always uppermost in their minds, many crabs unthinkingly fall into a harmful overindulgent pattern of behavior.

The sensitive crab is a softy at heart, but so self-protective that it is not easy to penetrate his shell and get to know the real person underneath. He excels at ferreting out other people's secrets, but rarely confides his own. In romantic relationships Cancer is loving and caring, but also tends to be extremely possessive. Like a real crab, once he gets a hold on something or someone, he would rather lose a claw than let go. It is a lot easier to *begin* a relationship with the Moon-ruled than it is to *end* one.

Myths and Symbols Associated with Cancer

The astrological ruler of Cancer is the Moon. The parts of the body ruled by Cancer are the breasts and stomach. Its symbol, ♋, is thought to denote the claws of the crab. The sign is classified as cardinal, water, and feminine (negative, indirect, yin, internal). Represented by the crab, Cancer's color is silver, its metal is silver, and its gem is the pearl or the moonstone.

The story most often associated with Cancer is the myth of the Greek mother goddess Demeter (Ceres) and her beloved daughter Persephone. Seduced by Zeus (Jupiter), Demeter gave birth to a daughter by him. The girl, who was extremely sweet and beautiful, grew up happily among the other daughters of Zeus.

After a time Demeter (goddess of agriculture and the harvest) and her lovely daughter Persephone came to live on the earth with human beings. Together they wandered the globe. Mother and daughter were gloriously happy in each other's company, and wherever they went, the land was blessed with abundance. The exquisite Persephone was desired by many suitors, mortal and god alike, but she found none to her liking, preferring to remain at her mother's side.

One day, while picking flowers in a field, Persephone wandered away from her companions and was spotted by her father's brother Hades (Pluto), god of the underworld. Hades, who was riding by in his golden chariot, had long been covetous of his fair niece. When he spied her among the flowers, he was seized by uncontrollable desire, and he grabbed hold of her and pulled her into the chariot. "Mother!" she screamed as the flowers fell from her apron onto the ground. The goddess responded to the cry, but before she could get to her daughter the ground opened up and dragged Persephone and Hades down to the underworld. When Demeter reached the meadow, she found no trace of Persephone or her abductor.

For nine days and nights the distraught mother wandered from one end of the earth to the other seeking news of her child, but no one could tell her where to find Persephone. On the tenth day she met Helios, the all-seeing sun god, and he told her everything that had happened. From Helios, Demeter also learned that Zeus approved of the marriage between his daughter Persephone and his brother Hades. When she heard this news, Demeter decided that until her daughter was returned to her she would abandon her own divine role as earth's goddess. Without her favors nothing prospered in the world, and mankind suffered through a terrible year of famine and starvation.

Zeus realized that if all the people died there would be no one to worship the gods. He sent the other gods and goddesses to plead with Demeter, but she gave the same answer to each of them: "The earth will not bear fruit again until my daughter is returned to me." Finally Zeus sent Hermes (Mercury) to Hades with a message commanding him to release his bride. Hades could not disobey his brother's order, but he tricked Persephone into eating a pomegranate and swallowing four of its seeds. Because she had eaten of the food of the dead, Persephone was forever linked in marriage to Hades. When her daughter was returned to her, Demeter discovered the deception and refused to lift her curse on the land. Ultimately a compromise was reached. For each pomegranate seed she had eaten, Persephone had to spend a month in the underworld with her husband. The rest of the year she could be with her mother on the earth. During the time Persephone spends in the underworld, winter covers the land as a sign of Demeter's grief during her separation from her beloved daughter.

The Cancer Man

If ever there was a paradox, the quintessential Cancer man is it—no one sends out signals that are more confusing. In love and romance, the Moon-ruled man will cheerfully wine you and dine you one night, then totally ignore you the next. In the blink of an eye he can change from outgoing and protective to withdrawn and self-protective. The crab is a very touchy fellow. When his feelings are hurt, which happens frequently, he retreats into his shell, usually refusing to come out until his mood improves. As a water sign he is sensitive, sympathetic, and anxious about everyone's problems, especially his own. As a cardinal sign, he is goal oriented and possesses a "go for it" mentality. However, being Moon-ruled, he has developed worry into a high art. One moment he is the initiator who is tenacious, resolute, and determined; the next he falls into a brooding fit of despair, certain that nothing will ever work out the way he's planned.

Cancer's need for security is so overwhelming that it often obscures his finer qualities. Papa crab is a nurturer who is always ready to extend a sympathetic ear to anyone in trouble. Cancers love to feel needed, and they're among the most compassionate and self-sacrificing members of the zodiacal family. Although they tend to be emotionally needy themselves, most crabs are better at counseling others than they are at sharing their own troubles. Many Cancers are *empaths* who can actually tune in to other people's feelings. They understand your pain because they feel what you feel, and they will do just about anything to help make the pain go away.

Cancer natives have a terrific sense of humor, but not about their own foibles. Never, ever, try to joke or kid him out of a bad mood. It will only cause him to retreat deeper into his shell. After the darkness passes, it is usually better not to refer to it unless he broaches the subject first. Those born under this sign often have a problem expressing anger. When overwhelmed by their emotions, they are prone to respond with passive-aggressive behavior, cutting comments, and sarcastic remarks. For the Cancer man, moodiness and difficulties dealing with emotions are part and parcel of his basic nature. If you absolutely can't put up with it, perhaps you need to rethink your relationship.

Sweet, gentle, caring Cancer likes to have his own way. When he does something, or helps someone, he wants it to be on *his* terms. Generous and loyal to a fault, he is always there when you need him. But when he performs a service for you, he wants to do it *his* way, not *yours*. Even when you pay him to do a job, the crab's inclination is to take over and act as if he is the one in charge, not you. Others may resent his proprietary attitude, and sooner or later his friends and associates stop calling on him when they need assistance. He doesn't mean to be bossy, or tell you how to do your job or run your life, he just can't help himself. What he is really doing is assuming the role of the *father*, and like the parent of a young child he expects to be obeyed.

Cancers love to eat as well as nourish others. Even the moodiest Cancerian usually perks up when the conversation turns to food and food preparation. Many great cooks and professional chefs were born under this sign. Since the moon rules the stomach, the quickest way to Cancer's heart *is* through his stomach. Food represents safety and security for the Moon-ruled man. He feels most comfortable when the pantry and the refrigerator are well stocked, and the dining table is laden with goodies.

The Cancer man is a wonderfully imaginative sweetheart who loves to kiss and cuddle. Romantic and sentimental, he is at once shy and sensual—a very appealing combination. Passionate on the one hand, affectionate and tender on the other, he is enough of a sexual athlete to please his partner fully. All he needs is a little encouragement to help him overcome his fear of rejection. The crab is conventional and conservative by nature, and prefers to idealize his lover. Typically Moon-ruled men are not comfortable with sexual experimentation. Any show of crudeness or vulgarity can be off-putting, especially early in a relationship.

Crabs are difficult to get to know, and almost impossible to understand. The Cancer man doesn't give his heart away easily, and he usually keeps his feelings under wraps until he's certain they are reciprocated. When he does find the love and affection he craves, he immediately starts worrying about losing it. No matter how much you tell him he is loved, he never feels totally secure. With his insecurities driving his imagination, he can become extremely jealous and possessive.

Unlike other signs of the zodiac, Cancer rarely loses his temper when either his anger or his jealousy gets the upper hand. Crabs are more inclined to express displeasure by withdrawing. While his frequent crabby moods don't really mean very much, when your Cancer lover turns on the deep freeze, he is seriously upset. Although he may never get to the point where he is willing to tell you what is really bothering him, you can be sure it has something to do with his deep-seated insecurities. The best you can do is leave him alone until he comes out of his funk, then try reassuring him of your love and devotion.

The Cancer Woman

Psychic and intuitive by nature, the Moon-ruled lady acts on instinct. She rarely stops to question her own motives or analyze her deepest feelings. The Cancer female is basically shy and reserved, but also extremely sexy and appealing although she is often unaware of her own sex appeal. Potential partners find themselves drawn to her femininity and charm, as moths are drawn to a flame. The typical Cancer woman is not bold or aggressive. Like her male counterpart she is deathly afraid of rejection. When she spots someone who attracts her, she doesn't approach her target directly. Instead she finds some way to catch the other person's attention without actually showing her own interest ("Oh my, I've spilled my drink all over you. How could I have been so clumsy? I'm really sorry! Can you ever forgive me?").

Cancer women are the world's most enthusiastic mothers. In fact they try to "mother" everyone they meet. The Moon-ruled female is a caring, nurturing, protective parent, a great cook, and an excellent homemaker. Although she takes care of her possessions, she doesn't fuss or throw fits when children or adults make a mess in her house. The neighborhood kids flock to her home because it's child friendly, with lots of children, toys, and pets to play with, and plenty of snacks and goodies to eat. Most Cancers absolutely love water. If she can afford it, and she usually can, Mama crab will have a swimming pool in her backyard.

Family welfare and security are everything to the Moon-ruled woman. Where money is concerned, she spares no expense to see that her children get the very best of everything. Cancer mothers need to be totally involved in their children's lives. They never miss a school or team event, parent–teacher meeting, or appointment with their child's doctor or dentist. Cancer moms are generally the first to volunteer in the classroom, make cookies for a bake sale, or chaperon a school field trip.

Many Cancers are full-time mothers. However, those who do work outside the home can usually be found in fairly demanding and high-paying jobs. Working Cancer moms never stint on their career responsibilities, but they also refuse to shortchange their kids. Somehow the female crab finds a way to do it all—and have it all.

Cancer women are generally attracted to careers that offer financial security and the opportunity to work in close contact with other people. On the job the Moon-ruled female may choose to fill the role of "office mother." She's the one who everyone comes to for advice and sympathy. She's also the one who brings in the homemade cakes and cookies. In spite of her willingness to counsel and nurture her co-workers, Cancer is no slouch when it comes to getting her work done. She's a team player and a nose-to-the-grindstone type of employee, devoted to the organization and those who run it. As a manger she's known for her ability to advise her staff and point them in the right direction. When the Cancer woman is the one in charge of the entire show, she leads her company with persistence and determination. Behind the soft voice and gentle manner there lurks a dynamo with a great imagination and the ability to mobilize all her forces and send them into action.

Was it a Cancer who first expressed the idea that it is as easy to fall in love with a rich man as with a poor man? If not, perhaps it should have been. Romantic, sentimental Cancer is not likely to be blinded by love if it means she's forced to live in poverty. When things get rough, her partner may be surprised to find she has been secretly hoarding money for a rainy day. Cancer won't end a relationship because money is tight, but she will find a way to supplement the family income. She's always willing to take on extra work in order to pump up the bank account.

If Taurus' favorite room in the house is the kitchen, then Cancer's must be the dining room. Cancer natives really do love to cook, but they also love to eat and entertain. Unfortunately the crab's tendency to equate food with love can sometimes have serious consequences. When lonely or disappointed, Cancer women often turn to food for solace. Female crabs have a tendency toward gaining weight and retaining water. A love affair gone sour can result in the loss of a lovely figure. It certainly doesn't help matters that the Moon-ruled generally avoid exercise whenever and wherever possible.

In love and romance the lunar lady cannot be rushed or coerced. Although it may seem as if she wants nothing more than a committed union with marriage and a family, her self-protective instincts keep her from jumping impulsively into new relationships. Crabs tend to be old-fashioned in the bedroom and outside of it. Cancer likes to be wooed before she is won. Most Cancers want to be cared for and cherished, and they like to care for and cherish their lovers. It is not unusual for a Cancer woman to be more concerned with pleasing her partner than she is about her own needs and pleasures.

Although moon ladies are passionate, they are not likely to engage in sexual adventures just for the thrill or the experience. Sex is definitely important to Cancer women, but love and romance are equally important or more important. If you want to make points with the female crab, remember that above all she wants to be romanced. This is one lady who can be won over with flowers and candy, a romantic dinner, or a few sweet words whispered in her ear. Given her love of water and moonlight, a romantic swim under the stars can take you a long way toward gaining her heart.

The Shadow Side of Cancer

The public face of Cancer is one of compassion and sympathy for everyone. Members of this sign always seem to find reasons to excuse other people's foibles ("Poor fellow, it isn't his fault, he just can't help himself."). Typically Cancers are full of compliments and kind words. On the surface they all seem to be firm believers in the adage, "If you can't say something nice, don't say anything at all."

However, the crab's hidden side is somewhat uglier. When in pain the Moon-ruled will strike out with any available weapon. At first the crab stews over an injury, real or imagined, holding back the floodgates of his anger as long as possible. Eventually the dam bursts, and he takes steps to retaliate. Like the goddess Demeter when her daughter was stolen from her, Cancer doesn't care who gets hurt in the fallout.

Cancers are capable of making enormous sacrifices, especially for those they love. However, their sacrifices usually come with strings attached. The Cancerian rarely gives you the option of saying yes or no. More often than not he jumps in uninvited with aid and support, even if you don't necessarily want his help. Then, when the crab decides that his efforts are not sufficiently appreciated, something deep inside him snaps and turns into resentment ("After everything I've done for you, this is how you repay me for all my sacrifices!"). But, the Moon-ruled native will never come right out and complain to the offending party. Instead, he contents himself with a cryptic or sarcastic remark to your face, then crabs about you to one and all behind your back.

Cancers like to work from behind the scenes, pulling the strings and manipulating the action. This is the sign of the typical stage mother who pushes her child forward without any thought as to whether or not the kid even wants a career. Sometimes the crab begins to define his own life solely in terms of his relationships with others, and their successes or failures. When he attempts to live through his loved ones in this way, Cancer's entire reason for being may eventually come through someone else's life. It's no wonder that if problems arise in this type of symbiotic relationship, the hapless crab will go to almost any lengths to hold on to the lover, mate, or child in question.

Crabs of both sexes are prone to "smother love," and they rarely realize that this type of behavior can be seriously destructive. Many Cancers, lacking sufficient interests of their own, prefer to do *everything* with their families. They get really offended whenever a spouse, child, or parent makes plans that don't include them. The crab considers holidays, anniversaries, and other occasions as sacrosanct, and there can be the devil to pay if any relative opts *not* to join in the traditional family festivities. The Moon-ruled native would never forget or forgo a special date, and he really can't understand why any of his relatives would rather spend Thanksgiving, Christmas, Easter, or any other special day with friends instead of family.

Cancerians are people who *need people*. They must have a sense of belonging because they can't stand isolation or rejection. As long as the Moon-ruled are part of a group such as a family, an organization, or a country, they feel loved and protected. It is said that Cancer is the first to laugh, the first to cry, the first to complain, but always the last to leave. When the crab gets involved with someone, he tends to want to stay involved for a lifetime. Most Cancers will put up with just about anything rather than let go of a relationship, job, or group membership. They tend to hold on long after the fun and the thrill have gone, and it is almost always the non-Cancer individual who is forced to end the association.

Cancer Romantic Dinner for Two

Cancer the cook

Only Taurus loves to cook as much as Cancer. A great many professional chefs, past and present, were born under the sign of the bull or the sign of the crab. Cancers tend to associate the kitchen, and all its wonderful memories of mother, home, and family, with sustenance, comfort, and security. Cancer cooks generally keep the larder well stocked with a variety of foods. Given their moody natures, they never know exactly what they are going to feel like cooking or eating tomorrow or the next day.

When Cancer does the family cooking, there's always more than enough food to go around. The Moon-ruled cook is anxious to please, and may prepare several different main dishes so that every member of the clan can have what they like best. One Cancer lady is a particular favorite in her office because she frequently brings in generous samples of her delicious homemade specialties. She says that cooking before work is not a problem for her, as she gets up early every day in order to prepare a daily ration of chicken wings for her dog's dinner ("He won't eat anything else!").

Since Cancer is a water sign, its members generally cook instinctively with a lot of imagination. They prefer to follow wherever their emotions and appetite lead them. The rigid rules of a recipe book appeal to them far less than the prospect of creating new and different dishes. However, they are also traditionalists, partial to many tried-and-true favorites from the past. Crabs love to travel, and most members of the sign enjoy an eclectic variety of foods and beverages. When a Cancer native cooks for you, you're treated to an array of tastes that feature a combination of old and new dishes and an interesting blend of national and international cuisine.

Cancer the dinner guest

When you invite a crab to dinner, be sure to prepare a variety of different foods. Cancer is not a finicky eater, but his tastes can be as capricious as his moody nature. He may suddenly decide that a dish he once loved is now passé. No matter what you serve him, the food must be superb and there should be lots of it. Many crabs are gourmets. They don't just eat, they *dine*. Typical Cancers enjoy a formal atmosphere, and they prefer to eat at a table set with beautiful linens and fine dinnerware.

If you want to impress your Cancer guest, don't skimp on ingredients or try to pass off a substitute as the real thing. The crab never considers money spent on food as an extravagance. Cancer always buys the very best he can afford for his own table. When he comes to your home for dinner, he expects you to provide the very best you can afford.

Moon children don't like to eat alone, and they

tend to treat any meal in congenial company as a festive occasion. Although the crab is home and family oriented, he can be very gregarious when out with friends and acquaintances. He loves parties, especially dinner parties. The average Cancer native is no fashion plate, but you can rest assured he won't show up for dinner in jeans and a tee shirt. Crabs look forward to special occasions, and they usually view them as a good excuse to dress up.

Above all, remember that the crab is a romantic to the core. When you invite him to an intimate dinner for two, don't forget the flowers, candles, soft lights, beautiful music. If possible, you might want to consider serving dinner outside on the balcony or patio. Cancers love to eat near the water. If you have no pool or spa of your own, think about surprising your special crab with a moonlight picnic at the beach.

Foods commonly associated with Cancer

Meat: pork, chicken, rabbit, frogs' legs

Fowl: duck, geese

Fish and Shellfish: all

Dairy Products: all

Vegetables and Beans: cucumbers, cabbage, potatoes, squash (all varieties), pumpkin, turnips, lettuce, endive, leeks, mushrooms, watercress, kale, seaweed

Nuts and Grains: barley, wheat, water chestnuts

Fruits: melons, pomegranates

Beverages: all liquids, beer, spring water

Herbs, Spices, and Miscellaneous: rosemary, poppy seeds, hyssop, eggs, bread

CANCER MENU

Honeydew Melon

*Baked Stuffed Lobster Tails

*Cheesy Potato Wedges

*Cucumber Salad

Crescent Rolls

Sparkling White Wine

*Italian Cheese Cake

Espresso

**Cancer Recipes*

**Baked Stuffed Lobster Tails*

2 lobster tails
1 cup flaked crab meat (fresh or pasturized)
½ cup whole baby shrimp
¼ cup bread crumbs
1 egg
  pinch salt
¼ cup white wine
1 tablespoon butter, cold

Split lobster tails down the back. Prepare stuffing by mixing together crab meat, shrimp, bread crumbs, egg, and salt. Stuff each tail with half of the prepared stuffing. Place the stuffed tails on a baking sheet lined with foil, and pour the wine over them. Cut the butter into small pieces, and dot it on the top of the lobster tails. Bake at 350 degrees for about 40 minutes, or until stuffing is crusty on top.

*Cheesy Potato Wedges

    2 large baking potatoes, sliced in wedges
       nonstick cooking spray
       salt
       pepper
       onion powder
    1 cup grated cheddar cheese

Preheat oven to 350 degrees. Parboil potato wedges until tender. Spray a shallow baking dish with nonstick cooking spray. Drain potatoes and place in baking dish. Sprinkle with salt, pepper, and onion powder. Spray the seasoned potato slices with nonstick cooking spray, and bake 30 to 35 minutes or until brown. Remove from the oven, and sprinkle with the cheddar cheese. Return to the oven, and bake 5 minutes more or until the cheese melts.

*Cucumber Salad

    1 large cucumber
    ¾ cup plain yogurt
    1 tablespoon fresh dill (or chives), chopped

salt
pepper

Pare cucumber. Run the tines of a fork down the sides of the cucumber, cut into thin slices, and transfer to a shallow bowl. Add the yogurt, dill (or chives), and salt and pepper to taste. Stir and chill in the refrigerator for at least 30 minutes.

*Italian Cheese Cake

2 eggs
½ pound cream cheese
½ pound ricotta cheese
¾ cup sugar
3 tablespoons flour
¾ teaspoon lemon juice
½ teaspoon vanilla
½ pint dairy sour cream
4 tablespoons butter, melted and cooled

All ingredients must be at room temperature for at least one hour. Preheat oven to 350 degrees. Generously grease a 9 × 2 spring form pan. Place the eggs in the large bowl of an electric mixer, and beat. Add the cream cheese and ricotta cheese together. Scrape the bowl and beaters with a rubber spatula. Add the sugar a little at a time, beating well after each addition. Add the flour and beat. Add the lemon juice and continue beating. Add the vanilla and beat some more. Add the sour cream a little at a time and beat.

Add the melted butter, and beat all ingredients until nice and creamy. Pour batter into prepared pan. Bake 45 to 55 minutes, or until the center is firm and the top of the cake cracks. Turn the oven off, and leave the cake in the oven with the door closed for 1 to 1½ hours. Refrigerate at least 4 hours before serving.

♌ Leo ♌

July 23–August 22

Symbol: The Lion   **Element: Fire**
Quality: Fixed   **Planetary Ruler: Sun**
Polarity: Masculine

Ay, every inch a king.

—William Shakespeare
King Lear

How to Identify Leo

As the Sun-ruled fire sign, Leo is synonymous with warmth and light. Its natives are impelled to seek the spotlight, and when they find it, they shine. Although the lion is often accused of being bossy, what he really wants is to be *the boss*. Leos like to make their own decisions, and they strongly resent being told what to do. When the proud cat receives his heart's desire—recognition as leader—he usually refrains from bossing others around or telling them what to do. Besides, once acknowledged as king, Leo is much too busy acting the part of the gracious sovereign—smiling, waving, dispensing boons to the admiring throng—to be bothered with petty details. The regal lion generally concentrates his attention on life's larger picture, and leaves it to the rest of the zodiacal signs to work out the finer points of living.

The famous, or infamous, Leo pride is no myth. If you want to get along with a lion, you won't step on his toes, hurt his feelings, or wound his ego. As long as you stick by him, and give him what he considers to be his due, he will repay you by doing whatever it takes to justify your loyalty and confidence in him. However, if you hurt his pride, disappoint him, or let him down in any way, you will definitely hear him roar.

When dealing with Leo, flattery will get you everywhere. The lion equates flattery with love and affection, and even your most obvious attempt to gain the cat's favor is virtually assured of success. Lions are smart, not easily fooled about most things. However, when you start piling on the compliments, lions respond to even the most ludicrous pronouncements with blushes, smiles, and bows and waves to an unseen audience ("Do you really think so? You are much too kind! Then again, you are probably right. After all I did do a great job, didn't I?").

Lions are inclined to mythologize their lives, and live out their own myths. Leos dearly love dramatizing their experiences. All lions, even the most timid ones—the pussycats—are actors at heart. Of course many Leos are professional entertainers, but even those who aren't tend to view themselves as star players in the drama of their individual existence. Typically Leo gravitates toward the limelight, and views his entire life as a movie in which he is not only hero but also writer, producer, and director.

The role that Leo assumes is a noble one. Naturally warmhearted and giving, he will open his purse and his heart without hesitation, and he despises anything that appears to be mean or petty. However, the generous lion expects generosity in return, not as recompense but because he believes it is the way things should be. Although he is not selfish, he can appear so because he loves comfort and luxury and he likes to be waited on and catered to. Without even realizing it, the Sun-ruled native may assume that everyone else is here to gratify his desires. Most lions have an abundance of charm. They possess a particular combination of personal magnetism and childlike innocence that often causes other people to spoil them in an attempt to please them.

Lions thrive on approval and appreciation. Many natives of this sign believe that fame and recognition are infinitely more important than money. However, for the typical Leo native, whose lifestyle seems to tread a thin line between lavish and excessive, money is an absolute necessity. The Sun-ruled lion has excellent taste and very little self-discipline when he sees something he wants. He adores the good life but disdains its persnickety little details, such as checking to see if there is enough money in his account to cover his extravagances. He flatly refuses to live on a budget, or deny himself or his loved ones anything they want. With his unquenchable optimism he feels certain that, one way or another, the bills will be taken care of. If you are the mate or partner of a free-spending lion, you may discover that much of the responsibility for finding a way to pay Leo's debts rests firmly upon your shoulders.

As the sign of kings and presidents, Sun-ruled Leo is about taking charge, no matter what the situation. Lions enjoy responsibility, and they can be quite fearless when it comes to managing large companies or directing major projects. As a born executive, the king of the jungle excels at inspiring others and motivating them to carry out his plans and follow his orders. The idealistic Leo native needs to be proud of the work that he does, but he must also enjoy it or he won't stick with it.

Lions are extremely creative. Many are drawn to the world of arts and entertainment where their talents can be showcased in front of an approving and appreciative audience. The Leo native invests himself emotionally in everything he does, and he views the success or failure of his endeavors as a matter of personal pride. When his efforts are not well received he feels hurt and slighted, and his disappointed roar can usually be heard for miles.

Leo is the sign of love and romance. You won't find many loners born under the sign of the lion. Leo is one of the signs most often referred to as "being in love with love," and perhaps that is not very far from the truth. Certainly most lions are in love with the drama that surrounds a romantic relationship. The idealistic lion tends to view his love affairs as somewhat larger than life. Because his dreams are so big and his expectations so high, he is often disappointed. However, even the most disillusioned lion is rarely alone for very long. His natural optimism, as well as the need to always be in love with someone, spurs him on in the search for his ideal lover. Typically he may engage in a number of affairs of the heart before finding his one true love.

Myths and Symbols Associated with Leo

The astrological ruler of Leo is the Sun. The parts of the body ruled by Leo are the heart, back, and spine. Its symbol, ♌, is thought to denote either the lion's tail or its mane. The sign is classified as fixed, fire, and masculine (positive, direct, yang, external). Represented by the lion, Leo's color is gold, its metal is gold, and its gemstone is the ruby.

The story most often associated with Leo is the myth of the Greek hero Heracles (Hercules) and the Nemean Lion. Heracles, son of Zeus (Jupiter) and the mortal woman Alcmene, granddaughter of Perseus, was the mightiest of all the Greek heroes. He was named Glory of Hera for Zeus' wife Hera (Juno) who was queen of the gods. Hera hated her namesake Heracles, as she did all the offspring of her husband by his mortal mistresses. She sent two serpents to destroy the infant in his cradle, but the baby Heracles strangled them with his bare hands.

Before Heracles' birth, Hera had gotten Zeus to promise that the firstborn prince of the house of Perseus would be named High King, and rule over all of Perseus' descendants. Zeus had agreed because he believed that Heracles would be born first. However,

Hera contrived things so that Eurystheus was born one hour before Heracles. Therefore Eurystheus was made king, and Heracles was forced to be his subject.

Great things were expected from young Heracles, and his mother's husband King Amphitrion saw to it that his powerful stepson was well schooled in the manly arts of war, boxing, and wrestling. To test himself Heracles set about fighting wild beasts and giants, and soon tales of his prowess and good looks were being repeated all over the country.

King Eurystheus began to realize that the young hero was even more famous than he was. Eurystheus schemed and plotted, and eventually came up with a plan to rid himself of Heracles by sending him on a series of extremely dangerous missions (the Twelve Labors of Heracles), reasoning that the young hero would surely be killed while performing one or another of the labors. At first Heracles refused because he did not think it fitting that a demigod should be commanded like a servant. However, Zeus intervened and told Heracles that he must obey the king's commands.

The first of the labors involved an order to kill and flay an enormous lion, with an invulnerable skin, which was terrorizing the hills around Nemea in the Peloponnese. The lion had been born of Echidna, the snake woman, and Typhon, a monster with a hundred eyes. It had been sent by the goddess Hera to wreak havoc upon Nemea, a plain sacred to Zeus.

Heracles met up with the lion on Mount Tretus. First he shot arrows at the beast, but they didn't even pierce its tough skin. Then he went after him with a club, which did little more than irritate the lion, who retaliated against these annoyances by biting off one of Heracles' fingers. Heracles followed the lion into a cave with two entrances. He blocked one of the doorways, and then went after the lion through the other. Heracles grasped the lion in his mighty arms, and managed to choke it to death with his bare hands. When he attempted to skin it, he found that the hide resisted his knife, but eventually he flayed it and wore its skin as armor through the remaining eleven labors.

Zeus was impressed by the bravery and courage of the noble Nemean lion, and honored it by setting its outline among the stars in the heavens, where it shines as the constellation Leo.

The Leo Man

Although the passion and energy of fire are what drive the lion to succeed, Leo is also a fixed sign. Like the other fixed signs (Taurus, Scorpio, and Aquarius), Leo has the determination to stick with a task and see it through to the end. Since his resolve rarely shows on the surface, some people may mistakenly regard the friendly, outgoing Leo native as frivolous or superficial. Typically those who don't know any better could refuse to take the lion seriously, and that would be a fatal error. Leos usually refuse to engage in underhanded tactics, and they're rarely found sneaking around behind your back. However, if you underestimate one, especially one who is your rival in love, politics, or business, you could be in for a very rude awakening. While you are confidently writing him off as a negligible force, the lovable lion may be off somewhere charming and winning over your voters, your clients, or the object of your affections.

The Leo man is an extrovert who expects to be noticed and admired, and even the shyest pussycat attracts attention upon entering a room. Lions are always *on*. They play to the crowd and glory in its adulation. Leo dearly loves to entertain and hold court, and he doesn't need to be rich or famous in order to be surrounded by an entourage of adoring fans. Like the sun, which rules his sign, the lion naturally positions himself at the center of any group.

Style and *drama* are two important keywords invariably associated with members of this sign. However, Leo's style is not necessarily the same as the current chic found in fashion magazines. His style is very much his own. Even lions who haven't a clue as to what's *in* and what's *out* manage to convey a distinctive personal flair. Sun-ruled natives love to dramatize their experiences. As natural actors, they adore the spotlight, and tend to view most of their activities as performances of one kind or another. Provide the lion with an audience, and he's off and running. Even in life's most intimate moments, Leo usually can't resist dramatizing his feelings and showing off his talents and abilities.

Most Sun-ruled natives excel in sports and games, and they can be extremely competitive. Like Aries, Leo really wants to win. However, unlike the ram, the lion knows how to turn a defeat into a seeming victory. When he loses at something, Leo's conduct and demeanor are generally so noble and magnanimous that he confuses onlookers into thinking he actually won, or he probably should have won. Although he may be seething with disappointment on the inside, Leo hides his pain and treats his loss as bad luck, or a soon-to-be-remedied accident of fate.

A caged lion is an unhappy lion, so Leo needs to feel free and unfettered. You will rarely find him in a job that keeps him tied to a specific place or to a dull, boring routine. Motivated by the creative energy of the sun, the lion is the classic superachiever. Although an occasional lazy and self-indulgent cat can be found, the majority are ambitious, hardworking, and tenacious. When he works for himself, Leo will shoulder any burden in order to succeed. He is also capable of working with great loyalty and devotion for an individual, company, or cause he admires and respects. Although the lion prefers to be boss, he is usually willing to put that need aside in favor of what he views as a greater good. Many members of this sign choose to enter politics, where they function quite effectively as servants of the people. Their innate idealism and strong social conscience motivate them to try to change the world, and make it into a better place. Of course, the appeal of the political life may come from more than just the desire to help others. The possibility of Leo ultimately attaining high public office is rarely overlooked as a consideration.

As befits a fire sign, Leo natives are strongly sexed, and they make ardent, passionate lovers. Lions need love and affection in their lives, which makes sense since Leo rules the heart. The big cat is not a loner, and he is almost always in love with someone or looking for someone to love. In the beginning of a romantic relationship, Leo has a tendency to sweep you off your feet. He comes across as Mr. Wonderful, and few are able to resist his magnetic charm. He can be a most generous, loving, and enthusiastic partner, but also an extremely demanding one.

The lion in love is not afraid to show his deepest feelings. However, he expects absolute loyalty and devotion in return. Leo requires a lot of attention, and is easily offended if he feels he is being slighted in any way. Because it is hard for a lion to take second place, the Sun-ruled man can become quite jealous—not just of potential rivals but of anyone who threatens to draw his partner's attention away from himself, including his own kids.

The typical lion's demeanor is one of innate cheerfulness. Gloom and doom normally have no place in Leo's life. On the rare occasion that he does appear dejected or depressed, it is usually because someone or something has hurt his pride or, worse yet, compromised his dignity. Failure of any kind scares the wits out of the Leo native, and he cannot bear to be put down or rejected. To the noble lion his image is everything. If you want to make points with him, you won't chip away at his ego or damage his reputation. If, in spite of all warnings, you threaten his self-esteem or self-respect, don't be surprised if you never see him again.

The Leo Woman

The lioness is versatile, artistic, and a natural entertainer. Her world is her stage. The Leo lady wants to be noticed, and her feminine charms are always on display for all to admire. The queen of the jungle is easy to recognize. She usually has a mane of beautiful hair and moves as gracefully as a cat. Her sense of style is evident. While some pussycat Leo ladies may choose understated elegance, the majority prefer dramatic attire and an unmistakably bold fashion statement. The Sun, Leo's ruler, also rules gold and goldsmiths, and it is a rare lioness who doesn't like to adorn herself with beautiful jewelry. Although confidence and self-esteem are part and parcel of her basic makeup, she thrives on the adulation of others. If you want to win her over, remember that she needs to feel cherished and appreciated. Flattery and compliments are never wasted on the Sun-ruled woman.

Traditionally lionesses have gotten some bad press, being variously characterized as egocentric, imperious, and domineering. However, many of the negative descriptions were written at a time when strong women were not generally admired. If Leo's manner is sometimes forceful and commanding, it is because she has confidence in herself and in her own methods and ideas. The Sun-ruled sign of Leo represents the emergence of the ego. One of the aims of its members is to build something that will serve as a testament to their unique talents and abilities. While Leo can be authoritative and commanding, she is also charismatic, greathearted, affectionate, and kind. She cannot bear hypocrisy or deceit. When she loves, she loves loyally and sincerely. When she gives, she gives of her whole self, holding nothing back.

Individualistic and competent, the lioness is perfectly capable of living life on her own terms. But she's not a loner and usually prefers the company of a mate or partner. Like her male counterpart, she is family minded and loves to be surrounded by children. While Leo may indulge herself and her personal whims from time to time, at heart she's a warm and caring woman who is exceedingly generous to others, especially her loved ones.

The typical Leo female is intensely alive and eager to make the most of every moment, and she succeeds at virtually everything she tries. It is not surprising that some people are envious of her successes or intimidated by her proud manner, elegance, and style. She needs to be the star of the show. Where family members and friends are concerned, she is often inadvertently guilty of causing them to feel as if they can't do things as well as she. She does have a tendency to give advice, even when it is not wanted. She needs to learn when to back off and let others, especially her mate and children, live their own lives in their own way.

The outgoing, self-assured lioness has a zest for life that is unmatched by any sign in the zodiac. She has a wonderful knack for living in the present moment, savoring its joys to the fullest. She rarely gets hung up on past regrets or future considerations. She wants the best for herself and her family, and she wants it *now*. Moreover, she knows exactly how to go about getting what she wants. She is ambitious and hardworking. Her stick-to-itiveness and strength of purpose allow her to triumph in virtually any endeavor.

As the sign that rules kids, Leo bestows a natural affinity for children. The Leo mom has a wonderful sense of fun. She enjoys her kids and everyone else's, and they invariably respond in kind. Although adult Leos can come off as smug or pompous with other adults, they rarely patronize children. The Leo mother is always "there" for her offspring. She is interested in everything they do, and they pick up on her warmth and affection. Typically the lioness is never too proud or dignified to get down on the floor and join the children in their play. She's often a willing volunteer when they need someone to help stage a drama, or even up the teams in a game or competition.

The female Leo is inherently proud of her children, but she can be a demanding mother. She willingly gives a great deal to her kids, but she also expects a lot from them. She puts her children first, treats them as individuals, nurtures their unique abilities, and encourages their personal talents. In return, she counts on her kids to always do their best, and to conduct themselves in a manner befitting children of royalty.

Leo, the fifth sign of the zodiac, rules love and romance. When the lioness loves you, she does so without reservations. Extremely magnanimous when it comes to expressing love and affection, she gives of herself emotionally, materially, and sexually. Her romantic nature is intense. When she meets the person of her dreams, her idealism causes her to view the romance as larger than life. If you are her lover, she'll probably set you up on a pedestal and make you the center of her universe. She will pamper you, inspire you, and love you. But she won't put up with disloyalty! And she's not shy about letting you know if you fail to live up to her expectations.

Lady Leo loves faithfully, and it takes a serious betrayal to make her break her commitment and walk away. When she is disillusioned or disappointed, her initial impulse is to stay and try to work things out. However, once she is convinced that a romantic relationship cannot be saved, she will leave and she won't look back.

The Shadow Side of Leo

When something bad happens, you can always count on a Leo friend (parent, boss, coworker, or lover) to come to your rescue. Sun-ruled natives love to be needed, and no sign is more generous or helpful. The lion is a magnanimous beast, and he won't think twice about offering time, energy, and material aid in an all-out effort to assist you. However, after he helps you solve your problem, he may offer to help you sort out your entire life. Since he has no trouble organizing his own life, the big cat is confident of his ability to organize other people's lives as well. The trouble is that he can be interfering and bossy. He expects you to take his advice whether or not you've asked for it, and whether or not you think you need it. If you reject or ignore his suggestions, he'll probably act hurt and may let you know that he thinks you are being ungrateful or unappreciative of his efforts on your behalf.

Whoever said, "It is better to give than receive" must have been a Leo. The proud lion loves playing the part of the generous benefactor, but he'd rather not be on the receiving end of someone else's benevolence. When he gives, he usually does so from a sense of noblesse oblige. He sees it as his obligation as a "royal personage" to help those who need help. If you happen to feel that his helping you puts you in the position of owing him something in return, that's fine with him. Like the proverbial Godfather of story and film, the lion dispenses his largesse, then allows the recipients to pay him homage (and owe him favors). However, Leo really hates being emotionally indebted to anyone. If he accepts your help, it puts you on equal footing with him and makes him feel obligated to you instead of the other way around.

Another manifestation of the Leo shadow is his inclination to show off and hog center stage. Nobody likes a know-it-all, but the typical lion fancies himself an expert on most subjects and acts as if he knows everything there is to know. He can't stand admitting ignorance on any subject, and he usually covers up for his lack of real knowledge with an assortment of quips, jokes, and quick-witted remarks. As a born showman, the Sun-ruled native strives to enlighten and entertain, but he also has a habit of seeking attention for its own sake. He generally spends more money than he should in a concerted effort to impress other people. He does this to get them to love him, but the harder he tries to dazzle them, the more likely it is that he will turn them off.

No matter what the situation, if it takes place in Leo's world he tries to make it about him. He hates being a bit player. Even when he's neither the "corpse" nor the "bride," the lion somehow manages to be the center of everyone's attention. He despises the humdrum, the ordinary drives him to distraction, and boredom is one of his least favorite words. He has a knack for attracting extremely colorful individuals and bizarre situations. Whenever he begins to feel that life doesn't supply enough excitement, he stages his own melodramas.

In love, as in life, the Sun-ruled Leo native never does anything halfway. He has a tendency to view his love affairs in mythical terms. To the typical lion every relationship is a grand passion, and every romantic encounter a high drama. He will shower his new love with gifts, attention, and admiration, convincing himself that this time he has found *the one*. However, when the individual in question turns out to be smaller than his dreams, Leo quickly falls out of love, gets on his white horse, and rides off into the sunset.

Leo Romantic Dinner for Two

Leo the cook

Although lions can be wonderful and inventive cooks, many of them don't especially enjoy cooking. They view the process as the means to an end. What Leos really love is entertaining. Dinner parties inspire the big cat, providing him with an excuse to show off his magnificent home and demonstrate his unique culinary skills. What the lion wants most is to impress his guests. When you're invited to his house for a meal, you may expect to be treated to a sumptuous and delicious feast. The presentation of the food will certainly be exquisite. The table will probably be adorned with flowers and candles, and beautifully set with the best china, glassware, linens, and silver that the Sun-ruled native has to offer.

When the king of the jungle prepares one of his special dinners, he does so for the benefit of other people. The lion loves an audience, and he rarely bothers to cook a meal for himself. Leo is not the least bit uptight or secretive about his recipes or methods, and he enjoys having company while he cooks. If you arrive early for dinner, you may find him holding court in the kitchen along with the other early birds he's charmed into assisting with the preparations. In all likelihood, the lot of you will soon be having a great time laughing it up and enjoying a little predinner celebration, while helping to get things ready for the upcoming meal.

Although everything Leo does is impressive, it is

not always formal. Lions love to cook over an open fire, and most have a passion for barbecues and picnics. When you eat outdoors with a Leo, you may eat from paper plates, but they will certainly be paper plates fit for a king's dinner and the very best money can buy.

Leo the dinner guest

Leo dearly loves to be catered to. It's always a good idea to find out his favorite dishes in advance, and include some of them on the menu. Although you won't go wrong if you greet him with champagne and caviar, the average lion is not a gourmet. He enjoys basic fare. A nice glass of wine with an assortment of cheeses, or a cold beer (imported, of course) and a few hot hors d'oeuvres should do very nicely.

The typical Leo native has an excellent appetite, is not a finicky eater, and thoroughly enjoys any meal that is well prepared and nicely presented. Although lions love to eat, they don't like to eat alone. They are usually more interested in their dining companions than in the food that is served. Nothing gives them more pleasure than dining with celebrities or other interesting and talented individuals who have something to contribute to the dinner conversation. As far as the lion is concerned, even children and pets are welcome to join in the festivities, and if you don't invite them to the table, he probably will.

When a Leo dines at your home, he expects to be pampered, but he doesn't expect you to spend hours toiling over a hot stove. Lions want to have fun. They believe that life's precious moments are to be enjoyed, not wasted fussing over details. If you possess the means to hire a cook or caterer, or order in from a fine restaurant, that is perfectly fine with him. However, if you should do all the work yourself in an attempt to please him, he's sure to notice and let you know that he appreciates your efforts. The most important thing to remember when you invite the lion to dinner is that he needs to feel that he is the center of your world. If he believes that the entire evening has been engineered for his pleasure, he's sure to relax and have a wonderful time.

Foods commonly associated with Leo

Meat: lamb

Fowl: chicken

Fish and Shellfish: none

Dairy Products: none

Vegetables and Beans: tomatoes, hearts of palm, olives, carrots, okra, vine leaves

Nuts and Grains: almonds, coconuts, walnuts, sunflower seeds, poppy seeds, cashews, barley, cornmeal, rice

Fruits: oranges, lemons, limes, tangerines, grapefruits, cherries, mangoes, bananas

Beverages: tea, herbal tea, gin

Herbs, Spices, and Miscellaneous: saffron, turmeric, sugar, mustard, ginger, rosemary, cinnamon, bay leaves, chamomile, mace, nutmeg, curry, dill, fennel, comfrey, angelica

LEO MENU

---

*Mozzarella Appetizer Platter

*Iberian Chicken in Garlic Sauce (Pollo al Ajillo)

*Saffron Rice

Crusty Bread

*Sangria

*Caramel Flan

Tea

*Leo Recipes

*Mozzarella Appetizer Platter

fresh mozzarella cheese
green olives
black olives
cherry tomatoes
marinated artichokes, drained
canned hearts of palm, drained and sliced

Cut the cheese into chunks, and arrange all the ingredients on a platter. Serve with crackers.

*Iberian Chicken in Garlic Sauce (Pollo al Ajillo)

1 small frying chicken, cut into eighths
  salt

paprika
¼ cup olive oil
1 head garlic, separated into cloves, peeled and sliced
1 cup dry white wine
1 bay leaf

Season the chicken pieces with salt and paprika. Heat the olive oil in a large pot, and add the chicken pieces. Brown the chicken, and add all the garlic. Continue cooking, turning the chicken pieces often, until the garlic slices are soft but not brown. Add the white wine and bay leaf. Cover and cook over a low heat for about 45 minutes, or until the chicken is tender.

*Saffron Rice

2 cups chicken broth or bouillon
½ teaspoon salt
¼ teaspoon onion powder
¼ teaspoon garlic powder
½ teaspoon saffron or turmeric
1 tablespoon olive oil
1 cup uncooked rice

Heat the chicken broth or bouillon and add the salt, onion powder, garlic powder, and saffron or turmeric. Set aside. Heat the olive oil in a saucepan over medium heat. Add the rice and sauté gently until the rice is translucent. Carefully add the seasoned chicken broth or bouillon and bring to a boil. Reduce heat, cover, and cook 12 to 14 minutes or until the rice is tender.

*Sangria

  1 bottle dry red wine
  1 ounce gin or vodka
  1 ounce cognac
  ¼ cup sugar
  ½ cup orange juice
  1 orange, sliced
  1 lemon, sliced
  1 banana, sliced
  1 apple, peach, pear, or nectarine, sliced
  ½ cup grapes or cherries

Pour the wine, gin or vodka, cognac, sugar, and orange juice into a large pitcher. Add the fruit and allow the sangria to sit outside of the refrigerator for four to eight hours, stirring occasionally. Discard the fruit. Add ice to the sangria just before serving.

*Caramel Flan

  ⅔ cup sugar
  3 eggs, beaten
  1½ cups milk
  1 teaspoon vanilla

Cook ⅓ cup of the sugar in a heavy saucepan over

high heat. When the sugar begins to melt, shake the pan occasionally but do not stir. Reduce the heat slowly and continue cooking until the sugar is golden brown, stirring frequently. Divide the melted sugar mixture among four 6-ounce custard cups. Tilt the cups to coat the bottoms.

Combine the eggs, milk, remaining sugar, and vanilla, and beat the mixture until well combined but not foamy. Pour the egg mixture into the custard cups. Set the custard cups in an 8 × 8 × 2 baking dish and pour boiling water into the baking dish to a depth of one inch. Preheat the oven to 325 degrees and bake for 30 to 45 minutes. To serve, loosen the edges of each custard with a spatula or knife, and invert onto a dessert plate. The flan may be served warm or chilled.

♍ Virgo ♍

Symbol: The Virgin   Element: Earth
Quality: Mutable   Planetary Ruler: Mercury
Polarity: Feminine

There is a great amount of poetry in unconscious
fastidiousness.

—Marianne Moore
Critics and Connoisseurs

How to Identify Virgo

The sign of the virgin, like that of the scorpion, is
frequently misunderstood. The common image of
Virgo is that of a chaste, compulsively neat, clock-
watching, nit-picking perfectionist. This characteriza-
tion persists despite the fact that some members of
the sign are messy, late for appointments, unconcerned with perfection, and somewhat less than vir-
ginal. Actually the typical Virgo's main goal in life
is to bring order out of chaos and confusion, and
one way he does it is by organizing and classifying
information. Virgo is ruled by Mercury. Like Gemini,
which shares Mercury's rule, Virgo is known for
mental agility and the ability to communicate
thoughts and ideas. However, the Virgo native gener-

ally delves deeper, and is more exacting, discriminating, and critical than his Gemini counterpart.

The astrological sign of Virgo reflects the qualities of the word "virgin" rather than its dictionary definition. In ancient times the word signified *purity of intent*, not chastity. A virgin was a woman who was considered to be whole unto herself—not someone who was without sexual experience. Modern natives of this sign do tend to be modest, shy, and somewhat insecure about love, sex, and romantic involvement. Their calm surface appearance often leads others to classify them as cold and unemotional. However, the exact opposite is probably closer to the truth. Despite the cool outer shell, on the inside Virgo is anything but cold and unfeeling. His emotions run very deep, but he sometimes has great difficulty expressing them. It can take a long time for Virgo to come to terms with his own feelings. Yet once he learns to trust and open up to another person, he makes a caring, steadfast, loyal, and giving lover.

Virgo is the sign of service. Individuals born under its auspices tend to use their skills and talents for the good of others. With the ability to work hard and stick at organized routine, industrious Virgo makes an excellent addition to any business. More at home with facts than abstract theorizing, the responsible, practical Virgo has the ability to see all sides of an issue. However, the virgin has a tendency to vacillate and may have difficulty arriving at concrete conclusions and decisions. Typically detail oriented and conscientious, he often gets so bogged down in the minutiae of a situation that he loses sight of the bigger picture. Although some Virgo natives can be found running major organizations, most function best in subordinate positions.

Since he is usually calm on the outside, the Mercury-ruled individual can fool you into thinking that he is equally relaxed on the inside, but nothing could be further from the truth. The typical Virgo native is a restless bundle of nervous energy, constantly on the lookout for problems that need solving or situations that need improving. Invariably conscientious, practical, and reliable, Virgo needs to feel that the work he does is useful. Because he is such a relentless worker, he generally measures his own successes by how much he can accomplish in a given day. Although he may not be handy like Gemini, and he probably can't service the car, tile the kitchen floor, or repair the leak in the roof, he always knows exactly who to call to get the job done properly.

Most Virgos are health-conscious and extremely fastidious about hygiene and cleanliness. They take good care of their bodies and may look years younger than the age given on their birth certificates. Virgo is acutely aware of the connection between what he eats and how he feels, and is often the first to try a new diet or health regimen. However, in spite of a predisposition to exercise and eat properly, many virgins suffer from acute anxiety with regard to their health and well-being. They worry about food contamination, air pollution, the ozone layer, global warming, the future of the rain forest, and just about anything else they can think of. Some of them are out-and-out hypochondriacs. It is an unusual

Virgo who doesn't live in fear of contracting or developing some dread disease. Because of their deep interest in health and illness, Virgos are often drawn to careers in medicine and other health-related fields.

Most Virgos have a great sense of style and a flair for clothes that can make them trendsetters. It is not unusual for a member of this sign to pursue a career in fashion. Although the average virgin's taste tends to be somewhat conservative, he is always ready to try new ideas when they make sense to him. While his approach to changing fashions may be cautious, Virgo has an innate understanding of what is worth keeping from the past and what needs to be discarded or changed. His wardrobe is generally elegant and well coordinated. His attention to even the smallest detail of style and color only serves to increase his sartorial splendor.

Although you will come upon a lazy Virgo now and again, the typical member of this sign has energy to burn. Fueled by the need for constant activity, he finds the concept of "hanging out and doing nothing" totally foreign to his nature. Virgo makes a great second in command. When you invite him to your home, he usually arrives ready to help and assist you any way he can. If you're cooking dinner, he'll probably offer to chop the vegetables, prepare the salad, set the table. When the meal is over, he will clear the table, stack the dishes, and take out the garbage. Of course the time may come when you begin to feel that your Virgo companion is a bit *too* helpful, especially if he starts reorganizing your cabinets and rewashing your dishes and glassware.

Myths and Symbols Associated with Virgo

The astrological ruler of Virgo is Mercury. The parts of the body ruled by Virgo are the intestines and the sympathetic nervous system. Its symbol, ♍, is thought to represent a maiden carrying a shaft of wheat. The sign is classified as mutable, earth, and feminine (negative, indirect, yin, and internal). Represented by the virgin, Virgo's color is navy blue, its metal is nickel, and its gemstone is the sapphire.

The story most often associated with Virgo is the legend of Astraea, the star maiden, who was the daughter of Zeus (Jupiter) and the Greek Titaness Themis, goddess of law and adviser to the other gods. Astraea was very sweet and beautiful, and she was revered by all as the goddess of truth, justice, innocence, and purity. She lived happily on the earth during the golden age when disease and unhappiness were unknown and the world was a peaceful place in which the gods dwelt among the human inhabitants.

After Pandora's box was opened and all the evils were let loose upon the world, humankind grew increasingly more violent. One by one the gods abandoned this world and retreated to the heavens. Ever patient, kind, and hopeful, Astraea remained on earth, preaching the ways of justice to the people. When the fighting and injustice became too much for the goddess to bear, she too left and went to live with the other gods. Astraea was the very last of the gods to leave the earth, and she took her stalk of wheat with her. When she reached the heavens, she broke it and scattered its grains across the sky, forming the stars. As a reward for her goodness and patience, Zeus placed Astraea among the stars where she was transformed into the constellation Virgo.

Over the centuries there have been those who believe that Astraea will return when earth once again reaches a golden age such as existed before the opening of Pandora's box. During the Renaissance it became commonplace for courtly poets to praise favored patrons and princes claiming guidance from the goddess Astraea. The literary cult of the goddess persisted into the sixteenth century when some writers compared Queen Elizabeth I of England (Sun in Virgo) to the goddess Astraea, and declared that the wise virgin queen would oversee the return of the golden age.

Another version of the Virgo myth relates to the legend of a poor girl named Erigone. Her father was a wine maker who introduced the intoxicating beverage to the people of their village. They had never tasted wine before and they got very drunk, and in their inebriated state they assumed that the wine must be poisonous. The angry villagers murdered the poor man, and buried him in an unknown place. Erigone, accompanied only by her faithful dog Maera, spent countless days searching for her father's grave. She finally found it. When she died, Zeus, king of the gods, honored her devotion by turning her into the constellation Virgo and setting Maera in the skies as the Dog Star.

The constellation Virgo is also associated with the

Greek god of medicine Asklepios (Aesculapius), son of Apollo and the mortal maiden Coronis. Apollo was in love with Coronis, who was carrying his unborn child. One day Apollo received a message from a white raven telling him that Coronis was romantically involved with another mortal, Ischys. Apollo became so enraged that he turned the white raven coal black. Then he decided to punish Coronis for her unfaithfulness by burning her on a funeral pyre. Hermes (Mercury) saved the baby by delivering him on the funeral pyre, then entrusted him to the care of the centaur Chiron, who trained him in the healing arts.

The Virgo Man

Although the typical Virgo man is not the most passionate lover in the zodiac, he's much more susceptible to love and sex than he is willing to admit. As natives of the most idealistic of the earth signs, most Virgos take their love relationships very seriously. However, they tend to feel that their heads should always rule their hearts, and strong emotions make them acutely uncomfortable. Sexually Virgo is earthy and sensuous, but emotionally he can be uptight and puritanical. Because he believes in *forever* and *happily ever after*, he is not apt to be swept away by impulse or desire.

Virgos can be loners. While they crave love and affection, they fear rejection and often hesitate before risking their hearts. The virgin's basic nature, which is intellectual, nervous, tense, and overly critical, makes it difficult for him to relax. The Mercury-ruled Virgo native is into working, thinking, and worrying rather than feeling and enjoying. The pleasures of the senses are all too often shoved aside, overlooked, or put on hold in favor of work and responsibility. Virgo's tendency is to analyze and overcomplicate everything, which means that it's hard for him to respond on a purely physical or emotional level. He needs to learn how to live in the moment and celebrate its joys.

Since he is more concerned with pleasing than being pleased, Virgo can be a wonderful, giving, caring, and thoughtful lover. However, if you hope to win him over, you must first engage his mind, then his heart, and last, but not least, his body. Virgo is no prude, nor is it likely that he is uninterested in love or sex. But he prefers to leave nothing to chance. When he finds himself attracted to someone, instead of immediately following up on his feelings, he may first stop to analyze them. He proceeds to the next step only after he's convinced himself that he is not making a mistake. While the Virgo man may not be a good bet for a brief, wild, passionate affair, once committed to an ongoing relationship he will do everything he can to please and accommodate his lover.

Virgo often obsesses over minor problems. On occasion he may act like a faultfinding, critical, sanctimonious prig. However, your Virgo lover turns into Mr. Wonderful when he senses that his help is needed. If you are sick, he will take care of you. When you need a favor, he willingly goes out of his way to see that it gets done. Just remember that his

132 *Sydney Omarr's Astrology, Love, Sex, and You*

fragile ego is easily crushed. Virgo's insecurity and tendency toward low self-esteem make him intensely jealous. In return for his kindness, love, and fidelity, he demands your absolute loyalty and total devotion.

Virgo truly enjoys work. Although he may secretly seek the approval of others, and he certainly appreciates the value and importance of financial rewards, nothing actually pleases Virgo quite as much as a job well done. He aims for precision. He feels happiest and most fulfilled when he's sure he has dotted all the "i's" and crossed all the "t's". Members of this sign don't do things by halves, and they tend to be extremely critical of their own labors as well as everyone else's. Shortcuts and shoddy work are just not acceptable in the virgin's world. The Mercury-ruled Virgo native strives to do things correctly the first time. If he is not entirely pleased with the results, he may chuck it all and start over.

This man takes his time when making a decision. No matter if it affects the future course of his life or only the next few moments, he is careful, painstaking, and critical in his judgment. In a world where many things are based on superficial values, Virgo explores every nuance, penetrates every secret, and uncovers every fault. Depending on the circumstances, Virgo's thoroughness can be either a blessing or a curse. In business, the Virgo caution, careful preparation, and good planning often lead to success over the long haul. However, in personal matters and work involving the creative process, inspiration and intuition often prove to be more beneficial than Virgo's extensive analysis.

Virgo's nature is kind and caring. He loves animals and children, especially when they are well trained and do not make a mess around the house. Although he sees himself as practical and pragmatic, he is actually more of an idealist than he realizes. The typical virgin is not extravagant by nature, has little sympathy for shirkers, and will probably tell you that he believes, "God helps those who help themselves." However he's a soft touch for a sob story. Unscrupulous types have been known to take advantage of him. Natives of this sign often join groups that promote animal rights, patients' rights, vegetarianism, clean air, clean water, and world peace. Whatever the cause, if he decides that its aim is just he will readily volunteer his money, time, and energy in an effort to help make the world over into his personal vision of a safer, more perfect place.

The typical Virgo is blessed with a quick wit and a wonderful sense of humor. Although his clever quips may be biting, they are rarely malicious. However, he's inclined to take himself too seriously. He may jest about his own flaws, but he does not take kindly to witticisms aimed at him by others. Like Leo, the sign that precedes it in the zodiac, Virgo is extremely proud. He places a great deal of importance on the good opinion of others, and absolutely dreads the thought that he might appear foolish or ridiculous. Because he is clever, articulate, and prone to hold a grudge, Virgo can react in a very spiteful manner if his feelings have been hurt. He expects his relatives, friends, coworkers, and acquaintances to behave with proper decorum in public. If you have a bone to pick with Virgo, it's best to not mention it until you are alone with him.

The Virgo Woman

If your impression of Virgo is that of a pure and innocent maiden, you are in for a surprise. The typical Virgo female is no angel. Although she may be shy, this woman is tough. When she's in love, she is seldom willing to settle for less than the real thing. In spite of her practicality, Virgo can be profoundly romantic. It is her purity of heart that impels her to seek the perfect mate. She waits for her knight in shining armor to come and sweep her off her feet. If she doesn't find perfection the first time around, she's perfectly capable of leaving in order to continue her search elsewhere. A disappointed Virgo wife will rarely stoop to cheating or sneaking around. But if she deems it necessary, she will put an end to an unhappy situation.

Although she herself is not superficial, where others are concerned the Virgo female can be quite superficial in her judgments. She has a tendency to disregard anyone who appears the least bit disheveled or unpolished. Because she judges potential lovers at face value, the Virgo woman may lose out on an opportunity to meet someone really terrific. In her quest for the partner who offers her the best chance of perfection, Virgo simply can't imagine getting involved with anyone who is uncultured, unrefined, or willing to appear in public looking less than his best. More Virgo women are unmarried than females of any other sign of the zodiac. This is because the virgin often prefers spinsterhood to the prospect of being in a relationship that does not live up to her high expectations.

The Virgo mother strives to be a model parent, and she begins by taking an active part in her child's life even before it is born. The virgin reads all the latest books on the ins and outs of prenatal and postnatal health, and only her doctor knows more about birth and pregnancy than she does. She prepares everything she will need for her baby well in advance. By the time the little tike arrives, the nursery is ready and so is the mom. As the baby grows, she takes care to see that the child is given every possible advantage. The health-conscious Virgo woman makes sure that her kids eat balanced meals and take their vitamins. Sometimes she may go too far. If she tries to impose her own Virgo eating habits on her non-Virgo progeny, she could end up with a minor rebellion on her hands.

At home and at the office, the typical virgin is a model of hard work and efficiency. She rarely makes mistakes, and when she does she catches them quickly. She also has a knack for catching other people's errors, and she doesn't hesitate to point them out. Even the boss is not immune from her criticism and assumption that his mistakes, like everyone else's, should be uncovered and corrected immediately. In business the virgin may step on a lot of toes. She is not likely to be awed by positions or titles, and perfection is the only thing she considers important. Virgo is no clock-watcher. When she is in the middle of something, she doesn't drop it and run out the door at five o'clock. She's totally dedicated to the task at hand, and willingly stays overtime whenever she feels it's necessary. She shines in any type of work that requires careful analysis and strict attention to detail. Virgos are often drawn to positions in scientific research, quality control, bookkeeping, accounting, publishing, pharmacy, and medicine.

Virgos like money. However, most natives of this sign don't view wealth as a status symbol, and are not into accumulating money for its own sake. Although they like nice things, they do not value the dollar for its purchasing power alone. Typically Virgo is deathly afraid of poverty. More than anything else, the Virgo woman is frightened by the idea that she may someday have to depend upon others to support or care for her. She will go to virtually any lengths to see that it never happens. Her goal is financial security, and she won't relax until she achieves it. Of course, no matter how much money she has, she never *feels* totally secure financially.

The Virgo woman is a loving though critical wife, responsible parent, dutiful daughter, dependable friend, and indispensable employee. Above all, she feels the need to be of service to others. She is not totally happy unless she is helping someone who desperately needs her help. In a world where many people are selfish and self-centered, she is one person who can always be counted on to come to your aid. Unfortunately, not everyone is as honest and caring as Virgo, and it is not unusual for others to try to impose on her good nature. Unless she learns when and how to draw the line, she may wake up one day to find that she and her family have been severely taken advantage of by someone who came to her for assistance.

Virgo women are among the best-looking in the zodiac. Most take excellent care of their bodies, are meticulous in their grooming, and look much younger than their years. However, Virgo doesn't especially care to be noticed or loved for her good looks. Like members of Gemini, the other Mercury-ruled sign, virgins would much rather be appreciated for their quick minds and scintillating wit. Because she's very much her own person, this lady sometimes projects an air of detachment, and her apparent aloofness may be misconstrued by some as coldness. Although her surface demeanor is reserved and undemonstrative, deep down she is warm and caring. In public situations she conducts herself like a lady, and keeps her emotions under control. However, in private moments with the right partner, the Virgo woman can be as warm, loving, and sensual as any member of the zodiacal family.

The Shadow Side of Virgo

Virgo's inclination is to judge everything against his own ideal of perfection, and it is very hard for him to accept life on its own terms. Virgins are among the most giving, caring, and helpful members of the zodiac. However, their help often comes with a price tag. The darker side of the sign manifests most often when Virgo begins to regard himself as someone who is here on a mission to resolve all the problems and clean up all the imperfections of the world. Yes, he will help you if you ask him—and even if you don't—but he will also fuss over you, criticize your actions, and meddle in your business. Moreover, he will expect you to do whatever he suggests and follow his advice to the letter (After all, how else can you get everything *exactly right*?). Before you are finished, you may be very sorry you agreed to accept his help or his advice.

Many of the elements that constitute the shadow side of Virgo relate to extremes of the typical Virgo virtues. Intelligent, balanced criticism turns into carping and nagging. Modesty and restraint become old-maidish fastidiousness. Normal concerns for health, safety, and fitness give way to obsessive behavior and hypochondria. Careful attention to detail is replaced by punctilious overspecialization. The ability to see and understand all sides of a question is overtaken by equivocation and indecision. The inclination to seek knowledge and to probe the depths of a subject or idea gives rise to a know-it-all attitude. Candor becomes an excuse for tactless remarks. The desire to always do the right thing is expressed as pompous self-righteousness.

The negative Virgo personality is inclined to look on the dark side of every issue. Typically Virgo is hardest on himself. His propensity toward fear, worry, and self-doubt can be extremely stressful. Apprehension and insecurity can lead to nervous complaints that manifest as internal disorders such as ulcers and digestive problems. Unfortunately, the virgin's propensity to worry about his health and safety can turn into self-fulfilling prophecy because negative energies and beliefs have a way of creating negative consequences.

Many members of this sign are health-conscious in the extreme, fixated on personal fitness, diet, and hygiene. However, there is the occasional Virgo who is messy and seemingly unconcerned about health or diet. On the surface this sloppy Virgo native appears to be nonchalant with regard to most sanitary conditions. If you probe a little deeper you will find that although he may be messy, this Virgo is exceptionally clean, and as worried about germs and disease as any other virgin. A Virgo of this type is often so afraid of illness that he buries his head in the sand, and absolutely refuses to consider the possibility that he might become ill. If he does get sick, he may refuse to consult a doctor. In the event that he decides to seek medical attention, he may ignore the doctor's advice and not take the prescribed medication (sometimes with disastrous results). Closing his mind to the possibility of disease and illness is this type of Virgo's attempt at coping with his deepest fears and anxieties. Instead of being obsessed with health and fitness, he becomes obsessed with the idea of avoiding any thought or discussion of illness, disease, or death.

The Virgo lover may be loyal and devoted, but his inclination toward low self-esteem can make him extremely jealous. He often shoots himself in the foot by creating a crisis where none exists, or allowing himself second thoughts about everything he does and says. With a partner who is so insecure about things, his significant other may begin to wonder if their relationship is really worth all the doubts and problems that it engenders.

Virgo Romantic Dinner for Two

Virgo the cook

The Virgo native associates cooking with good health and a comfortable life. He thoroughly enjoys preparing meals for friends and family. A start-from-scratch cook, the virgin favors homemade dishes, fresh vegetables and herbs, and healthful, wholesome ingredients. Virgo's kitchen, like that of his Gemini counterpart, is usually filled with the latest laborsaving gadgets. But you won't often find the Virgo chef using prepared mixes or frozen, freeze-dried, or pre-packaged foods.

Typically meticulous in planning and execution, Virgo wants each meal to be perfect, and will take great pains to see that it is. The practical, earthy virgin is not overly extravagant. Unlike Taurus or Leo, Virgo doesn't automatically choose the most expensive foods available. However, everything he serves is sure to be of the very best quality. His kitchen is clean and orderly. Virgo's approach to cooking is the same as to everything else in his life. He is fastidious, measures all ingredients with care and precision, and follows new recipes with exactitude.

When Virgo cooks for you, be sure you arrive on

time because the virgin abhors tardiness. However, it might be a good idea to stop for a snack on your way to Virgo's house. Although the virgin expects you to arrive on time, his dinner is usually late. Virgo will spend as long as necessary getting everything just right, even if it means that hungry guests are sometimes kept waiting. No matter, the final result will invariably be a culinary treat definitely worth waiting for. The presentation of the meal will be spectacular, with the centerpiece, table linens, dishes, silverware, and glassware gleaming and as close to perfection as possible. The dinner itself will be positively delicious.

Virgo the dinner guest

When Virgo comes to your home for dinner, it is best not to invite him to join you in the kitchen while you prepare the meal. Either he will discover something on the menu he is sure won't agree with his "delicate constitution," or he will try to tell you a better way to prepare the entire meal. If you want to spend a pleasant evening with your fussy Virgo guest, remember that the less he knows about what is going on in your kitchen, the better it will be for all concerned.

In spite of their cautious natures, Virgos are usually open to new ideas about food and nutrition. In the virgin's eyes, presentation is as important as flavor. If you want Virgo to truly enjoy his meal, it must look as good as it tastes. Virgos like to eat, and enjoy sampling different types of exotic dishes.

However, to be safe you should stick to seasonings and flavors that are interesting yet not too wild or outrageous.

Most virgins dislike heavy dinners, preferring lighter meals and smaller portions or even just nibbling throughout the day. Always be sure to check with your Virgo guest before planning your dinner menu because many Virgos are either vegetarians or followers of specialized diets. Members of this sign tend to be food faddists. It is not unusual for Virgo to suddenly switch from an ordinary diet to a special health regimen such as a microbiotic or macrobiotic diet. One day he may announce he has given up dairy products, and the next he swears off red meat, wheat, corn, and refined sugar.

Shy yet intensely sociable, the typical Virgo native likes people, and is a witty conversationalist. At dinner he may show more interest in the company than in the food. This doesn't mean he is not enjoying his meal. It is just that most Virgos, like their Mercury-ruled cousin Gemini, would simply rather talk than eat.

Foods commonly associated with Virgo

Meat: beef tongue, venison, hare
Fowl: game birds
Fish and Shellfish: mullet
Dairy Products: none
Vegetables and Beans: broccoli, beans, cauliflower, celery, mushrooms, parsnips, turnips

Nuts and Grains: pistachios, hazelnuts, pecans, walnuts, wheat, oats, all whole grains
Fruits: apricots, pomegranates, mulberries
Beverages: herbal tea, tea
Herbs, Spices, and Miscellaneous: herbs in general, aniseed, caraway, dill, lavender, fennel, licorice, marjoram, parsley, bread, rolls, pastries

VIRGO MENU

*Virgin Mary

*Roast Beef, Avocado, and Goat Cheese Salad

*Marge's Irish Soda Bread

Rosé Wine

*Apricot Fool

Herbal Tea

*Virgo Recipes

*Virgin Mary

16 ounces tomato juice, chilled
 2 tablespoons lemon juice
 1 teaspoon Worcestershire sauce
¼ teaspoon of celery salt
    dash of hot pepper sauce
¼ teaspoon grated horseradish (optional)
 2 celery stalks

In a pitcher stir together tomato juice, lemon juice, Worcestershire sauce, celery salt, hot pepper sauce, and horseradish. Serve in a tall glass over ice. Garnish each glass with a celery stalk.

Roast Beef, Avocado, and Goat Cheese Salad

    6 ounces mixed salad greens
    1 large avocado, ripe
    8 ounces rare roast beef, sliced
    ⅓ cup sunflower seed kernels, roasted and salted
    ½ cup crumbled goat cheese
    ¼ cup olive oil
    2 tablespoons balsamic vinegar
       salt
       pepper
       garlic powder

Wash and dry the salad greens, and tear into small pieces. Place the greens in the bottom of a large serving bowl. Pit and peel the avocado, and cut into chunks. Shred the roast beef into small pieces. Put the avocado chunks, roast beef, sunflower seeds, and goat cheese into the bowl with the salad greens. Prepare the balsamic vinaigrette dressing in a small bowl. Combine the olive oil, balsamic vinegar, salt, pepper, and garlic powder. Whisk together or mix with a fork. Pour the dressing over the salad and toss. Serve immediately.

*Marge's Irish Soda Bread

- 3 cups all-purpose flour
- 5 teaspoons baking powder
- ½ teaspoon salt
- 2 tablespoons sugar
- 1 tablespoon caraway seeds
- 2 eggs
- ¾ cup milk
- 1 cup raisins, rinsed in warm water

Preheat the oven to 375 degrees. Lightly grease and flour two round baking pans. Place the flour, baking powder, salt, sugar, and caraway seeds in a large bowl and mix together with a wooden spoon. Beat the eggs and milk with a fork, and add to the dry ingredients. Drain the raisins, add them to the dough, and knead lightly. Separate the dough into two balls. Dust the top of each ball with flour. Shape each ball into a round loaf and slash a cross on the top (to keep the bread from bursting during baking). Bake in prepared pans for 45 minutes, or until bread is lightly browned and a toothpick inserted in the center comes out clean. Cool on a rack.

*Apricot Fool

- ½ cup dried apricots
- 3 tablespoons orange juice
- 2 tablespoons apricot jam
- ½ cup heavy cream, chille
- 1 tablespoon sugar

Place the apricots in a small saucepan and cover with cold water. Bring to a boil and simmer for ten minutes. Drain, but reserve the liquid. Puree the apricots, orange juice, and jam in a food processor or blender. Add enough of the reserved cooking liquid to make a thick puree. Beat the cream and sugar in a chilled bowl until the mixture forms stiff peaks. Fold in the fruit puree. Spoon the fool into individual glass serving dishes and chill for at least one hour before serving.

♎ Libra ♎

Symbol: The Scales   Element: Air
Quality: Cardinal   Planetary Ruler: Venus
Polarity: Masculine

> Who would give a law to lovers?
> Love is unto itself a higher law.
>
> —Boethius
> *The Consolation of Philosophy*

How to Identify Libra

The typical individual born under the sign of the
scales is refined, with excellent taste, delicate sensibil-
ities, and an innate dislike of things or people that
are boorish, crude, or vulgar. Libra is a cardinal sign,
so its natives are initiators of action and activity. Unlike those born under the other cardinal signs (Aries,
Cancer, and Capricorn), Librans would rather not
work alone and usually seek the partnership and cooperation of others. Since Libra is an air sign, many
of its members are drawn to literature, mathematics,
science, and the study of human relations. Libra's
ruler, Venus, bestows a love of beauty, music, and
art.

Libra is the sign of paradox. Those born under the

147

scales generally have several distinctly different aspects to their personalities. As the prime diplomat of the zodiac, Libra is like the gentle dove of peace spreading a message of love, balance, and harmony. Naturally inclined toward collaboration and teamwork, the Venus-ruled Libran often bends over backward to avoid controversy and conflict. However, any depiction of Libra solely as a statesman and mediator imparts only a portion of the truth. Remember, Libra is the sign ruled by the scales, and scales are not always in perfect balance—they dip back and forth. Like the scales, Librans have their ups and downs. When Libras are down, they can be as sulky, bad-tempered, and quarrelsome as any Aries.

Libra is sometimes referred to as "the iron hand in the velvet glove." Beneath the smiling face there lies a steely will. Libras may be amiable and agreeable, but they are not pushovers. Typically these Venus-ruled natives won't do anything they don't want to do. Although he may have difficulty making up his mind, once Libra decides what it is that he really wants, he knows exactly how to go about getting it. Intelligent, clever, charming, and usually good-looking, the typical Venus-ruled Libran can get around just about anyone, and get away with almost anything. He knows how to get others to do his bidding, and he is not above using his considerable charm and diplomatic skills for his own benefit.

More than anything Libra needs love and companionship. Most individuals born under the sign of the scales are not truly happy without a partner. Scales enjoy group participation. Even those rare Librans who are athletically inclined often shun individual activities in favor of team sports. Sociable Libra can get along with almost anyone he meets, but tends to gravitate toward those who share his cultured interests and refined tastes. If you are searching for a Libra lover, you are much more likely to find him at an art gallery or concert than at a wrestling match.

In a working environment Libra seeks balance and harmony, and has a special knack for bringing people together and synthesizing the many parts into a comprehensive whole. Cooperation is one of Libra's assets, persuasion is another. Although it goes without saying that those born under the scales of justice make excellent lawyers, judges, diplomats, and statesmen, they also excel as teachers, psychological counselors, artists, musicians, writers, interior designers, architects, fashion consultants, feng shui practitioners, hairdressers, makeup artists, publicists, and advertising executives. Libra is sure to succeed in any career that allows him to combine his love of beauty with his sense of fair play and desire to please.

The Libran abode is invariably a lovely place, luxuriously furnished with a variety of art objects and other beautiful things. Libras, among the great hosts of the zodiac, love to entertain. They seek to fill their homes with music, laughter, and the scintillating conversation of interesting, intelligent people. The Venusian native is usually an excellent cook who knows how to set a romantic mood and complement it with fresh flowers and a colorful, attractive table. His signature dinner party is generally a candlelit affair with music playing softly in the background.

Libran natives are extraordinarily romantic. Some actually seem to prefer the courtly rituals of love and romance to the unbridled passion of earthy sexual encounters. "Love" is the all-important keyword for these members of the zodiac sign who tend to think in pairs. Many an airy Libra has been accused of being more in love with the *idea* of love than with the actual person who serves as the object of his affection. The typical native of this Venus-ruled sign just doesn't feel complete without a partner. When happily involved with someone, the scales' conversation is invariably peppered with terms such as *we*, *us*, and *our*.

In a committed union, Libra is a model mate who does not forget birthdays, anniversaries, or other special dates. Libra has a knack for doing the right thing at the right time. No other lover knows how to make you feel more adored. Venus-ruled individuals like to be admired by others. Libras enjoy flirting, but are rarely found entangled in messy extramarital affairs. Unfortunately, Librans tend to fall *out* of love almost as easily as they fall *in* love. Since airy Libra responds more easily to ideas or ideals than to feelings, when the scales' partner no longer fits his idealized version of a lover, the romance may fade. When romance fades, Libra has a way of disappearing. Suddenly a love affair or marriage that appeared to be happy and solid becomes a thing of the past. To an outsider Libra's termination of the alliance may appear to be rather sudden and superficial.

Myths and Symbols Associated with Libra

The astrological ruler of Libra is Venus. The parts of the body ruled by Libra are the kidneys and lower back. Its symbol, ♎, is thought to represent a pair of scales. The sign is classified as cardinal, air, and masculine (positive, direct, yang, and external). Represented by the scales, Libra's color is indigo blue, its metal is copper, and its gemstone is the opal.

Libra is the only constellation of the zodiac represented by an inanimate object—the scales. The Romans believed that the sign of the scales symbolized the autumn equinox because it divided and balanced the two halves of the year. However, there is an earlier association of the scales with Libra that has been passed down from ancient Babylon. The scales and Libra were connected in the Babylonian myth of the last judgment and the weighing of the souls.

The scales figure prominently in the Egyptian *Book of the Dead*, playing a large part in the story of the soul's passage from this life to the next. Anubis, the jackal-headed god, and his brother Apu-at, the opener of the ways, watched over the two roads that led to the Underworld. Anubis used the scales to weigh the souls of those who had died, and to judge their value based on what they had done on earth. The judgment ceremony took place in the Hall of Double Justice in front of an assembly of Egypt's gods and goddesses. Anubis weighed the dead person's heart on one side of the scale, balancing it against a feather representing *truth*. The gathering was presided over by Osiris, ruler of the Underworld, and the ibis-headed moon god Thoth, who faithfully recorded the results. If the deceased was found worthy, he was admitted to eternal life in the kingdom of Osiris. If not, his heart was consumed by a beast known as the Devourer.

Although there is no single Greek myth or tale specifically associated with the astrological Libra, the sign's alliance with the idea of justice and balance probably relates to the Greek Titaness Themis, goddess of order, law, oaths, and justice, and adviser to the other gods. Usually depicted as blindfolded, Themis carries the scales of justice in one hand and a sword in the other. Almost always draped in flowing robes, she symbolizes fair and equal administration of the law without corruption, avarice, prejudice, or favor. The daughter of Uranus (Heaven) and Gaia (Earth), Themis was Zeus' (Jupiter) second consort, and remained as his constant companion on Mount Olympus even after his purge of the old pantheon. She sat by Zeus' side and helped him deal with ceremonial matters and judgments concerning law and order. One of the daughters of Zeus and Themis was Astraea, the star maiden, who was also known as a goddess of justice.

The ruler of Libra (and Taurus) is Venus, named for the Roman goddess of love. Venus is known as "the morning and evening star" because it can only be seen shortly before sunset or just before dawn. Libra is considered the masculine or day aspect of

Venus, while Taurus is the feminine or night aspect of the planet.

The Greeks associated Venus with Aphrodite, their goddess of love. Venus was unhappily married to the blacksmith god Hephaestus (Vulcan), and she was less than faithful to her homely husband. Numbered among her many lovers were Aries (Mars), Dionysus (Bacchus), Hermes (Mercury), and Adonis, who was so handsome that Aphrodite hid him in a chest that she entrusted to Persephone. When Persephone beheld Adonis' beauty, she refused to give him back to Aphrodite, and the case had to be tried before the court of Zeus. Zeus divided the year into three parts: Adonis would stay by himself for part of the year, spend part with Persephone and part with Aphrodite.

The Libra Man

No one is more willing to compromise and cooperate than Libra. Although he loves to debate and discuss things, Libra hates to quarrel and will rarely be caught displaying anger in an overt fashion. Since the Venus-ruled native has amazing powers of persuasion and an uncanny knack for understanding all sides of an issue, he doesn't need to resort to yelling and screaming in an attempt to win an argument. Instead he employs more subtle means of communication to help him make his point. He may not have Gemini's glibness or Scorpio's hypnotic magnetism, but the Libra man is charm personified. He knows how to use all of his diplomacy and charisma to get you to see things his way.

Although the popular image of Libra as lazy is a blatant exaggeration, it is true that in his leisure time he seems to have less energy than most other signs. The fitness craze appears to have bypassed many Librans, who would much rather visit with friends than go out and run a marathon. The sociable Venus-ruled male likes to be with people, and typically will follow an exercise schedule only if he can do it in the company of others. Although he may agree to join his mate or partner in a fitness program at the neighborhood gym, if left to his own devices he would rather go to a movie or stay at home and read a good book. Even though Libras are not lazy per se, they do tend to work in spurts, and will often follow a period of intense activity with one of unqualified rest and relaxation.

Even in old age most Librans consider love and companionship to be of paramount importance in their lives. An eighty-five-year-old Libra man who recently lost his wife (they were married for more than fifty years) can talk of nothing else. Although he cares deeply for his children and grandchildren, without his lifelong companion at his side he's lost his zest for living. Some elderly Venus-ruled males are so lonely and desperate to be part of a couple again that they fall for the first available female they meet. This can lead to a very bad situation, especially if Libra is wealthy and the chosen one turns out to be a fortune hunter.

Libra's desire for beauty and luxury impels him to

seek only the best. He is always on the lookout for ways to improve his life by making it more graceful and harmonious. In some ways Libra can be as much a perfectionist as Virgo. Whether searching for the perfect partner or just the right decorating touch, he takes his time and weighs all the options before coming to a decision. He naturally gravitates toward others who share his love of beauty, art, and music, and who don't demand immediate and decisive answers to all their questions.

Money is usually not a prime concern for these airy natives. Many Librans are incredibly naive about financial matters. The Libra man considers good taste to be much more important than the prospect of a balanced budget. Where his bank account is concerned, he is often extravagant and unrealistic. Credit card companies love those born under the scales. A typical Libra will charge anything because lack of ready cash is no reason to show up at a party in a tacky outfit, and a cheap gift is looked upon as worse than no gift at all.

Libra strives to keep in touch with all his acquaintances, and generally puts a lot of effort into maintaining good relationships with friends and family. Libra's home is likely to be a hub of social activities, and the Venus-ruled native rarely runs out of novel ideas for great parties or cozy little get-togethers. Librans throw the best parties because they know lots of people, and their expertise at mixing and matching individuals makes for some of the liveliest, most interesting conversation on the planet. Although the typical Libra-inspired gathering may come off as informal and spontaneous, a good deal of serious planning usually goes into making every detail of the festivities as perfect as possible.

Children are part and parcel of Libra's ideal of a happy marriage. As a father the Libra male is typically loving, affectionate, fair, and equitable. It is unlikely that you will find a number of untrained and unruly kids running around Libra's harmonious abode. One way or another the scales will find a way to incorporate his kids' needs into his own life with a minimum of disruption and discord. As a member of an air sign, Daddy Libra is keen to read to his children, and teach them to share his love of art and music. However, since kids cannot be counted on to always behave as their parents would prefer, when unexpected things happen to upset Libra's carefully crafted routine, he is easily upset and thrown off balance. When this happens, the scales may well hand the children off to his mate or the baby-sitter and take off for calmer surroundings.

As a lover the Libra male is patient and caring. Courtship is his forte, and he will generally go the whole nine yards in order to provide a satisfying romantic and sexual experience for his partner. He hates to hurt anyone's feelings, and is unusually generous with flattery and compliments. Libra also likes to be on the receiving end of compliments and flattering remarks. If you want to make points with him, make sure to respond in kind. Librans, like the natives of other air signs (Gemini and Aquarius), typically feel more through thoughts than emotions. Any successful relationship with the scales requires that you strike a delicate balance of body, heart, mind, and spirit.

The Libra Woman

Venus-ruled females are among the loveliest in the zodiac. The typical Libra woman comes across as the embodiment of feminine elegance. Always agreeable and charming, this graceful lady is sure to be noticed and admired wherever she goes. With all that sweetness and warmth, it is easy to forget that her sign, Libra, is *masculine* in nature. The sweet-natured and amiable Libran woman is an interesting mixture of masculine strength and feminine sensitivity, and not nearly as easygoing as she appears. While the scales may have a hard time coming right out with a definite "yes" or "no" answer, Libra is a smart cookie who rarely does anything she doesn't want to do. As the personification of that old saw about catching more flies with honey than with vinegar, she invariably knows the best way to get others to do her bidding—while still allowing them to think that everything they do is their own idea.

Because she has a deep aversion to anything unattractive, the female Libran is frequently accused of being vain or shallow. While the personification of Libra as narcissistic is unfair, it is not entirely incorrect. Most Venus-ruled ladies have a tendency toward self-indulgence. They love to surround themselves with beautiful things and beautiful people. Libra women are fastidious. They prefer to avoid anything and anyone ugly, crude, or vulgar. Libra lives to be admired. She is sometimes called fickle because she has a tendency to test her powers of attraction on every good-looking man she meets.

Libra generally makes an excellent wife and mother. Because of her feelings about romantic love, she tends to put her spouse before all else, and her children can sometimes feel shortchanged. It's not that the Venus-ruled don't love their kids, it's just that they have a tendency to revolve their lives around their partner's needs and desires. Actually the Libra female is the type of mother who (like her airy sisters Gemini and Aquarius) knows how to engage her children's minds and keep them entertained. She takes them to museums, art galleries, movies, and the theater. She teaches them to love books and music. It's a rare child of a Libra mother who doesn't grow up learning how to do arts and crafts or play a musical instrument. Her children tend to be proud of their lovely Libra mom, and they will usually try to emulate her creativity and social graces.

No matter how much Libra loves her home, her family, and her social life, she generally requires a more viable outlet for her executive abilities. Stay-at-home Libra wives and mothers tend to become bored and disenchanted without a job or creative project to keep them on their toes. Libra's cardinal qualities mean that members of this sign are highly motivated, ambitious self-starters who possess what it takes to succeed in many different types of endeavors. In business Libra has the gentle touch and the ability to convey a message or build a relationship. The typical member of this sign is people oriented with a wonderful way of relating to everyone on an individual basis. Harmony and companionship in the workplace are a necessity for the scales to do her best work. Libra is a team player. When she is on her own for extended periods of time, she may lose interest in what she is doing and become downcast or discontented.

Librans have a strong sense of justice. They do everything they can to see that the fair play they seek for themselves is enjoyed by all. When family problems arise, Libra prefers to resolve them through discussion and will go to almost any lengths to avoid a head-on confrontation. The Venus-ruled female wants to look good to the world. She worries about what the neighbors think, and has a tendency to try and keep a lid on her troubles rather than dealing with them directly.

As the seventh sign of the zodiac, Libra is the first one to focus on the interaction among individuals. The first six signs concentrate on personal development, the remaining six represent turning outward toward other people. Librans like to put their minds to good use. Like Aquarians, Librans enjoy communicating and exchanging thoughts and ideas with others. However, Aquarius is mainly concerned with abstract ideas. The scales' main purpose is to get to know *people* better. Like Gemini, Libra wants to pick your brain. Unlike Gemini, she is not as interested in finding out what you *know* as she is in discovering *who* you are. Typically she will use what she learns about you to improve your relationship with her and make it more harmonious. However, under certain circumstances she may use her knowledge of how you think to gently but firmly persuade you to see things her way.

The Venus-ruled woman believes in giving her all for love. She's usually not happy unless she is involved in a permanent relationship. Libra's sensitivity and romanticism make her extremely vulnerable in intimate relationships. If she is let down by her lover, she can become seriously distressed. Disloyalty or disaffection upsets her emotional equilibrium, and can cause her normally loving nature to turn bitter and resentful. Because the Libran female looks to her spouse or partner to give meaning to her life, when hurt or abandoned she naturally feels as if the meaning has gone from her existence. When Libra marries and says, "For better, or worse," she really means it. Consequently those born under the scales usually have a greater tolerance for putting up with problem partners than do the members of most of the other zodiacal signs.

The Shadow Side of Libra

Characteristically Libra wants to be all things to all people. The question Libra needs to ask himself is: "Can I be all things to all people, and still be true to myself?" In *Power Astrology*, author Robin Mac-Naughton states, "Powerful people are directed from within. They trust their own intuition and they rely on their own judgment." Libra's shadow side emerges most often when, through indecision or the desire to please, he consigns his power over to others. In his need to please everyone else, Libra often forgets to please himself. When the craving for love and approval gets to the point where Libra becomes more concerned about what other people think than about what he feels, it is easy for him to fall into a pattern of *reacting* to outside pressure rather than *acting* on his own initiative. If this happens, Libra may flounder around like a rudderless ship. His motor is running, but he really isn't going anywhere.

It certainly is no secret that indecision is the major bugaboo of this sign. In a search for harmony and perfection, Libra splits hairs, hems and haws, and finds it extremely difficult to form a policy, fix a viewpoint, or chart a direction. The Libra native has the ability to see all sides of every issue, but this tendency does not always serve him well either in business or in personal matters. The paralyzing effect of indecision often causes the Libran to miss out on many of life's best opportunities. He is so intent on weighing each side of an issue that he finds it virtually impossible to come to a single concrete conclusion.

Another side of the Libran shadow is that which Liz Greene in *Astrology for Lovers* terms, "the Coy Maiden syndrome." In this case Libra is so intent on getting love and approval that he or she turns all relationships into competitions in which the object is to get the other person to fall in love with him or her. In this situation the Venus-ruled native uses all his or her charm to make the victim feel like the one and only, but the declarations of love are actually nothing more than a seductive ploy with no real feeling behind it. Once the prey is caught in the trap, attentiveness quickly fades and Libra takes off in search of a new pigeon.

Another manifestation of this sign's shadow comes from Libra's ability to play one person off against another, and use his seductive charm to manipulate his many admirers. Libra hates being alone. In his search for companionship he may stir up a false sense of competition among prospective partners. The Libra individual innately understands how much attention and admiration to give each person in order to win him or her over. He also knows how to drop certain subtle hints that will make it seem as if the Venus-ruled native is the only one who can be relied upon or trusted. Although it may start innocently enough, if carried too far this little game can lead to bad blood between friends, family members, and even business associates.

Worst of all the Libra shadows is the inclination to suppress hurt, anger, and disappointment in order to avert battles and confrontations. Librans willingly put up with a lot of guff because they hate to rock the boat or disturb the status quo. By pulling his punches and avoiding direct confrontation, the typical Libran manages to maintain his sense of balance and harmony. However, he often pays a very high price for the peace he so avidly seeks. He may not *act* on his negative feelings, but neither does he release them. He pushes them down and tries not to think about them, and there they stay until they grow into full-fledged obsessions. After awhile the negative feelings may resurface as a strong sense of anxiety and discontent, the source of which is no longer identifiable.

Libra Romantic Dinner for Two

Libra the cook

Librans are fond of good food, fine wine, and convivial company. The majority of those born under the sign of the scales love to cook and entertain. Although your Libra host may appear to be in a super-relaxed mode when you arrive, he is probably just replenishing his energy for the evening ahead. The scales has probably spent much of the day in spurts of frenzied activity in an all-out out effort to make sure everything on the table appeals to the eye as well as the palate. The Venus-ruled individual is an imaginative perfectionist who enjoys experimenting with the various colors, flavors, and textures of each dish. When you're invited to Libra's home for a meal, you can be sure everything on the menu has been carefully thought out and planned well in advance.

The Venus-ruled native generally chooses ingredients that are fresh and natural. The herbs may come from the scales' own garden, the bread and pastries will be homemade, and the meats, fish, vegetables, and fruits used in each dish are sure to be fresh rather than frozen. However much airy Libra loves to plan and cook the meal, he resents the drudgery of the preparation and cleanup. His kitchen is generally well organized, replete with expensive cooking utensils and laborsaving gadgets and devices. To the Libra cook, presentation is as important as taste. The setting and appearance of the food must be equally impeccable. Subtlety and variety are the keywords that apply to most of the foods prepared by the scales. Libra's touch is delicate, and he usually shuns anything coarse or heavy. Librans seek balance when they cook, so no one flavor or theme is allowed to dominate the overall presentation.

Libra the dinner guest

Typically Librans are not heavy eaters, unlike the Venus-ruled Taurus. But Librans do love to sit down to a good meal, especially in the company of others. Appearance is paramount to Libra. The scales usually consider pleasant settings and congenial conversation to be as important, or more important, than the actual food served. When you invite the scales to dinner, think in terms of symmetrical, harmonious surroundings. The dining area should be tastefully lit, the table beautifully appointed and set with your very best dinnerware. Fresh flowers and soft, romantic music, or a small fountain playing in the background, will serve to further enhance your meal and enchant your romantic Libran guest.

The food you serve the scales should be relatively light, pleasantly presented, and easy to digest. To Libra, food is a work of art and a feast for the eyes as well as the stomach. Most members of the sign would rather leave the table a little hungry than feel stuffed and bloated. They tend to think of themselves as connoisseurs of food and wine. They can be a bit snobbish about what they eat, also where and with whom. Given a choice of restaurants, the typical Libran prefers elegant establishments that serve haute cuisine, continental dishes, and imported delicacies. The Venus-ruled are famous for their love of sweets, and all candies, cakes, and other confectioneries come under this sign.

To Libra, good taste implies a lot more than flavorful food. It is important for him to dine in a relaxing atmosphere. When the Venus-ruled are feeling tense, food and drink tend to lose their appeal. Typically Libra responds best to a harmonious atmosphere, animated by scintillating conversation and garnished with a touch of love and romance.

Foods commonly associated with Libra

Meat: veal, beef, venison, kidneys
Fowl: chicken, partridge, pigeon
Fish and Shellfish: shellfish
Dairy Products: butter, ice cream, eggs
Vegetables and Beans: artichokes, potatoes, green beans, spinach, lentils, chickpeas
Nuts and Grains: walnuts, pecans, wheat
Fruits: apples, strawberries, raspberries, peaches, pears, grapes, persimmons, blackberries, cherries, kiwi, nectarines, plums, figs, gooseberries, dried fruits
Beverages: tea, wine

Herbs, Spices, and Miscellaneous: thyme, coriander, mint, honey, catnip, candy, cakes, bread, pastry, sugar

LIBRA MENU

Veal in Sherry Sauce

Buttered Egg Noodles

Green Beans with Almonds

Flaky Drop Biscuits

Sparkling Rosé Wine

Chocolate Peanut Butter Bark

Espresso

Libra Recipes

Veal in Sherry Sauce

    2 tablespoons olive oil
    1 small onion, chopped
    1 clove garlic, minced
    1 pound veal, trimmed and cubed
    1 can (8 ounces) tomato sauce
    ½ cup dry sherry
       salt and pepper to taste

Heat oil in a heavy pot. Add the onions and garlic, and cook and stir over medium heat until the onion is soft but not brown. Add the meat and brown evenly. Stir in the tomato sauce and sherry. Season with salt and pepper. Bring the stew to a boil, reduce heat to low, cover and simmer for 1½ hours or until veal is tender. Serve over hot buttered egg noodles.

*Green Beans with Almonds

½ pound fresh green beans
2 tablespoons slivered almonds
1 tablespoon butter
1 teaspoon fresh lemon juice

Wash the green beans and cut into inch-long pieces. Steam or cook covered in a small amount of boiling water for 15 to 20 minutes, or until tender. Drain and set aside. Melt butter over medium heat, add slivered almonds, and cook and stir until golden. Stir in lemon juice. Stir the almond mixture into the cooked green beans and serve.

*Flaky Drop Biscuits

2 cups flour
1 tablespoon baking powder
2 teaspoons sugar
½ teaspoon cream of tartar
¼ teaspoon salt
½ cup butter
1 cup milk

Place all the dry ingredients in a bowl and stir

together. Cut in butter until mixture resembles coarse crumbs. Make a well in the center and add the milk all at once. Stir just until the dough clings together. Drop the dough from a tablespoon onto a greased baking sheet. Bake in a 450 degree oven for 10 to 12 minutes or until golden. Serve warm.

*Chocolate Peanut Butter Bark

    18 ounces semisweet chocolate chips
    ½ cup creamy peanut butter
     5 tablespoons confectioners' sugar, sifted
    ¾ cup salted peanuts

Line a 9 × 13 pan with aluminum foil. In a double boiler, melt the chocolate chips over hot water. Place the peanut butter in a small bowl and gradually beat in the sugar. Add the peanut butter mixture to the melted chocolate, and stir until blended. Allow mixture to cool slightly. Stir in the peanuts and spread the mixture in the foil-lined pan. Smooth the top. Chill in the refrigerator until firm, and then break or cut the bark into pieces.

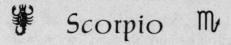

Scorpio ♏

October 23–November 21

Symbol: The Scorpion	Element: Water
Quality: Fixed	Planetary Ruler: Pluto
Polarity: Feminine	

A man's most open actions have a secret side to them.

—Joseph Conrad
Under Western Eyes

How to Identify Scorpio

Ruled by Pluto, the planet that represents transformation and death, Scorpio is known as the sign of rebirth and regeneration. Its element is water and its quality fixed, indicating still waters that run very deep. As the eighth sign of the zodiac, Scorpio rules sex, death, and the beginning and ending of all things. More concerned with feelings than appearances, people born under this sign tend to respond to the world through their emotions rather than through intellect or physical activity. Scorpios are constantly probing the depths in order to see what lies beneath the surface. One of the scorpion's main interests is in ferreting out other people's feelings and emotions and observing their reactions to different situations. Naturally intuitive and blessed with an excellent memory, the scorpion's inquisitive mind and investigative abilities may lead to a career in psychology, detective work, medical research, or mystery writing.

Represented by the scorpion, an animal that hides in dark places and when threatened inflicts a painful sting on its enemies, this sign is among the most feared, misunderstood, and maligned in the zodiacal family. Although the perplexing Scorpio native may be as much a mystery to himself as to everyone else, his intensely secretive, suspicious nature tends to attract a lot of bad press. The story most often told in conjunction with the astrological Scorpio is that of the scorpion who convinces a reluctant frog to carry it across a river. At first the frog refuses, "If I take you across you will sting me." "Nonsense," says the scorpion. "If I sting you, *both* of us will die." So the frog agrees to carry the scorpion on its back, and halfway across the scorpion stings the frog. As they are sinking the frog asks the scorpion, "Why did you do that?" and the scorpion replies, "Because it is my nature."

The Scorpio native is courageous, strong-willed, and determined. Unlike Aries, he is not openly combative, but when he's feeling threatened or vulnerable he can deliver a painful sting. The members of this sign are often accused of imposing their will on people, but they take control because they are mortally afraid of being controlled by others. Scorpions make vehement adversaries because they will protect themselves at all costs. However, their emotional vindictiveness can serve as a double-edged sword that poisons them along with their enemies. Prone to cutting off their noses to spite their faces, at times Scorpio natives can be positively self-destructive, not unlike their symbol the scorpion, which will kill itself rather than allow someone else to kill it.

Typically Scorpios are complex and difficult to understand. The Pluto-ruled are generally strong-willed and stubborn. It is always a mistake to count them out because they refuse to give up on their desires. Long after everyone else has gotten bored and abandoned a cause or project, the tenacious scorpion holds on and continues the fight. As a result Scorpios often accomplish things that others consider impossible. Even when you think he is beaten, Scorpio rises phoenixlike from his own ashes and begins again.

The scorpion lives in a black-and-white world of fixed ideas and opinions. If you try to get him to change his mind about something or someone, you will probably run into a wall of resistance. Scorpio is stubborn, passionate, intensely loyal, and rarely indifferent or indecisive. Like all fixed sign natives, once he has made up his mind it is difficult to get him to change it. Secretive Scorpio has his own way of doing things. Sometimes even those close to him have great difficulty understanding either his agenda or his true motivation.

The quintessential Scorpio struggle is that of attaining mastery over desire. It is with good reason that Scorpio has been dubbed, "the sign of the saint and the sinner." Despite his reputation for passion and smoldering sexuality, the scorpion is generally able to sublimate his strong physical and emotional desires when it suits his purposes. More than any other sign, Scorpio understands the power wielded by sexual overindulgence, but he also understands the power of celibacy, and at times may alternate between periods of intense sexual activity and periods of total abstinence.

Typically Scorpio is not promiscuous nor is he a loner. The scorpion longs to establish a close loving relationship, and when he finds it he pledges his undying devotion. Scorpio's love is limitless, and his commitment is such that it can easily turn into obsession. When he feels rejected or betrayed, the scorpion rarely accepts defeat graciously. The love that once burned like a fire can turn cold as ice in the blink of an eye. When scorned, the scorpion seeks vindication and revenge. He may lash out blindly against the object of his affection. Or, in a puritanical need for self-punishment, he may turn his pain and anger inward on himself.

When it comes to lovemaking, no other sign is as passionate as Scorpio. Although not romantic, scorpions typically live up to their reputations as superior lovers who are capable of gratifying their partners and providing them with a great deal of sexual pleasure. With Scorpios most things are *all or nothing at all*. The Pluto-ruled are capable of reaching the highest highs and sinking to the lowest lows. Scorpio tends to dominate in any union. He can be notoriously jealous, but also quite protective of his mate and family. When he feels secure and in control, the scorpion leads with his heart and invests one hundred percent in the relationship. He expects no less in return.

Myths and Symbols Associated with Scorpio

The astrological ruler of Scorpio is Pluto. The parts of the body ruled by Scorpio are the genitals. Its symbol, ♏, is thought to represent the scorpion's tail. The sign is classified as fixed, water, and feminine (negative, indirect, yin, and internal). Represented by the scorpion, Scorpio's color is dark red, its metal is iron, and its gemstone is topaz.

The story most often associated with Scorpio is the Greek myth of Orion the Hunter, whose father was the sea god Poseidon (Neptune) and his mother, Euryale, one of the Gorgons. Orion was a very handsome man of gigantic proportions and exceptional talents. From Poseidon he had the power of walking on the sea floor without getting his head wet. He was also a great hunter who boasted that he could kill any animal alive. He fell in love with Merope, the daughter of Oenopion, king of Chios, who was the son of Dionysus (Bacchus), god of wine, and the mortal woman Ariadne. Orion cleared the island of Chios of wild beasts, and brought the spoils of his hunt to his beloved Merope.

Orion wished to marry Merope. When the king withheld his consent, the impatient lover got drunk and attempted to take her by violence. Oenopion appealed to his father, Dionysus, to punish the hunter. The god put Orion into a deep sleep, and Oenopion blinded him and threw him onto the seashore. The wounded hero wandered around blind until he came to the forge of Hephaestus (Vulcan), who graciously provided Orion with a young boy to guide him east toward the rising sun. After the rays of the sun restored his sight, the angry hunter went off in search of Oenopion. Hephaestus, having foreseen this probability, had built an underground chamber for the king to keep him safe from Orion's vengeance.

Eventually Orion gave up the search for Oenopion and went to Delois to live with the dawn goddess Eos, an inveterate collector of handsome young men. In Delois Orion bragged of his sexual conquest of the goddess, and continually boasted of his capabilities as a hunter. He threatened to use his hunting skills to exterminate all the wild beasts in the world. This boast severely angered the god Apollo, who was responsible for guarding the herds.

Ultimately Orion left Delois for Crete, where he worked as a hunter to Apollo's twin sister, the goddess Artemis (Diana). Artemis fell in love with Orion and was planning to marry him, which greatly displeased her brother who regarded the match as highly inappropriate. Apollo appealed to Gaia, the earth goddess, who sent a giant scorpion with an impenetrable armor to sting Orion to death.

Artemis was so grief stricken at the death of her lover that she placed Orion and the scorpion as constellations among the stars. She set them far away from each other so that Orion would be eternally out of danger. When the constellation Scorpius is rising, chasing after Orion, the hunter is already starting to disappear behind the western horizon.

Another scorpionic myth can be found in the Sumerian Gilgamesh Epic. The twelve tablets of the Gilgamesh cycle tell of the many feats of the legendary king, and are a mirror of the sun's journey throughout the year. After the death of his friend Enkidu, Gilgamesh searches for the sage king Utnapishtim who reputedly has the secret of immortality. In order to find the ancient wise man, Gilgamesh has to first confront the Scorpion men—the half man and half scorpion creatures who are guardians of Mount Mashu, the great mountain that safeguards the rising and setting of the sun.

The Scorpio Man

Scorpio is the one sign that doesn't skim the surface of life. Its members typically delve deeply and probe into regions of the psyche that most other signs would prefer to ignore. The Scorpio man loathes weakness, hypocrisy, superficiality, and sham. His perceptions and intuitions about people are uncommonly strong. When he turns his penetrating stare in your direction, you may feel as if he has X-ray vision. Although the scorpion usually hides his own inner self behind a mask of mystery and enigma, he rarely grants anyone else the same privacy. With one piercing glance he seems to see into the very depths of your soul, while divulging very little of his own nature. The scorpion does not like to reveal anything until he feels safe and secure in a relationship. He generally feels secure only when he's the one who is in control of the situation.

Although Scorpio may sometimes be hard to live with, he is fiercely loyal to those he loves. When he makes a commitment, he sticks with it "in sickness and in health" and through good times and bad. This man is no fair-weather friend who will run out on you at the first sign of trouble. The scorpion is intensely possessive. Part of his stick-to-itiveness has to do with his inability to let go of even a bad situation or relationship. He absolutely hates to lose anything or anyone. No matter what the challenge, his inclination is to hold his ground and see it through to the bitter end.

Scorpio is arguably the least laid-back sign in the zodiac. The Pluto-ruled find it virtually impossible to live spontaneously. Most feel compelled to organize every facet of their lives in terms of some sort of master plan. Although he may appear cool on the surface, this fellow is generally consumed by his driving need to manipulate every aspect of every situation. He simply cannot believe that things can ever be simple, direct, or to the point. Because of his knack for making things more complicated than need be, he tends to wear out himself and everybody else with all of his many self-created dramas. When his pride has been wounded, Scorpio can go to great lengths to appear as if nothing is bothering him—at least until he can crawl into some dark corner to sulk, brood, obsess over the hurt, and plot his revenge.

Often difficult, tiresome, and irritating, the typical Scorpio man is not the easiest person to get along with. As a hardworking perfectionist, Papa Scorpio seeks to impose his own high standards on family members and close friends. He is so good at mind games, and puts so much time and energy into trying to outwit others, that he sometimes doesn't know when or how to stop. Because he equates information with power, the scorpion strives to gain as much information as he can about the various people and situations in his life, a trait which doesn't always sit well with those nearest and dearest to him.

With the right person, and in the right time or circumstance, Scorpio can be a loyal, passionate, caring, and considerate lover. But when hurt or disappointed, the scorpion's love has a way of turning into hatred or obsession. The wounded scorpion may strike out at the person he blames for his pain. Or he may try to escape from his own intensely disturbing emotions by immersing himself in work, alcohol, or mindless sexual activity.

In business and career the Scorpio man is goal oriented, and an excellent strategist with a strong desire to prove that he can "make it" in the world. Determination, willpower, and the ability to focus on his objective give him the power to accomplish virtually anything he sets his mind to. Reversals of fortune do not faze this man because he is a master at turning adversity into opportunity. The Pluto-ruled do not like to be supervised, and generally work best on their own or at the head of a small team. Their fixed nature gives scorpions the stability and tenacity to stay the course, no matter how long it takes to achieve their objectives.

Shrewd Scorpio is prized in the business world for the ability to take over during a crisis and turn things around. No one has a better grasp of what it takes to rescue a struggling company from the jaws of disaster because no other sign has Scorpio's knack of getting to the *source* of a problem. The scorpion will snoop around, turning over rocks and looking into dark corners, until he uncovers every pertinent bit of information. Once he knows the cause, it is relatively easy for him to come up with viable solutions to a company's difficulties. Although his colleagues and coworkers may resent Scorpio's cagey and clandestine methods of ferreting out the truth, they can't argue with his results.

Control is the major issue in the life of most Pluto-ruled natives. In love the Scorpio man needs to feel that he is the one in charge of his own destiny. This can be quite a problem for him because of his tendency to become totally consumed by his own feelings and desires. If he thinks he is losing control over his love life, he will stoop to sexual power games. He is not above using sex as a means of manipulating and controlling his mate or partner.

When the scorpion loves you, his passionate intensity in bed and out can take your breath away. Although he may be jealous, possessive, and controlling, Scorpio is also loyal, sympathetic, intuitive, and understanding, capable of deep love and long-lasting devotion. If you are the one in love with a complex Scorpio man, be prepared to accept him as he is—because you will never be able to change him.

The Scorpio Woman

Scorpio is the intriguing female who, like the High Priestess in the tarot deck, knows but doesn't tell the secrets of life and death. She exudes an aura of mystery and sensuality that fascinates, and sometimes frightens, those around her. Although some people are put off by her seemingly cool and detached manner, most are drawn to her as if by some unknown magic. She aims high. Once she sets her mind or heart on something or someone, she does not rest until she has achieved her objective. Possessed of a good deal of charisma, the female scorpion attracts power and powerful people into her circle. At her very best she is similar to the heroines of old who served to inspire others to greatness. At her worst she's a cold manipulator who uses her power and connections to further her own interests and agenda.

Like the members of the other water signs, Cancer and Pisces, Pluto-ruled Scorpio natives are extremely intuitive. Their emotions and instincts generally govern most of their actions and reactions. The Scorpio woman often feels impelled to delve into the deepest mysteries of life and death. Whether she is attempting to get to the bottom of a murder mystery, saving a life with her surgical skills, researching a new drug, auditing financial records, or pursuing a personal spiritual journey, she seeks to uncover the truth that lies hidden beneath the façade of basic facts and figures.

Scorpio can be ruthless when betrayed, biting and sarcastic when hurt, calculating and manipulative when seeking control. But when she feels loved and secure, she can be the most loyal, devoted, and caring person you know. As a wife and mother she strives to create a home atmosphere that serves her family as a comfortable refuge from the outside world. The process of procreation fascinates the Pluto-ruled. Many Scorpio women actually look forward to pregnancy and birth. Mama Scorpio goes through each prenatal stage with total preoccupation regarding her baby's growth and development. After her child is born, the Scorpio mom is fiercely protective and totally devoted to her little bundle of joy. Although hard on everyone else, Scorpio parents can be notoriously indulgent softies where their own kids are concerned. They will do everything possible to provide their children with all the advantages that life has to offer.

Like her male counterpart, the female Scorpio smolders with sexuality and enjoys her reputation as the most passionate woman in the zodiac. This Pluto-ruled lady is a master of nonverbal communication who mesmerizes potential lovers with the mystical intensity of her gaze. Romantic partners do not choose her—she chooses them. She intuitively picks up on someone's interest in her, then she silently gives a red or green light. Depending on her mood, she can come across as ethereal and unattainable or bewitchingly erotic and totally available.

When an otherwise intelligent scorpion female becomes sexually obsessed, she will typically throw all caution to the winds and follow wherever her physical and emotional desires lead her. Although she is generally attracted to potential partners who are successful and can help her get ahead in the world, when caught up in a passionate affair the Scorpio woman invariably thinks with her heart, not with her mind. In this situation she may totally immerse herself in an unsuitable obsessive-compulsive relationship, with little hope of extricating herself until her unholy passion has run its course. This is one reason that smart, beautiful Scorpio females are often found in inappropriate alliances that cause their friends to ask, "Whatever does she see in that one?"

In love and romance the Scorpio female does not wear her heart on her sleeve. She may not mean to be mysterious, but she certainly comes off that way most of the time. She can be a demanding partner because of her high standards and little patience with those who do not measure up. Like the male scorpion, the female is rarely spontaneous. All of her moves are well thought out and carefully planned in advance. She knows what she wants, and she is not afraid to go after it. She is stubborn about getting her own way. Although her actions are rarely overt, she has a way of zeroing in on the thing or person she wants, and drawing it to her. Few can resist the power of her formidable presence or the combined force of her magnetic personality and captivating sensuality.

If you are the one who is in love with a Scorpio

woman, you better be totally honest with her. If you lie to her or hurt her in any way, prepare to pay the piper—there's no fury like a Scorpio scorned or betrayed. When frustrated or thwarted, the Pluto-ruled woman can become vengeful and destructive, and she makes a formidable and very dangerous enemy. Her rage takes many forms. She has few scruples when it comes to seeking revenge on someone who proves unworthy of her trust.

When she cares for someone, Scorpio is capable of making great sacrifices and treating her lover royally. However, do not attempt to subdue her or make her feel she is dependent on you. She despises weakness in herself and others, and will never submit to pressure or allow anyone to tell her what to do. Living with a Pluto-ruled woman often involves walking a very thin line between taking what she dishes out and resisting her more forceful and outrageous demands. Life with Scorpio can be either heaven or hell. If you are faint of heart, perhaps you better steer clear altogether.

The Shadow Side of Scorpio

The main thrust of the scorpion's shadow comes from the fact that Scorpio is a water sign and also a fixed sign. From the water element comes the tendency to concentrate on feelings rather than facts. For the water sign native, what actually happened in any given situation is not nearly as important as how he *feels* about what happened. Because Scorpio is a fixed sign, most of its members are very strongly opinionated. They have great difficulty seeing things from an objective point of view. This subjective picture of the world can make the Pluto-ruled individual seem downright fanatical and self-righteous. Because the scorpion rarely understands the other person's point of view, he is frequently unable to give him or her the benefit of the doubt.

Many of the scorpion's problems stem from his inclination to always look on the dark side of every issue and situation. Members of this sign often suffer from bouts of severe depression, usually brought on by their decidedly negative outlook. When things get really bad, the scorpion plummets to the depths of despair. His friends and associates may have a hard time understanding and dealing with the bleak despondency that is an essential part of Scorpio's nature.

Although he sinks into darkness on a regular basis, Scorpio instinctively knows that he can fight his way back to the light. It seems to be part and parcel of the scorpionic character to wander around in the psychic mists until he comes face-to-face with his own deepest fears. Eventually he uncovers the answers he seeks, after which he transforms himself again and again. Like the scorpion that regenerates a new stinger whenever it loses a tail, the Scorpio native may be reborn many times over.

Scorpio's inclination to repress his feelings and emotions can cause a number of potentially serious problems. When unable to forget or forgive perceived slights and insults, the scorpion typically becomes vengeful and vindictive. Instead of talking about his negative feelings, he resorts to sarcasm and spite. His refusal to discuss what is really bothering him can lead to gross misunderstandings as well as health problems, both physical and mental. It is very important for the members of this most secretive sign to try to get in touch with their deep emotions and learn how to talk about their feelings with a friend or counselor.

Two important aspects of the Scorpio shadow are jealousy and lack of trust. The Pluto-ruled native is naturally possessive. Since he finds it impossible to play second fiddle, when he suspects that his mate or partner is fooling around with someone else—or even *thinking* about another person—the scorpion quickly convinces himself that his suspicions of disloyalty or infidelity are completely valid. Because he truly believes that people are not to be trusted, it is extremely difficult to get Scorpio to change his way of thinking. Since his jealousy is based on his idea that everyone is basically rotten, when the scorpion gets the idea in his head that his mate or partner is being unfaithful no amount of logic or even proof will serve to change his mind.

Control and manipulation are the final manifestations of the scorpion's shadow. Always aware of the advantage of not putting all his cards on the table at once, Scorpio will conceal his true intentions for as long as possible. He holds back until he is sure the other person has been completely won over, then he makes his move. Scorpio is the consummate player of power games. He often uses sex as a means of control, including the withholding of sexual favors in order to gain the upper hand.

Scorpio Romantic Dinner for Two

Scorpio the cook

When Scorpio invites you to dinner, consider yourself lucky—you are in for an extraordinary treat. Most scorpions are extremely fond of good food. They know what they like, and they have great instincts in the kitchen. Scorpio is all about intensity. Most members of this sign are born gourmets who strive for perfection in everything they do. However, when Scorpio cooks for you, you better stay out of his kitchen. The scorpion likes to work alone. He especially enjoys creating an air of mystery and surprising his guests with unusual culinary treats. Scorpions are intuitive cooks. Even when they follow a recipe, they will usually add their own little touches.

Scorpions tend to be homebodies who enjoy every aspect of meal preparation from planning to serving. They dearly love experimenting with complicated new recipes. The scorpion rarely takes shortcuts when it comes to cooking. Everything he serves you is likely to be homemade and freshly prepared. Most Pluto-ruled natives prefer powerful, exotic foods that are highly seasoned and bursting with flavor. The typical menu at Chez Scorpio consists of a variety of interesting dishes that are not only tasty but also unusual and mysterious.

Money is no object when the scorpion throws a dinner party. The foodstuffs are always the best available, the presentation generally lavish and appealing. Many scorpions are collectors of pewter, silver, china, and crystal, and they are not afraid to use their most precious objects on the dinner table. They are often gifted artistically with a well-developed sense of color. Everything from the flower arrangements to the finger bowls reflects their impeccable taste.

Scorpio the dinner guest

When you invite a Scorpio to dinner, don't skimp on the food and drink. Most members of this sign have healthy appetites. They enjoy hearty meals, especially when they are well presented. Scorpio's taste often runs along unorthodox lines, with definite feelings about various foods. If possible, you should check with your Pluto-ruled guest in advance and ask about his likes and dislikes. Of course, you may not get a direct answer. The scorpion loves surprises and can be quite mysterious about his personal preferences. When in doubt, serve something unusual, exotic, or foreign that has a real kick to it. Herbs, spices, and other flavorings should be strong, interesting, and genuinely representative of the particular cuisine you have chosen.

The scorpion absolutely abhors food or conversation that is bland, dull, and tasteless. Although secretive about himself, he simply adores gossip. He delights in ferreting out every last intimate detail of other people's lives. When Scorpio cooks for you, don't expect him to share his treasured secret family recipes with you. However, when you cook for the scorpion, if you tell him that the recipe for a dish he just enjoyed is your "secret," he will probably probe and question you until he figures out exactly how it was prepared.

Scorpio natives are extraordinarily aware of aromas. The scorpion's sensuous nature is easily aroused by the smell of good food. Because of the strong relationship between their sign and human sexuality, the Pluto-ruled tend to be fascinated by those foods said to contain aphrodisiac powers such as oysters and chocolate. The scorpion also enjoys alcoholic drinks and foods cooked in wine or brandy. To score extra points with your Scorpio lover, don't forget his before-dinner cocktail and after-dinner liqueur.

Foods commonly associated with Scorpio

Meat: aged meat, goat, pork, snake, frogs

Fowl: aquatic birds, game birds

Fish and Shellfish: all shellfish, shark, pike, eel

Dairy Products: aged cheese, yogurt, sour cream, buttermilk, blue cheese, sour milk, limburger cheese, Roquefort cheese

Vegetables and Beans: all root vegetables, carrots, onions, garlic, peppers, pimentos, radishes, shallots, leeks, asparagus, truffles, brussels sprouts, beans, sauerkraut

Nuts and Grains: pine nuts, dark breads

Fruits: black cherries, sour cherries, blackberries, rhubarb, cactus apples, figs, prunes, blueberries, gooseberries, pineapples

Beverages: coffee, red wine, blackberry tea

Herbs, Spices, and Miscellaneous: basil, cayenne, ginseng, salsa, molé, curry, mustard, fermented foods, aged foods, chocolate

SCORPIO MENU

Stuffed Shrimp Wrapped in Bacon

Lima Beans

Salad with Roquefort Dressing

Savory Corn Bread

Red Wine

Cherry Crumble with Vanilla Ice Cream

Coffee

Scorpio Recipes

Stuffed Shrimp Wrapped in Bacon

1 pound large shrimp, peeled and deveined
1 15-ounce can white clam sauce
¼ cup bread crumbs
1 teaspoon parmesan cheese

1 pound thin-sliced bacon strips, cut in half
1 bottle honey smoked barbecue sauce

Butterfly the shrimp. Drain the clam sauce in a colander and discard the liquid. In a small bowl mix the minced clams with the bread crumbs and parmesan cheese. Put some stuffing on the top of each shrimp and roll each one in a bacon strip. Dip the wrapped shrimp in honey smoked barbecue sauce, and place on cookie sheets. Preheat the oven to 350 degrees, and bake 25 to 27 minutes, or until the bacon is cooked. For crisper bacon place the baked shrimp under the broiler for an additional 1 to 2 minutes before serving.

Salad with Roquefort Dressing

1 small head romaine lettuce
1 small red bell pepper
1 cup watercress sprigs (optional)
2 ounces Roquefort (or other blue cheese), crumbled
1 cup dairy sour cream
1 tablespoon fresh lemon juice
1 green onion, finely chopped
  salt and pepper to taste

Tear the romaine lettuce and cut the bell pepper and watercress into bite-size pieces. Toss together in a bowl. In a smaller bowl, mix the Roquefort cheese, sour cream, lemon juice, chopped green onion, and salt and pepper until well blended. Just before serving, spoon the dressing over the salad and toss again.

*Savory Corn Bread

1½ cups flour
2 tablespoons sugar
4 teaspoons baking powder
2½ teaspoons salt
1½ cups yellow cornmeal
2 teaspoons dried sage
1 teaspoon dried thyme
¼ cup onion, finely chopped
¼ cup celery, finely chopped
¼ cup pimento, finely chopped
3 eggs, beaten
1½ cups milk
⅓ cup shortening, melted and cooled

Sift flour, sugar, baking powder, and salt into a large bowl. Add cornmeal, sage, thyme, onion, celery, and pimento and stir to blend. Combine eggs, milk, and shortening and add to dry ingredients. Stir the mixture until blended. Line a 10-inch ovenproof skillet, or a 9-inch square pan, with aluminum foil and grease lightly. Spoon the corn bread mixture into the prepared pan. Preheat the oven to 400 degrees and bake the corn bread for 35 to 45 minutes. Cool on a rack. Remove the corn bread from the pan, peel off the foil, and place on a serving plate.

Cherry Crumble with Vanilla Ice Cream

    1 16-ounce can pitted sour cherries, drained
    ¼ cup sugar
    1 teaspoon flour
    ¼ cup rolled oats
    ¼ cup flour
    ¼ cup brown sugar
    ¼ teaspoon cinnamon
    ¼ cup butter or margarine

Preheat the oven to 325 degrees. Lightly spray a shallow baking pan or pie plate with cooking oil. Combine the cherries, sugar, and teaspoon of flour and pour into the prepared pan. In a small bowl combine the oats, flour, brown sugar, and cinnamon, and cut in the butter or margarine until crumbly. Sprinkle the topping over the cherries, and bake 20 to 25 minutes or until the cherries are bubbly and the top is browned and crisp. Serve warm with vanilla ice cream.

Sagittarius

November 22–December 21

Symbol: The Archer   Element: Fire
Quality: Mutable   Planetary Ruler: Jupiter
Polarity: Masculine

I shot an arrow in the air,
It fell to earth, I know not where.

—Henry Wadsworth Longfellow
The Arrow and the Song

How to Identify Sagittarius

The archer is the wanderer and truthseeker of the zodiac whose gaze is always fixed on the far horizon. Knowledge and freedom are the key themes of Sagittarius' world. Together these keys help him to probe the true meaning of life and transcend the petty limitations that other people readily accept. His basic character is comprised of a combination of the enthusiasm of fire, the versatility and restlessness of mutability, and the broad-minded generosity and wisdom of Jupiter.

Sagittarius is about action and getting things going, so its natives are more process oriented than goal oriented. Archers see life as an ongoing adventure, and, like Aries, they are generally better starters than finishers. Sagittarius loves to initiate projects. While his intentions may be grand and impressive, he often loses interest in the race before reaching the finish line. The wide-ranging Sagittarian mind comes well equipped with intelligence, foresight, and intuition. Members of this sign are not loners, and they tend to do their best work when teamed with others.

The Jupiter-ruled love to gamble and take risks. They are generally very lucky at games of chance and in the game of life. Sagittarians tend to expect everything to go their way, and it usually does. Typically they want the freedom to do whatever they feel like doing and to learn things as they come along. Sometimes Sagittarius' optimistic belief that everything always turns out for the best causes him to act in a careless or impulsive manner. Sagittarius is not a long-term planner. Yet no other sign is better equipped to go with the flow than the freewheeling, independent archer. If something seems like a good idea at the moment, he usually jumps right in without thinking too much about where it may lead.

Sagittarius' ultimate aim is to broaden his vision. He views his existence as an exciting journey in which adventure and experience are much more important than stability and security. His optimism and enthusiasm can make him blind to the practical necessities of life. He invariably concentrates his attention on the big picture, is easily bored or annoyed by small details, and sometimes comes off as irresponsible and undependable. Overconfident archers often overextend themselves financially. However, they are very resourceful. One way or another, usually through a combination of good luck and clever ideas, they find a way to get back on their feet.

Archers love to party and most enjoy a very active social life. Naturally outgoing, playful, and flirtatious, no one is better at working a crowd than the charming, gregarious Sagittarian. Like his opposite, Gemini, Sagittarius is a witty conversationalist. Although he is rather opinionated, his mind is constantly open to new dimensions of thought. The archer loves to connect with people in order to chat, explore thoughts and ideas, and exchange knowledge and information.

Some members of this sign are instinctive comedians, actors, and storytellers whose tales of personal exploits and adventures may be exaggerated for dramatic or comic effect. However, Sagittarians in general are honest to a fault. They have a reputation for being frank and forthright to the point of tactlessness. Because he has never learned how to tell the proverbial white lie, this master of the left-handed compliment can suffer from a severe case of foot-in-mouth disease. ("You look great today. I love your new dress. Those vertical stripes sure do make you look a lot less dumpy than usual. Now, if you would only do something about your hair, you would be absolutely perfect.")

Sagittarian natives usually love the outdoors. Archers are rarely sedentary. Many Jupiter-ruled natives are gifted sports enthusiasts who continually push the envelope of their inherent athletic abilities. During leisure time Sagittarius may enjoy horseback riding, hunting, deep-sea fishing, skydiving, flying airplanes, racing (horses and cars), and any other activity that causes him to stretch himself to the limit of his physical capacities. When he is not challenging himself physically, you may find him engaged in debates and discussions designed to test his mental capabilities. More than anything Sagittarius enjoys travel, especially to foreign lands. Nothing appeals to the archer quite as much as meeting interesting new people and discovering and exploring exotic new places.

Sagittarians make charming, sexy lovers who are affectionate, straightforward, and sincere. If you are out for a good time, look no further—no other sign is as much fun as Sagittarius. The idealistic archer truly believes that each and every affair of the heart is going to last forever. However, Sagittarians tend to love their freedom and independence more than anything or anyone, so these free-spirited souls don't really take love or sex all that seriously. Archers are natural hunters. Although they mean to be faithful, when they find someone more appealing they are likely to go off in pursuit of their new interest. They can be faithful partners in a happy, successful relationship, but only if they are allowed to *feel* free. Archers are generally easygoing, magnanimous, and forgiving, but they will not put up with anyone who tries to keep them chained to hearth and home. The secret to dealing with the Jupiter-ruled native's innate restlessness is to provide a comfortable home base for him to return to when his travels are over. But if you are the emotionally demanding, possessive type who tends to cling to your lovers, a devil-may-

care Sagittarian is probably not the best partner for
you.

Myths and Symbols Associated
with Sagittarius

The astrological ruler of Sagittarius is Jupiter. The
parts of the body ruled by Sagittarius are the hips
and thighs. Its symbol, ♐, is thought to represent
the archer's arrow. The sign is classified as mutable,
fire, and masculine (positive, direct, yang, and external). Represented by the archer, Sagittarius' color is
light blue, its metal is tin, and its gemstone is
turquoise.

The Greek mythological figure most often associated with Sagittarius is the centaur, a being that is
represented as half man and half horse. Sagittarius
is usually referred to as a dual sign. Like the centaur
with the upper torso of a man growing out of the
body of a horse, this sign combines the rational
human mind with earthy animal instincts and intuition. Also like the centaur, the Sagittarian archer has
his feet on the ground and his bow and arrow
pointed upward toward the heavens. The two renowned centaurs most often identified with the zodiacal sign Sagittarius are Crotus and Chiron.

Crotus was the son of the god Pan and the nymph
Eupheme, who was nurse to the Muses. The nine
Muses, daughters of the god Zeus (Jupiter) and
Mnemosyne, were the Greek goddesses that presided
over the arts and sciences. Eupheme raised her son
Crotus with the Muses, and Crotus grew up sensitive

to all the arts. Skilled in the hunt, he was known as a great archer and is sometimes credited with having invented archery. It is said that upon his death the Muses begged Zeus to memorialize Crotus by transporting him to the stars. Zeus honored Crotus as the constellation Sagittarius, which portrays the centaur as an archer drawing back a bow.

According to another legend it is Chiron, not Crotus, who is the centaur depicted in the constellation Sagittarius. Chiron was the son of the god Cronus (Saturn) and Philyra, a sea nymph. Instructed by the twin gods Apollo and Artemis (Diana), he was renowned for his skill in hunting, medicine, music, and the art of prophecy. Known for his exceptional goodness and wisdom, he tutored a number of famous Greek heroes including Heracles (Hercules), Achilles, Jason, Asclepius, and Actaeon. He founded the Chironium, a healing temple on Mt. Pellius where he instructed his pupils and helped them learn the best ways to fulfill their highest potential.

In an attempt to wipe out some vicious centaurs that were plaguing the countryside, Heracles accidentally shot Chiron with a poison arrow. The arrow was tipped with the deadly venom of the Hydra, which instantly killed any victim it touched. However, Chiron was immortal and was not killed, but he was in terrible agony. He used all his great medical skills on the wound, but it proved to be incurable. Chiron's suffering was so profound that he wanted to die, but he could not. The Titan Prometheus took pity on Chiron and allowed him to renounce his immortality. After his death Zeus placed Chiron, the most just, gentle, and wisest of the centaurs, among the stars as the constellation Sagittarius.

Some tales associate Sagittarius with Artemis (Diana), goddess of the hunt. When her father, Zeus (Jupiter), asked Artemis what gifts she would like, Artemis requested a bow and arrows like Apollo's, so that she and her twin could hunt together. She also told Zeus that she wanted to retain her youth and never have to get married. Zeus granted all her wishes—and more. As mistress of the hunt, Artemis acted as game warden, and with her sharp arrows she killed anyone who hunted pregnant animals or their young.

The Sagittarius Man

The appeal of the Jupiter-born man is broad and comprehensive. Although some Sagittarians have decidedly hot tempers, most archers view the clash of ideas as much more invigorating than the clash of guns and are generally less combative than members of the other two fire signs, Aries and Leo. Sagittarius tends to think of himself as a citizen of the universe, and he hates being pigeonholed or typecast in any way. With his eye always on the larger picture, the archer is a natural humanitarian and reformer who is fervent about his dreams and ideals.

Sagittarius enjoys playing a role, and he has a natural gift for demonstrating and illustrating his plans. Because they love the spotlight and strive to influence others through their philosophy, thoughts, and publications, archers are generally well suited for positions as politicians, teachers, actors, reporters, news analysts, publishers, or writers. In their roles as visionaries who know how to make things happen, Sagittarians often leave a profound imprint on their time and on the people around them.

In the workplace the typical archer is considered a great asset because of his optimism, enthusiasm, and long-range vision. Although natives of this sign may be universally praised for their inspiration and expertise at understanding the complete picture, they are not known for either long-term endurance or hard work. Sagittarians are "idea men" who become quickly bored with the petty details involved in carrying their ideas through to completion. As a lifelong learner, the archer is constantly seeking to expand his horizons. When a project or job becomes routine or boring, the Jupiter-ruled native usually begins to feel antsy and ready to move on to something newer and more exciting.

The Sagittarius man is a bundle of contradictions. As a fire sign native, he can be quite impulsive. But just when you think he is going to spring into action, he stops to procrastinate and question his own actions. When his freedom is on the line, he usually thinks twice before committing himself to a specific direction or course of action. He loves to be consulted. Sagittarius truly wants to help others, but is usually better at advising people than taking his own advice. In spite of the fact that they give the impression that they are liberal or radical in their thoughts and ideas, the Jupiter-ruled are basically traditionalists. Although well known for its connection to spirituality, Sagittarius is more often associated with the trappings and rules of organized religion than with the mystical and occult leanings of a truly ethereal sign like Pisces.

Although not a dreamer in the true sense of the word, Sagittarius is a visionary and an optimist. When he wants something, he is generally able to convince himself he will get it no matter what the obstacles. The archer is the quintessential fool who rushes in where angels fear to tread. He is usually so lucky that even his failures tend to pay off big time. (He buys an old farm with hopes of converting it into a dude ranch. His plans for the ranch fall through, but a few months later oil is discovered on the property.) When he does suffer a crushing defeat, the Jupiter-ruled native bounces back quickly. The only exception to this is the occasional embittered archer who allows himself to concentrate on past triumphs and disappointments instead of future goals. When he focuses on what was, or what might have been, Sagittarius can forget his true purpose, which is to live in the moment and learn from the experience.

Despite all their warmth, friendliness, and popularity, Sagittarius natives try to avoid true intimacy. Although there is usually a crowd around him, many of the archer's so-called close friends are actually what most people think of as acquaintances. The typical fire sign native doesn't have a subtle bone in his body, and Sagittarius is no exception. Archers tend to miss many of the little clues and inferences that help the other signs understand the deeper needs and vulnerabilities of their friends and lovers. Even when he tries his very best to be helpful and comforting, the typical Sagittarian has a predilection for saying and doing exactly the wrong thing at the worst possible time.

The fiery Sagittarius man is strongly sexed. However, sex alone rarely fulfills him. What the archer really cares about are friendship and the *experience* of love. Sagittarians are adventurous in all areas in life, and this naturally carries over to their love lives. Whereas the youthful archer may become involved in affairs with several different partners, the older Jupiter-ruled native can settle down with one person—as long as it is the right person. By then, he has experimented enough to know what works best for him sexually and romantically. Later in life Sagittarius may forget about sex altogether, especially if his attention is totally focused on an interesting project or hobby.

One of Sagittarius' major faults is his tendency to believe he is *always right*. This know-it-all side to the archer's personality can be extremely irritating to anyone who loves him. Although he seems to be a good listener, his mind tends to wander, so friends and associates often have to work extremely hard to get and hold his attention. The archer needs the liberty to pursue his goals and interests, and hates being tied down to inflexible schedules. When he feels hemmed in, his inclination is to take off and seek stimulation elsewhere. Thus, Sagittarians are not the most dutiful friends or lovers in the zodiacal family. Although their promises and commitments are easily made, they are often just as easily forgotten.

The Sagittarius Woman

The Sagittarius woman is a citizen of the world and natural-born adventurer who tends to view life as an endless series of exciting experiences. Superprotective of her personal freedom, the female archer may postpone marriage and motherhood until later in life, or take a pass on domestic responsibilities altogether. Often this is not a conscious decision on her part as much as something that just happens. She is generally too busy transversing the globe, climbing mountains, interviewing foreign dignitaries, or exploring the rain forest to settle down in one place.

When she does have kids, this lady is a fun-loving, unselfish mother who relates to her children as a friend as well as a parent. Since she's never quite grown up herself, she has a genuine gift for understanding young people and remembering what it felt like to be a child. The archer is a likely candidate for single motherhood, and she generally has little difficulty raising her children alone.

Given her natural empathy with kids, the Sagittarian mother may not even realize how great a mom she really is. One Jupiter-ruled mother was truly surprised when her grown daughter mentioned that her happiest memories of childhood were the wonderful times she and her mother had at the movies, museums, shows, and restaurants they frequented on weekends and holidays when her dad had to be at work. "I'm amazed you would say that," this archer told her daughter, "because we went on most of those outings when I was feeling restless and eager to get out of the house."

The typical Sagittarian woman loves being in love almost as much as she loves her freedom. However, when push comes to shove, most female archers choose freedom over love. After all, in addition to her romantic partner, Sagittarius also "loves" her friends, animals, children, studies, ideas, crusades, and travel. More than anything the female archer yearns to test uncharted waters, meet new people, and try new things. Although she will tell you she wants to put down roots and stay in one place, when she hears the call of the open road you may find that she cannot resist its seductive allure. Like Aries and Leo, the Sagittarius woman is impatient and has a low tolerance for the petty details of everyday life. Because she is easily suffocated by dull routine and unimaginative companions, Sagittarius is frequently happier alone than in a boring or restrictive relationship.

Although she may not be the most diligent worker in the company, Sagittarius' capacity for seeing the total picture and understanding the far-reaching ramifications of virtually any plan give her a decided edge over the competition. The archer makes contacts easily. Her gift for bringing people and ideas together, combined with her sense of humor and optimistic nature, readily charms bosses and clients alike. The versatile female archer is likely to be successful in any career field that she views as interesting and fun.

Jupiter, the ruler of Sagittarius, is known as the

planet of "greater fortune," generously bestowing the gifts of protection and good luck on the members of this sign. Sagittarius women are smart and optimistic. They think big and they like to be where the action is. These ladies are among the most imaginative members of the zodiac, and their restless, probing minds demand constant employment.

Contrary to nasty rumors, the Jupiter-ruled female is not lazy, but she dearly loves a good time. The archer's keen mind and aptitude for getting the job done with a minimum of fuss generally allow her the necessary freedom to pursue her after-hours pleasures. And pursue them she does! Whoever said "Life is a beach" must have been a Sagittarian. Unlike some of her workaholic sisters, the Sagittarius gal is a party animal and she does not feel at all guilty about going out and having a ball. While her career may be an important part of the archer's life (and a convenient way to pay the bills), she rarely lets her work get in the way of having a good time.

In the book *Sexual Astrology*, author Martine refers to the Sagittarian female as "the Dona Juana of the zodiac." While this is something of an exaggeration, it is true that it's impossible to possess the female archer, for she cannot be caged. Like her mythological counterpart Artemis (Diana), the Sagittarian female is extremely independent and very much her own person. She desperately needs a partner who is willing to allow her to be herself. Sexually this beguiling, fiery female is exciting, responsive, and willing to experiment. However, the Sagittarian gal is typically more interested in her potential lover's friendship and ability to exchange ideas than in his sexual prowess. She can be something of a tease, and the warm friendship she offers is often misconstrued and mistaken for love.

The Jupiter-ruled woman is attracted to individuals with wit and brains. She enjoys fun and games, and likes to have a fantastically good time. However, she is also something of a romantic who is always on the lookout for a knight in shining armor to come and rescue her from the banality of everyday life. When she's involved with someone, she may stray from time to time either literally or in fantasy. But if left to her own devices, she will come back again. Although she seems to prefer relationships that do not tie her down, when the archer is truly in love with the right person she is capable of fidelity and a life-long commitment.

The Shadow Side of Sagittarius

You meet an interesting archer at a cocktail party, and afterward he takes you out for a wonderful dinner. You have a great time, and you would like to see him again. You are quite sure he feels the same way. He says he will call you soon for a date, but you never hear from him. Or a Sagittarian buddy assures you he will lend you the money you need for an important purchase or project. However, when you stop by his house to pick it up, you find out that he's left on a trip to the Far East and no one knows when he will be back. Perhaps you mention an upcoming seminar to a Sagittarius friend. You explain that you would like to attend, but your car is in the shop. "Hey, don't worry about it," the archer says, "I'll go, too, and we can take my car." After you sign up for the class, he calls and tells you he can't go because he has to work that weekend.

Sagittarius cuts right to the chase. Because he rarely reads the fine print, he often skips important and necessary steps when doing a job or building a relationship. Even when he stays with something long enough to reach his goal, once he's there he often loses interest and seeks to change direction. If you are the one who has been counting on a restless archer, you may find that he's run off and left you out on the proverbial limb. Part of Sagittarius' problem is that he has great difficulty accepting limitations, especially the ones imposed on him by day-to-day reality. He often promises more than he is able or willing to deliver.

Another manifestation of the dark side of Sagittarius stems from the archer's seemingly noble belief in religious and political causes. In his ongoing search for the "truth" the Sagittarian can become rather preachy about his discoveries. When he believes that he is in the right, which is most of the time, the archer acknowledges no view other than his own because he can no longer conceive of other possibilities. Then the dogmatist emerges from the shadows. Instead of becoming an inspiration to others, the pedantic archer acts like a blowhard and a bigot who glorifies his particular faith at the expense of other people's ideas and beliefs.

Jupiter, the planet that rules Sagittarius, has to do with traditional religious beliefs, law and order, the courts, and all the outer trappings of ethics and moral principles. One telling aspect of the Sagittarian nature is a propensity for following the letter, rather than the spirit, of the law. The dark side of the archer's belief system surfaces when he concentrates on rules and regulations while totally disregarding the universal truths that they symbolize. Typically the archer has a strong sense of right and wrong, at least where other people are concerned, but he doesn't always think that the rules apply to him. He may continue to pay lip service to a religion or political party long after he has ceased to believe in its basic message because the outward forms of the organization continue to fulfill a basic need.

One particularly ugly aspect of the archer's shadow relates to his penchant for showing off and name-dropping. Some Sagittarius natives are so afflicted with the "groupie" syndrome that they can barely get through a conversation without mentioning several well-known persons with whom they claim "intimate" familiarity. This type of Jupiter-ruled native tends to be so impressed with celebrity that he will go so far as to write off those of his friends "who just don't hang out with the right people." Worse still, some of these shallow groupie types will brush off anyone they view as unimportant, and not think twice about hurting that person's feelings. ("No, I never see Ted anymore. He's a nice guy and all, but he's a nobody who hasn't a clue to what's really happening.")

Sagittarius Romantic Dinner for Two

Sagittarius the cook

Sagittarians are not generally ranked among the most accomplished cooks in the zodiac, but they definitely qualify as the most congenial hosts. Archers have better things to do than to spend an entire day in the kitchen. When they invite you for a special meal, you may find that the delicious repast was actually catered by a nearby restaurant. Or Sagittarius may skip the pretense of cooking altogether and simply take you out for a fabulous dinner. Whether or not he prepares it himself, everything the Jupiter-ruled archer serves or orders will be well made, appetizing, and highly unusual.

Most Jupiter-ruled natives are endowed with healthy appetites. They love to eat and have a tremendous curiosity for foods that are new and different. Thanks to their love of travel, when they do feel like cooking, foreign dishes usually appear on the menu. The archer adores shortcuts because they get him out of the kitchen faster, but he refuses to sacrifice quality or taste in order to save time. Sagittarius is a daring and intuitive cook who would much rather experiment with a recipe than follow it with exactitude. Archers are fond of fresh fruits and vegetables, freshly baked breads, game birds, smoked meats, and outdoor picnics and barbecues. Typically Sagittarian cuisine is comprised of a strange and intriguing mix of rustic, exotic, and traditional dishes.

Any dinner hosted by the archer is sure to be an

experience you won't soon forget. However, if you hope to eat any time before midnight, make sure to keep out of the archer's way while he's preparing dinner. It's not that he doesn't crave the company, he loves it. But Sagittarius is easily distracted, especially when he has an audience, so when he is cooking it's best to leave him alone to concentrate on the task at hand.

Sagittarius the dinner guest

When you invite a Sagittarian to dinner, always ask him to arrive early. Like Gemini, his zodiacal opposite, the archer tends to go off on tangents and is often notoriously late for appointments. When he does arrive, put Sagittarius in charge of entertaining the other guests, and he will keep them and himself amused and out of your hair until you are ready to serve the dinner. Try to keep your Sagittarian friend away from your kitchen. Archers generally see themselves as experts on every subject. Even the nicest of them is sure to be something of a know-it-all. Of course, you may not mind having him explain the "proper way" to prepare the meal.

Archers make rewarding dinner guests. They appreciate good food and drink, and thoroughly enjoy being surrounded by friends and acquaintances. Sagittarius is a wanderer who believes that variety is the spice of life, and he generally regards dining as just another source of fun and adventure. Typically archers are not overly concerned with matters pertaining to good health and proper diet. Many members of this sign are accomplished athletes who work out on a daily basis. Despite a tendency to eat whatever they want, most of them do not have serious problems with obesity.

No matter where he happens to find himself, the Jupiter-ruled native likes to experiment with new foods and different flavors. Some archers have tasted the great cuisine of various countries in their native settings. Even those Sagittarius natives who haven't been to faraway lands are sure to have sampled their share of exotic and unusual foreign fare. Sagittarius can be expensive to feed. Naturally extravagant himself, he expects to be served only the very best, and he won't hesitate to tell you if he has any complaints.

Foods commonly associated with Sagittarius

Meat: game animals, venison, rabbit, liver

Fowl: game birds, partridge, pheasant, Cornish game hens

Fish and Shellfish: tuna, shark

Dairy Products: cream, cheese

Vegetables and Beans: olives, asparagus, endive, tomatoes, beets, clover, dandelion

Nuts and Grains: chestnuts

Fruits: apricots, currents, raisins, figs, juniper berries, limes, strawberries, blueberries, mulberries

Beverages: peppermint tea, spearmint tea, ginseng tea

Herbs, Spices, and Miscellaneous: cloves, sage, nutmeg, cinnamon, balm, peppermint, spearmint, myrrh, ginseng, maple syrup, honey, sugar, sugar cane, wheat

SAGITTARIUS MENU

Cranberry–Orange Cornish Game Hens

Long Grain and Wild Rice Pilaf

Broiled Tomatoes

Dinner Rolls

White Wine

Baked Apples and Cheddar Cheese Wedges

Peppermint Tea

Sagittarius Recipes

Cranberry–Orange Cornish Game Hens

1 cup fresh cranberries, chopped
1 cup orange marmalade
¼ cup water
1 teaspoon lemon juice
2 Cornish game hens (10 to 12 ounces each)
   salt and pepper to taste
2 wedges fresh lemon

Preheat the oven to 375 degrees. Prepare the sauce by heating the cranberries, marmalade, water, and lemon juice in a saucepan over medium heat. Cook for 5 to 8 minutes, or until the cranberries have released their juices. Set sauce aside. Season the two game hens with salt and pepper, place them in a baking dish, and roast for 45 minutes. Remove the hens from the oven. Spread the cranberry–orange sauce over the top and sides of the hens. Save extra sauce to serve with the finished dish. Return the hens to the oven and bake for another 10 to 15 minutes. Remove from the oven, and spoon remaining sauce over the hens. Garnish each hen with a lemon wedge.

*Long Grain and Wild Rice Pilaf

   1 package (6 ounces) long grain and wild rice mix
2⅔ cups chicken broth
   1 tablespoon butter or margarine
   1 tablespoon olive oil
   ⅓ cup green onions, sliced
   ½ cup dried figs, diced
   ½ cup pine nuts

Prepare the wild rice mix with 2⅓ cups of the chicken broth and the butter or margarine, according to package directions. While the rice is cooking, heat the oil in a medium skillet. Sauté the green onion, dried figs, and pine nuts approximately 2 to 3 minutes, or until nuts are golden. Stir in the remaining ⅓ cup broth, and heat through. Toss the fig mixture with the cooked rice and serve.

*Broiled Tomatoes

2 large, firm tomatoes, cut in half
  salt and pepper to taste
2 teaspoons butter, melted
  parsley for garnish

Sprinkle tomato halves with salt and pepper, and broil under medium heat for about 10 minutes or until tender. Pour the melted butter over the tomatoes, garnish with parsley, and serve at once.

*Baked Apples and Cheddar Cheese Wedges

¼ cup raisins
2 large Rome Beauty apples
1 small lemon, cut in half
1 tablespoon honey
½ teaspoon ground cinnamon
⅓ cup apple cider

Plump the raisins by rinsing in hot water. Drain and set aside. Preheat the oven to 375 degrees. Cut a slice, ½ inch thick, off the top of each apple. Core and seed the apples, and squeeze a little lemon juice inside each one. Arrange the apples in a small baking dish. Mix together the honey, cinnamon, and raisins, and spoon half of the raisin mixture into each apple. Pour the apple cider into the bottom of the baking dish. Cover the top of the baking dish with aluminum foil. Bake the apples for 50 to 60 minutes or until very tender. Serve warm or cold with wedges of cheddar cheese on the side.

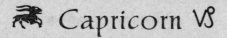
Capricorn ♑

December 22–January 19

Symbol: The Goat   Element: Earth
Quality: Cardinal   Planetary Ruler: Saturn
Polarity: Feminine

There's life alone in duty done,
And rest alone in striving.

—John Greenleaf Whittier
The Drovers

How to Identify Capricorn

In nature, goats are creatures that survive under almost any conditions. Surefooted, even on the steepest mountains, they will eat anything and can endure practically any type of bad weather. The "human goat" is very much like his animal counterpart. Although he is placid and cooperative most of the time, when he gets upset he loses his temper and tries to butt everyone else out of his way.

Capricorns are the most practical members of the zodiacal family. "Life is earnest, life is real," could be their motto. Of all the astrological signs, goats are the ones most likely to have their feet planted firmly on the ground and their eyes focused on the main chance. Purposeful and determined, Capricorn is se-

214

rious about everything he does. No one is more aware of the fact that there are goals to accomplish, rules to respect, deadlines to be met, and guidelines to follow. The Saturn-ruled individual refuses to sit around and wait for things to come to him. First he decides exactly what it is he wants, then he formulates a plan to get it.

Although most natives of this sign seem to have been born successful, they actually must work very hard to get to the top. Many goats have a five-year, ten-year, and twenty-year plan always in place. Willing to wait as long as it takes, they will do whatever necessary to "make it"—as long as it's not illegal or immoral. They win because they refuse to quit, and if knocked down they bounce right back up again.

Determined climbers and naturally hard workers, Capricorns are industrious, efficient, and disciplined. They really resent it when they see others slacking on the job. Easily impressed by the outward signs of success, the Saturn-ruled individual is quite materialistic by nature, mainly because he feels naked and insecure without a strong financial base. Actually the goat prizes power more than money or fame. A born executive, Capricorn is most comfortable when he or she is the one in charge. When not in command, he proves to be a loyal, steadfast employee, who is generally considerate of his underlings and always respectful of his superiors.

Old when they are young, goats generally come into their own after age forty. They often appear younger than their years when they are old. Many Capricorns suffer with health problems during their youth, but gain in strength and vitality as they age. One of the reasons Capricorns strive for money and security is that theirs is a very long-lived sign. Many of their frugal instincts are the result of a desire for security in their later years, and their inclination to accumulate riches can make them seem stingy and greedy.

Capricorns make caring, devoted parents. Traditional in every sense of the word, the typical goat is well aware of the offspring's place in the family dynasty. Capricorn parents are thorough and responsible. No aspect of their children's welfare is ever ignored or glossed over. Because they care what other people think, goats will usually make sure that the neighbors know they're doing a good job raising their kids. Although they may come off as excessively reserved and controlled in public, in the privacy of their homes Capricorn parents are generally loving and affectionate with their children. In return they expect their kids to be well behaved, dutiful, and responsible. If they are not, the typical Capricorn parent can be a strict disciplinarian.

On a personal level Capricorn wants to be the boss, and he can be genuinely dictatorial and demanding. However, as a friend or lover, no one else is as loyal, faithful, or reliable. Built to last, the goat does not jump into a serious relationship without giving it lots of thought. Once he makes a commitment, he sticks to it. He doesn't play the field or flirt. Although he may not bring you roses and chocolates, he always seems to be there when needed. The typical Capricorn is not outwardly romantic, but beneath his restrained exterior there is an individual who is deeply passionate, extremely sensitive, and very much in need of love and friendship—although he would probably rather die than admit it.

Some claim that natives of this sign are cold and calculating. However, the truth of the matter is that no other member of the zodiacal family is as much in need of love as the seemingly cool Saturn-ruled goat. Capricorn actually ranks among the most strongly sexed of the zodiacal signs. Where sexual passion and prowess are concerned, many of its natives could give Aries and Scorpio a run for the money. As a representative of the last of the earth signs, the typical Capricorn is also extremely sensual. More than most, goats need love in their lives, but they have a difficult time expressing their true emotions. They especially dislike feeling vulnerable or at the mercy of someone else's whims and desires.

Capricorn's feelings run deep, but most of the time he keeps them hidden beneath a hard, protective shell. Typically goats have a tendency toward depression, loneliness, and melancholy. Worry is the big Capricorn bugaboo, and members of this sign always seem to find something to fret about. No matter how successful he is at work, or how wonderful his life is at home, the goat never feels he has it made. He does his homework and takes all possible precautions, but still he is sure there is something he has forgotten to do. He lives in fear that everything he built will come tumbling down. Although he needs to learn how to slow down and relax, inertia is an anathema to this tightly wound workaholic.

Myths and Symbols Associated with Capricorn

The astrological ruler of Capricorn is Saturn. The parts of the body ruled by Capricorn are the bones, joints, knees, and teeth. Its symbol, ♑, is thought to represent a goat. The sign is classified as cardinal, earth, feminine (negative, indirect, yin, and internal). Represented by the goat, Capricorn's color is dark brown, its metal is lead, and its gemstone is garnet.

The Greek mythological figure most often associated with Capricorn is the demigod Pan, who was the son of Hermes (Mercury) and the nymph Penelope. Pan, whose name means "all," eventually came to be revered as the personification of nature. He was one of the Satyrs, and had the upper half of a man's body, but the horns, ears, legs, and feet of a goat. According to legend, when Penelope saw her baby, she shrieked in fear and ran away. However, Hermes truly loved his strange son, and he took him to Mount Olympus to be raised in the company of the gods and goddesses.

From his father, Pan inherited the responsibility for flocks, and became the god of the shepherds. He did not stay long on Olympus, preferring instead to dwell among the caves, trees, and mountains of the earth. The feelings of loneliness that can afflict those who travel alone through wild or inhospitable terrain were attributed to the presence of Pan. When the mischievous god wished to scare off travelers who passed through his beloved woods at night, he ut-tered a loud shout, which caused the unwelcome visitors to experience a sudden terrible fright that gave rise to the term "panic."

Pan was a noisy, merry god who liked to amuse himself by chasing nymphs through the woods. One of his attempted seductions, that of the nymph Syrinx, failed when the earth goddess Gaia turned her into a clump of reeds to protect her from Pan's amorous advances. When the god clutched at the reeds, he became enchanted by the sound that the wind made through them. He selected the best of the hollow reeds and turned them into his famous panpipes, or syrinx. The music produced by the pipes was so sweet that on one occasion Pan challenged Apollo, the god of music, to a competition.

The Greeks also related Capricorn to Amalthea, the goat nymph who served as baby nurse to Zeus (Jupiter) on the island of Crete. His mother Rhea had hidden the infant god there to save him from the wrath of his father Cronus (Saturn), who intended to swallow him as he had swallowed his siblings. Amalthea, half goat and half nymph, was sister to the god Pan, who was half goat and half human. She fed the baby Zeus on her magical nanny goat's milk. When he grew up, Zeus broke off one of Amalthea's horns and turned it into the "cornucopia." Just as the goat nymph could produce milk rich enough to feed a young god, so the cornucopia could provide magical nourishment for all the children of the earth. As a reward for her nurturing and devotion, Zeus placed his one-horned nanny in the heavens as the constellation Capricorn.

The sign Capricorn is also associated with an older

zodiacal creature, the goat fish of the ancient Babylonians. The god Ea was one of the major deities of the old Babylonian pantheon. He was sometimes depicted as half man, half fish, and also as a man cloaked in a cape of fish skin with a fish head over his head and the bottom of his cloak trailing in the form of a fishtail. He ruled wisdom and the water beneath the earth. He kept the Tigris and Euphrates rivers flowing, thus making it possible for life to exist on the land. It is said that he rose out of the water during the day in order to teach wisdom and the arts of civilization to the ancient Sumerians, and that he returned to its depths at night.

The Capricorn Man

The Capricorn man is among the most stable and reliable of the zodiacal types. His element is earth. Earth sign natives are generally dependable individuals who relate to the world through practicality and materialism rather than physical action, intellect, or emotion. Although goats are models of useful achievement, they also exhibit a decided desire for power and control. As a cardinal sign, Capricorn is a natural leader who needs to be the one in charge calling the shots, and expects to be well compensated for his efforts. Capricorn has been referred to as the master builder of the zodiac. When this Saturn-ruled native creates something, he wants it to last for a very long time. Goats are innovators, but they are also traditionalists who prefer to build on what has gone before instead of tearing it down and replacing it with something totally new and untried.

Goats are goal-oriented workaholics who have the grit and determination to succeed in any job or profession they choose to follow. They are the major finishers of many of the projects started by the "pioneering" signs, and can quickly become the backbone of any organization. Capricorns have good memories and the ability to think things through to a logical conclusion. They rarely take risks or act on impulse. The goat's intellect is deep and profound, and he likes to explore all possibilities before deciding among various alternatives. When in doubt, he usually chooses the safest and most secure path to his objective.

Goats make determined managers who set the highest standards for themselves and everyone else. The Saturn-ruled native is generally considered a perfectionist who is constantly on the lookout for something or someone to criticize. Although he may be too busy too realize it, members of his staff often resent the goat's blind adherence to by-the-book rules, rigid schedules, and tight deadlines. Although the typical Capricorn supervisor isn't likely to win any popularity contests, he can be as fair as he is demanding. However, sloppy work habits and indifference in the workplace really set the goat's teeth on edge. When Capricorn notices something that needs improvement, he can't resist calling attention to it.

The Capricorn male tends to be careful in financial matters. When he goes shopping, the goat demands a lot of bang for his buck. He can be a frugal, penny-pincher with regard to everyday expenses. But he can also be quite lavish when it comes to the big-ticket items that serve to strengthen his self-image, which he will go to almost any lengths to enhance. Capricorn loves to make an impression, but he refuses to go into debt in order to keep up with the Joneses. However, because he is extremely status-conscious, the goat will usually purchase an elegant home, a fancy car, and well-tailored clothing as soon as he feels he can afford them. During courtship he may not bring you the usual flowers or candy, but when he does buy you a gift or an engagement ring it's sure to be something that will dazzle you—and impress the neighbors.

In business Capricorn usually appears confident and in control, but in his personal relationships he may seem nervous and ill at ease. The goat has a wonderful knack for treating business acquaintances with diplomacy and tact, and he thrives wherever he has the authority to manage and organize others without too much intimacy. However, in love and friendship the Saturn-ruled are often shy and insecure. Where commitment is concerned, they tend to be cautious and overly wary. Many goats find it extremely difficult to relate to others on an emotional level, and as a result they usually have few close friends. When Capricorn does choose to enter into a close relationship, he is intensely loyal and loving but also somewhat jealous and possessive.

The goat's approach to love and commitment is cautious and conservative. He rarely falls in love at first sight, and may take considerable time deciding whether or not a likely candidate is even worthy of his time and attention. Capricorn is no fair-weather friend. Although he may not be the most romantic or exciting man around, once he determines that you are the one for him, you can depend on him to stick with you no matter what the circumstances. True, he will demand your total attention and expect you to put him ahead of everyone else, and at times he can be rather insensitive to your needs and feelings. However, if you are willing to put up with his failings and foibles, and know how to make him feel loved, admired, respected, and appreciated, he will reward you with his undying love and devotion.

Determination, persistence, and tenacity are the outstanding characteristics of the typical Saturn-ruled male. Of all the guys you meet, the goat is the one that truly refuses to take "no" for an answer. Turn him down tonight, and tomorrow night he will be back to try again. A believer in that old saw about faint heart never winning fair lady, he keeps coming back, again and again, until he wears down your resistance. He may be sensitive to rejection, but he rarely allows hurt feelings to stand in the way of getting what he wants. Deep down he believes it is only a matter of time until he can overcome all obstacles and win his heart's desire. The problem is that he forgets, or perhaps he never knew, the basic premise of relating: It involves *two* people, both of whom must be mutually attracted to each other and equally interested in building a relationship.

The Capricorn Woman

The Capricorn woman projects an air of aloofness that can make her seem distant and unapproachable. The typical female goat is naturally reserved. If you are involved with one, it may be up to you to try to penetrate her coat of armor. At first glance she can appear as tough as an elephant's hide. But the truth is that she is not tough at all, just serious and restrained. She sets up emotional boundaries that she refuses to cross, and she may not let you cross them either. However, under her cool facade there lurks a woman capable of giving a great deal of love and affection, but she won't give it to just anyone. First you will have to prove yourself deserving of her regard. Then you will have to reassure her that you truly care for her, and that you will be there for her when she needs you. When and if she finally makes a commitment, the Capricorn female can open up emotionally and physically in ways that may truly amaze you.

Casual affairs are generally not this lady's cup of tea. When she is in love, she plays for keeps. Because she is not a romantic, she's able to distance herself from emotional considerations long enough to consider the long-term implications of her actions. Love alone is usually not enough to influence her. She carefully weighs all the pros and cons before coming to any decision about a prospective relationship. She may expect you to demonstrate your worthiness before she agrees to a liaison that could affect her entire future. Capricorn will not allow anyone to derail her dreams and ambitions. If she happens to fall in love with someone she considers unsuitable, she would rather give him the boot than modify her plans for the future.

Many Capricorn women are career women, but they rarely let their jobs keep them from marrying and having a family. For this virtual Wonder Woman, managing a job, a home, a husband, and a couple of kids is usually only part of what she does each week. In her "leisure time" she may be found doing volunteer work at her church, helping out at her kids' school, stuffing envelopes for a political candidate she admires, taking a computer class, or painting the trim on the outside of the house. The Capricorn lady hates to see time wasted, and she generally manages to cram sixty busy minutes into every hour of her day. This busy gal truly believes that "time is money." She so prides herself on her efficiency that even when she can't actually be *doing* something, such as when she's commuting to and from work, her mind is generally busy *planning* her next move.

Determined to have it all, the Capricorn woman wants money, prestige, and security. As a member of the hardest working of all the signs, this gal is as far from lazy as you can get. She's willing to work as hard as necessary to get everything she wants. She generally has very little trouble incorporating the people she loves into her overall life scheme, so no area of her existence is given short shrift. Somehow she manages to have enough time and energy for career, home, and family. In fact, if anyone in her world is in danger of being shortchanged it's her. The lady goat is usually so busy doing her duty, fulfilling all her commitments, and taking care of all her responsibilities that she forgets to take time out to relax and enjoy herself.

Goats rarely forget an unkindness, insult, or slight. They tend to harbor deep resentments that can smolder for years before surfacing as part of a vengeful plan. When she's hurt, it takes a long time for the Capricorn woman's wounds to heal. While they are healing, she may seek out ways to pay back the hurt. The lady goat does not believe in luck, and she rarely leaves anything to chance. One of the keywords for this sign is *control*, and the Saturn-ruled are among the more manipulative members of the zodiacal family. At times Capricorn may come off as a puppet master who keeps trying to move everyone else around according to some grand design of her own. What's really happening is that the Capricorn woman lives in mortal fear of being manipulated by others, so she endeavors to take control of each and every situation before anyone else can.

One of the most endearing and unexpected characteristics of goats of both sexes is their wry sense of humor. Even the most serious minded Saturn-ruled native can be extremely witty and fun to be around. There is generally a dark side to every joke or clever remark because Capricorns are absolute masters of the art of black humor. Although she finds it mortifying to be made the butt of someone else's jokes, Capricorn is very good at poking fun at herself and at others. Goats are not above mining their own lives for laughs, and many of their funniest observations are self-deprecating. The Capricorn woman has a sharp eye for human foibles, her own included. Her particular brand of humor tends to be dry, sardonic, satirical, cynical, and sometimes a little desperate.

Like her male counterpart, the female Capricorn tends to be emotionally cool and somewhat brittle on the surface, but she's warm and sensitive underneath. She may be basically shy, but she's also strongly sexed and sensual. Once aroused, she's capable of intense and sustained physical passion. Loyalty and fidelity are everything to her. Where love is concerned, she is not into games. She won't flirt or pursue possible suitors, preferring to wait for them to come to her. If she does flirt, she'll do so in a subtle way that allows her to back out gracefully if she sees that her interest is not reciprocated. Not one to fall in love at first sight, this gal likes to take things one step at a time. She builds trust slowly, but when she accepts you she's yours for life.

The Shadow Side of Capricorn

One manifestation of the Capricorn shadow is the puritanical disciplinarian. Through its connection to the planet Saturn, Capricorn relates to the tyrannical patriarch or matriarch who thinks that he or she knows better than anyone else what is best for the children, spouse, relatives, friends, business associates, employees. It also relates to well-meaning but pompous religious leaders, greedy bosses and politicians, and inept managers, supervisors, and teachers who repeatedly stifle talent and initiative in the name of protocol, propriety, convention, social order, rules, and customs.

The dark side of the Saturn-ruled personality is closely associated to the issue of control. At his worst the goat believes that he has not only the right but also the obligation to provide you with a detailed plan on how to run your life. It doesn't really matter what type of relationship you have or whether or not you've asked for his advice. The negative goat is convinced that he knows what's best for you. At some level he is sure that he can help anyone improve themselves or their situation—if only they would heed his counsel. Refuse his advice, and he will be deeply offended. Worse yet, if you don't respond to his suggestions in ways he considers appropriate, he may resort to manipulation and deception in order to get you to go along with his plans and ideas.

No matter what his politics, the typical goat is a natural-born conservative. The Saturn-ruled native is often the loudest opponent of progress of any kind. If something has always been done a certain way, he sees no reason to make changes ("If it was good enough for my father, it's good enough for me."). Many Capricorns have an innate mistrust of dreams and imagination, and they tend to write off most visionary ideas as impractical and unrealistic—and much too expensive.

Some goats believe that sacrifice, hardship, and deprivation build character. Real problems can arise in relationships if the head of the family insists that his spouse or offspring keep to a tight budget, even when they have the means to live quite comfortably. This type of father or mother may insist that the kids work their way through college, or may even push them out of the nest as soon as they reach legal age, with strict instructions for "making it" on their own. In extreme cases the goat may believe that inherited money spoils people, and so will cut the kids and spouse out of his will altogether. This kind of parent often withholds love and affection unless his every word is obeyed. In his most negative guise Capricorn is analogous to Cronus (Saturn), who ate his children because he was afraid that one of them was going to supplant him.

Another aspect of Capricorn's shadow is a tendency to always play the martyr. The workaholic goat thrives on duty and responsibility. When taken too far, this can mean that he insists on shouldering all of the burden himself and absolutely refuses to ask for help or delegate any part of the load. When things become too much for him, he suffers in silence, or complains to everyone except the one person who can actually offer him some help and relief.

In romantic relationships the goat seeks comfort and security over excitement and romance. When a union goes sour, it's unlikely that Capricorn will just pack his bags and move out. Although the goat is not inclined to leave when things go wrong, he usually retreats into himself. It is difficult for him to open up emotionally, and he doesn't take kindly to suggestions that include psychological counseling. Goats cling, and they keep on clinging even when there is nothing left to cling to. Like as not, he'll hang in there hoping that things will get better, which in his mind means that the other person changes, not him.

Capricorn Romantic Dinner for Two

Capricorn the cook

Where cooking is concerned, Capricorn has a dual personality. When preparing a dinner for himself or his immediate family, the typical goat carefully considers cost along with taste and nutrition. No one is better at creating great meals on a budget. Typically Capricorn prefers to eat less of something good than a lot of something that is not quite as good. The mountain goat, which symbolizes his sign, can live on practically nothing, and the "human goat" is a master at stretching food and dollars. Capricorn can make a delicious meal out of pasta, beans, or leftovers that will feed the entire goat clan.

When the status-conscious goat entertains, he does so formally and with style. He'll spare no effort or expense in an attempt to dazzle and impress his guests. As efficient and controlled in the kitchen as he is everywhere else, he makes sure that his menus are well planned and painstakingly executed. Although the goat enjoys experimenting and mixing basic ingredients in new ways, he is essentially a conservative host who steadfastly follows the rules and adheres to traditional practices, such as always serving white wine with fish and red wine with meat.

The Saturn-ruled native approaches cooking in much the same way he approaches life. In the kitchen he's organized and determined. Even when serving a large group, he holds up amazingly well under pressure. With so many demands on his time, the Capricorn cook is a clock-watcher who prefers to prepare part of the meal in advance, as long it does not adversely affect the finished product. He plans everything carefully down to the last detail, so that when his guests arrive he can be cool and collected. He greets them at the door with a smile, then ushers them into his home with ceremonial pride.

Capricorn the dinner guest

Chances are that when you invite the goat to dinner, he will put you off with excuses about how busy he is and how much work he has waiting at the office. When this happens, it's up to you to tempt him with promises of a festive meal and good company. It's a good idea to issue a somewhat formal invitation, so that he can check his busy schedule in advance and "pencil you in" for the appropriate date and time. Goats don't like to waste time, either theirs or yours, so make sure that the dinner is ready to serve when your Capricorn guest arrives. Although he doesn't like it at all when meals are delayed, this workaholic often gets held up at his job, and he may be late for dinner.

When the Saturn-ruled native arrives at your home, he's likely to be keyed up and stressed out from the day's activities. Get him to relax with a drink, then serve him a good meal along with some interesting conversation. Chances are that he will have a wonderful time in spite of himself. Rest assured that the goat appreciates your culinary efforts, even if he doesn't openly applaud your efforts or give you rave reviews and flowery compliments. Capricorns like to eat, but they are often more interested in the social aspects of dining than in the actual food itself. The typical goat is a good listener. Once he relaxes and gets into the swing of things, he's also a fine conversationalist and an excellent dinner companion.

Capricorn expects the evening to be well organized and well presented. He's no great fan of casual dining, so be sure to set your table with your best linen, silver, and china. If things are not going smoothly in your kitchen, do not, under any circumstances, allow Capricorn to help out. If you do, he will come in and take over, tell you what to do and how to do it— and then proceed to finish the cooking for you.

Foods commonly associated with Capricorn

Meat: goat, aged steak, pork
Fowl: turkey
Fish and Shellfish: shellfish, carp, herring
Dairy Products: goat cheese
Vegetables and Beans: parsnips, spinach, onions,

beets, olives, potatoes, cabbage, rutabagas, artichokes, lentils

Nuts and Grains: barley

Fruits: quince, black currants, blackberries, black
figs

Beverages: coffee

Herbs, Spices, and Miscellaneous: comfrey, cumin,
sage, tarragon, rue, sorrel, vervain, carob, vinegar, sour pickles, whole wheat bread, gelatin

CAPRICORN MENU

Sun-dried Tomato and Goat Cheese Salad

Capellini Pasta with Pesto Sauce

Whole Wheat French Bread

White Wine

Jorge's Chocolate Raspberry Layer Cake

Coffee

Capricorn Recipes

Sun-dried Tomato and Goat Cheese Salad

½ teaspoon dijon mustard
2 teaspoons balsamic vinegar
1 tablespoon olive oil
  freshly ground black pepper
½ cup radicchio
1 cup bibb lettuce

2 ounces goat cheese
2 sun-dried tomatoes

Place the mustard in a small dish, and add the vinegar. Beat with a fork or wire whisk. Add the oil slowly, and continue beating. Add the pepper. Tear or cut the radicchio and bibb lettuce leaves. Put them into a bowl, add the dressing, and toss well. Divide the salad mixture between two plates. Cut the goat cheese and sun-dried tomatoes into pieces and distribute evenly on each plate.

Capellini Pasta with Pesto Sauce

2 cups fresh basil leaves, firmly packed
¼ cup toasted pine nuts
¼ cup grated parmesan cheese
2 garlic cloves, minced
½ cup olive oil
½ cup red or yellow peppers, chopped
1 tablespoon margarine
2 canned artichoke hearts, diced
½ cup pitted black olives, sliced
½ pound capellini pasta

First prepare the pesto: puree the basil leaves, pine nuts, parmesan cheese, garlic, and olive oil in a food processor or blender until smooth. Season to taste with salt and pepper. Set aside.

Sauté the peppers in margarine in a heavy skillet.

Stir in the artichoke and olives, and continue cooking until heated through. Set the skillet aside.

Cook and drain the capellini pasta according to package directions. Stir the pesto into the hot skillet mixture and toss with the pasta.

*Whole Wheat French Bread

    1 cup water, lukewarm (98 degrees F)
 1½ teaspoons dry yeast
    ½ cup bread flour
 1½ cups whole wheat flour
    ½ teaspoon salt

Pour the water into a large mixing bowl, and add the dry yeast. Stir together until the yeast dissolves. Mix the bread flour, wheat flour, and salt together. Add half the flour mixture to the yeast mixture, and stir well for about 3 minutes. Add the rest of the flour slowly, because the amount of flour needed may vary. The bread dough should form a ball, but still be wet and sticky to the touch. Knead gently for about 4 minutes. Shape the dough into a ball, place it in a lightly greased bowl, and cover with a towel. Let the dough rise for about 20 minutes or until double in bulk. Punch the dough down, knead slightly, and divide into two pieces. Form each piece into a loaf by shaping it into a flat rectangle and then rolling it up like a jelly roll. Close the seams carefully. Place the loaves, seam down, on a cookie sheet that has been lightly sprayed with oil and dusted with flour. Cover with a towel and allow the bread to rise once again until double in bulk. Cut diagonal lines across the top of each loaf and place the bread in an oven that has been preheated to 375 degrees. Bake for 20 minutes or until the loaves sound hollow when tapped lightly on the bottom. Cool on a rack.

Jorge's Chocolate Raspberry Layer Cake

2 9-inch layers prepared from any devil's food cake mix
8 ounces semisweet chocolate
1 can sweetened condensed milk
5 ounces raspberry preserves
fresh raspberries (optional)

Bake cake layers and set on a rack to cool. Melt the chocolate in a double boiler. When thoroughly cool, add the sweetened condensed milk and beat well. Divide the mixture in half. For the filling, add the preserves to half the mixture and stir until blended. Place one layer on a serving plate and spread the filling on top. Cover with the second layer and spread the remaining chocolate mixture on top of the cake. Decorate with the fresh raspberries.

Aquarius ♒

January 20–February 18

Symbol: The Water Bearer   Element: Air
Quality: Fixed   Planetary Ruler: Uranus
Polarity: Masculine

We stand for freedom. That is our conviction for
ourselves: that is our only commitment to others.

—John Fitzgerald Kennedy
Message to Congress, May 25, 1961

How to Identify Aquarius

There is an elusive, airy quality to the Aquarian
personality that is difficult to pin down or define.
Water bearers love freedom, detest oppression in any
form. Many are nonconformists who chafe at restrictions and consistently march to the beat of a different
drummer. Most are intellectuals who live more in the
mind than in the body. Emotionally they can come
off as somewhat cool and reserved. Although the
water bearer is genuinely friendly and outgoing, he
is not an extrovert. Aquarius is a group person, but
he's also something of a loner who periodically needs
space and periods of solitude.

Although some water bearers are obviously eccentric by nature, others consciously cultivate eccentric-

237

ity as a lifestyle. The herd mentality that is so prevalent in our society usually doesn't sit well with the Uranus-ruled native. Aquarians love to shock people, especially if they can knock the wind out of the sails of those self-righteous, hypocritical folks who've appointed themselves to membership in the moral police squad. On a physical level most Aquarians are not especially adventurous, but these unique thinkers are always searching for new and better ways to broaden their mental horizons. Motivated by an ongoing search for the truth, the typical water bearer is a genuinely compassionate humanitarian whose humanity and compassion stem more from his head than his heart.

Typically Aquarians are among the most broadminded members of the zodiacal family. But once their minds are made up, these fixed sign natives can be unbelievably stubborn, intractable, and dogmatic. When he's set on something, it's never easy to get him to change course ("My mind is made up, don't confuse me with facts."). If a problem arises, Aquarius may take his time arriving at a conclusion, but once he does he hates having to adjust his thinking. However, when he changes his mind about something he can be as obstinately defensive of his new belief as he was of the old one. The Uranus-ruled Aquarian may appear calm on the surface, but underneath his cool facade he is often anxious, nervous, and apprehensive. When he seems detached and impersonal in his interactions with people, it's usually because his thoughts are somewhere else. Perhaps he has allowed himself to become distracted by some larger-than-life new theory or idea, or by a challenging puzzle he has been trying to solve.

In his desire to help humanity Aquarius often feels the need to "pour forth" something of himself. He tends to envision the world as he believes it could be, and he may have great difficulty accepting it as it is. Nearly always intelligent, logical, and original in their thinking, Aquarians are also strongly imaginative and psychically intuitive. They like to use their minds to "push the envelope" of human capability. The Uranus-ruled have been responsible for many of the major advances in science. Since water bearers seek to explore the limits of human understanding, they make excellent psychotherapists, teachers, writers, artists, and astrologers.

Of all the signs, Aquarius is the one that has the most difficulty staying focused in the here and now. The typical water bearer is a future-oriented visionary whose head is crammed with thoughts and ideas about tomorrow. Always one step ahead of his time, Aquarius is fascinated with every aspect of new technology from aviation to space exploration to the latest discoveries in computers. The Uranus-ruled are the innovators of the zodiac. Their ultimate goal is to make the world a better place through study, invention, and social change. When he's not dreaming about the future, the water bearer enjoys studying the past. Members of this sign can also be found working in fields connected to history, archaeology, and anthropology.

Aquarius' emblem is the water bearer, pouring the water of originality and idealism onto the parched earth of materialism and conformity. Uranus-ruled natives often stand at the vanguard of liberal thinking and tolerance. Since they appreciate many kinds of people, it is not unusual for Aquarians to seek partners from other races and cultures. They generally treat everyone they meet as they expect to be treated, which is basically with respect and acceptance. Because he has a tendency to form odd alliances and favor unorthodox living arrangements, the Aquarian's domestic setup may differ quite a bit from the accepted norm. In fact many water bearers actually seem to prefer a nonconformist union that flaunts convention and thumbs its nose at legal ties.

Although the water bearer has many acquaintances, he usually has few close friends. Where feelings are concerned, the doggedly independent Aquarius may feel he is stumbling around in the dark. Members of this sign can't quite figure out how to relate to others in a close alliance without giving up their own individual rights. So they tend to substitute intellectual kinship for emotional ties. When they give love, it has to be on their terms. In general this means that even in the midst of a close relationship, Aquarius needs to retain enough space and breathing room to keep from feeling hemmed in.

Although his sex drive is not particularly strong, the free-spirited water bearer's unconventional nature makes him open to most forms of sexual experimentation. His deepest need is for a relationship that satisfies him mentally as well as physically. With the right person Aquarius can be an uninhibited, passionate, giving lover, as well as a faithful, caring, and understanding life partner.

Myths and Symbols Associated with Aquarius

The astrological ruler of Aquarius is Uranus. The parts of the body ruled by Aquarius are the ankles and circulatory system. Its symbol, ♒, is thought to represent waves of water (as well as sound waves, light waves, electricity). The sign is classified as fixed, air, masculine (positive, direct, yang, and external). Represented by the water bearer, Aquarius' color is electric blue, its metal is aluminum, and its gemstone is amethyst.

The Greek mythological figure most often associated with Aquarius is the Titan Prometheus, who stole fire from the gods and gave it to the mortals of the earth. Zeus (Jupiter) assigned to Prometheus and his brother Epimetheus the task of populating the earth. Epimetheus immediately jumped in and created the animals, and he gave them great gifts including strength, courage, cunning, and speed. Meanwhile Prometheus set about creating man out of the elements of earth and water. But when Prometheus finished shaping man, who was to be superior to all the animals, he discovered that his brother had already handed out all the best gifts to the animals, so there was nothing left for man.

Prometheus went to Zeus and asked if it would be okay for his mortals to have some of the sacred fire, which would make them more than a match for the other animals. With fire they could make weapons and tools, defend themselves, and cultivate the earth. They could also warm their dwellings so as to become relatively independent of the climate. Zeus was very jealous of any power other than his own, and he told Prometheus that fire belonged to the gods alone. He said that he thought mortal men would become arrogant if they possessed this wonderful blessing.

Prometheus felt that Zeus' attitude was wrong and unfair, so he rebelled and stole some of the fire from Zeus' hearth and gave it to man anyway. Zeus was enraged, but once the gift was made it could not be taken back. The father of the gods took vengeance on Prometheus by chaining him to a rock on Mount Caucasus. Each day a vulture came and gnawed at his liver, which grew back as fast as it was devoured. Prometheus hung in his chains and suffered, but he did not regret what he had done nor did he submit to the will of the tyrant Zeus. Prometheus' agony continued until rescued by Heracles (Hercules) who came to kill the vulture and set the Titan free.

Another Greek myth commonly associated with Aquarius is that of Ganymede. The original Olympian cup bearer was Hebe, goddess of youth and future wife to Heracles. However, one day she slipped and twisted her ankle while pouring water for the gods, and was no longer able to serve them as cup bearer. Zeus spotted Ganymede, the son of King Tros, tending sheep in the mountains near Troy. Ganymede was said to be the most beautiful boy alive, and Zeus fell madly in love with him. Zeus changed himself into an eagle and carried Ganymede up to Mount Olympus. After that Ganymede replaced Hebe as cup bearer to the gods, but he poured wine, not water, from his golden bowl. When King Tros protested his son's abduction, Zeus sent him two fine horses as compensation and promised to grant Ganymede eternal youth. As a reward for its help, the king of the gods turned the eagle into the constellation Aquila. In the sky Aquila appears to be flying down toward Aquarius.

Aquarius and Ganymede are usually seen as one and the same, a deity credited with bringing rain to the earth. Once Aquarius–Ganymede caused so great a downpour that only Deucalion, son of Prometheus, and his wife Pyrrha survived the deluge.

The Aquarius Man

Aquarius serves as witness and observer in our society, and it often seems as if he prefers watching life from afar to actually joining in. He is a curious fellow who finds endless fascination in everything that is going on around him. In his detached and impersonal way he would like to commune with all the forces of the universe, and he usually spends much of his life trying to do just that. One of his favorite activities is getting into other people's heads and finding out exactly what makes them tick. His profound interest in everyone else's peculiarities can make it seem as if he is more interested in their lives than he is in his own. His ongoing love affair with thoughts and ideas can give the impression that he spends more time theorizing about life than living it.

Although he is open and friendly toward everyone he meets, Aquarius is usually truly close to only a few select individuals. While he may be emotionally detached, the water bearer is not unfeeling. However, his claustrophobic nature causes him to quake at the thought of being closed in by either circumstances or people. He tends to become frustrated when things don't go his way, and his nervous anxiety can make him react with anger. However, as the archetype for the absentminded professor, Aquarius rarely stays angry for long, and he *never* holds a grudge—because he usually can't remember why he was mad to begin with.

Astrologers toss around a lot of descriptive terms in their attempt to characterize the behavior of the typical water bearer. Revolutionary, maverick, avant-garde, crazy genius, mad scientist, absentminded professor, space cadet, eccentric, and weird are just a few of the nicer terms. Aquarius serves society as a paradigm buster and prophet of progress and innovation. However, saner, more sensible individuals tend to place Aquarius' attempts to challenge the status quo in the same category as dangerous experiments done by a crazy kid with a chemistry set. Although Aquarius has his head in the clouds, don't be fooled by the faraway look in his eyes. The water bearer generally has both feet firmly planted on the ground. His forward-looking ideas may seem like pie in the sky to some, but they are carefully thought out and well grounded in reality. Aquarians are idealists and dreamers, but they are *practical* idealists who usually know or can find out exactly what they need to do to make their dreams come true.

Aquarius is generally an asset to any company he works for. Aquarius is all about change and progress. The Aquarian man loves all the latest gizmos and gadgets of next generation technology. Most water bearers are highly intelligent, creative, and analytical. They possess a special talent for uncovering trends and introducing new methods into the workplace. Although his idea of success is rarely the same as everyone else's, Aquarius usually manages to move up the corporate ladder fairly quickly. The Uranus-ruled are not particularly materialistic. Most water bearers are more concerned with turning their dreams into practical realities than with becoming rich or famous. However, riches and fame often do come to members of this sign as a result of their groundbreaking ideas and practical inventions. Although he doesn't usually put wealth at the top of his list of things he considers important, Aquarius likes money for the freedom that it brings, and he usually earns a good living in spite of himself.

If there is an Aquarian creed, it's probably the old maxim that says, "Rules are made to be broken." Although most people don't realize it, when Aquarius wants to do something he doesn't take "no" for answer. The water bearer may not stand around and argue about it, but if he thinks it is important he will usually go ahead and do whatever it is he wants to do, even without permission. Like Prometheus when Zeus refused his request to give humans fire, if the

Uranus-ruled native thinks he is in the right, nothing can stop him from carrying out his plans, especially when he believes they will benefit humanity.

The enigmatic Aquarian man has a courtship style like no other. Although he wants to know everything about everyone else's feelings, he is never in a hurry to reveal his own. The only thing that's for sure in a relationship with a Uranus-ruled man is that he views you as a friend as well as a lover. Even in his most intimate relationships, his first connection is sure to be a mental one. It's virtually impossible to arouse his romantic interest without some type of mind-to-mind contact. One nice thing about Aquarius is that he invariably sees his lover as an individual, not as a sex object. In fact the sex act, although important to him, is rarely the first thing on his mind.

The water bearer lives in the realm of ideas. Feelings frighten him, and he's more comfortable repressing his emotions than expressing them. On a physical level he's naturally low-key, and he may leave it up to his partner to take the initiative. However, any sexual approach must be subtle and tactful. While the Aquarian man can be seduced, he resists being dominated. It's not easy to pin him down. If you ever force him to choose between love and freedom, don't be surprised if he picks freedom.

Romantically Aquarius may be a slow starter. Once he gets going, he's a passionate, imaginative, and considerate lover. Because he is easily bored and drawn to the new and unusual, it can be difficult to get him to commit to a long-term arrangement. However, Aquarius is a fixed sign. If and when he finds the right person, he actually makes a surprisingly devoted, loyal, and faithful marriage partner.

The Aquarius Woman

Everything about the Aquarian woman is paradoxical. If you ever hope to understand this predictably unpredictable female, you may have to adopt a totally new frame of reference. Although she possesses all the loyalty and faithfulness of the fixed signs, she also displays the cool emotional detachment of the element of air. A logical, intellectual, linear thinker most of the time, Aquarius is also incredibly intuitive. Her hunches are usually right on target. Social, friendly, tolerant, and often extremely political, the female water bearer desperately wants to help make the world a better place. However, she's a secret elitist who is more at home in the ivory tower of her mind than working in direct contact with masses of needy people.

There is no such thing as a typical Aquarian woman. Each of them goes out of her way to be as different as possible. While the ladies of other signs are following fashion trends and striving to be as alike as possible, the water bearer is busy cultivating her various eccentricities. Because she is a loner who hates to be alone, this freedom-loving gal usually ends up being surrounded by family and friends. Actually Aquarius needs to *feel free*, but she doesn't actually need to *be free* in the sense that the other freedom-loving signs (Aries, Gemini, Sagittarius) need freedom. She can be at home with a half dozen kids and all the work and responsibility that goes with a family, and as long as no one is telling her what to do or when to do it she's perfectly happy.

Aquarius is not naturally a homemaker in the true sense of the word, but her home is always a nice place to visit. Drop by and she will welcome you with a cup of coffee, some interesting nibbles, and a few hours of scintillating conversation. She may not be a housekeeper in the traditional sense, as the Uranus-ruled female likes to live in a spacious, comfortable, pleasant place decorated in her own inimitable style. Some Aquarian women are neat and tidy, others actually seem to prefer living in a mess. Either way the Uranus-ruled woman orders her priorities so that some areas of her life can be almost obsessively organized while other areas are more or less neglected.

Although she's not one to coo and fuss over her children, the water bearer makes a caring and attentive, though somewhat detached, mother. She tends to relate to her kids as small adults. She is particularly interested in teaching them how to be independent and think for themselves. She believes that children are never too young to start learning. Her greatest pleasure is sharing what she knows with her little prodigies. While other moms are shepherding their offspring to play groups, Scout meetings, and ball games, Aquarius takes hers to libraries, museums, and planetariums. Although she will do everything she can to help her children succeed, she can switch off and become rather distant if they become too emotionally demanding.

Lady Aquarius invariably needs a job or interest of her own. Her family, if she has one, is important to her, but she rarely allows them to become her entire universe. When the Uranus-ruled female is otherwise engaged, her mate and kids had best learn how to fend for themselves. No matter what her job, cause, or project, the Aquarius woman is whole-hearted about getting it done, and she's not likely to drop something she considers important in order to run home and prepare dinner. If her children and her mate are smart, they will learn how to cope on their own, at least some of the time.

Social justice is a vitally important concept to natives of this sign. A world where everyone is free and equal is a true Aquarian ideal. These individual-istic folks want to be free to be themselves, and they graciously extend their desire for freedom to every-one on earth. As instigators of revolution and radical change, Uranus-ruled women are big on causes, and will join any organization from Amnesty Interna-tional to the Sierra Club that protects people, ani-mals, and the environment. Some Aquarius females have been known to sacrifice personal relationships in order to pursue the greater good. While seeking the very best for humanity as a whole, this dedicated lady can easily lose sight of the needs of individual human beings.

Although she has a streak of unpredictability, the Aquarian female usually keeps her wits about her. Even in the throes of passion, she never totally loses her head or her heart. In love, as in everything else, she is a contradiction. A devoted and faithful lover, she usually won't end a relationship without a good reason. If the relationship does end for whatever reason, she may not even bother to try to find someone new. If she does meet someone in spite of herself, she may pull back when things begin to get too serious. Aquarius enjoys having love and companionship, but she also enjoys being on her own with no one to question what she does or doesn't do.

Sexually the Uranus-ruled female is open to suggestion. The *idea* of sex turns her on sometimes more than the act itself. Some women born under this sign seem to prefer casual attachments without commitment. Others seem to enjoy love and sex in a safe, comfortable partnership. The Aquarius female is not especially sentimental or romantic, but she is ever *idealistic*. Forget the flowers, forget the candy, forget the jewelry, and don't worry if you forget a wedding anniversary—your absentminded Aquarius partner probably won't remember it either. But don't ever lie to her or disappoint her in ways that matter to her, or she may never forgive you.

The Shadow Side of Aquarius

"I know" is a key phrase associated with this sign. One aspect of the Aquarian dark side is the water bearer's presumption that he knows everything. Although he detests snobbery based on race, gender, economic circumstance, or physical ability, Aquarius can be remarkably snooty where the intellect is concerned. Many Aquarians genuinely believe that their unique combination of mental dexterity and intuition makes them special. Some project an attitude of intellectual superiority that others find insufferable. Aquarians tend to be abstract thinkers and often have great difficulty translating their ideas into words other people can understand. Because of this fixed sign's stubbornness and inflexibility, Aquarius often feels as if his ideas are the only ones that are valid, and he becomes greatly annoyed when people fail to understand or accept them.

The water bearer is proud of his prodigious store of learning. He expects to be respected and rewarded more for what he *knows* than for anything he actually accomplishes. Although he loves to teach, write, and lecture, Aquarius lacks patience. He can come off as pompous, patronizing, and condescending if his audience doesn't "get it" the first time around. The water bearer's propensity for talking without actually communicating a whole lot of information comes from a tendency to go off on tangents and make things more complicated than they need to be. The scientific, technology-oriented, Uranus-ruled native often fails to make himself understood simply because he insists on using technical language that goes over his listeners' heads.

Aquarius' financial style is often a weird mixture of frugality and extravagance. Another of the great Aquarian paradoxes is his overall attitude toward money and possessions. Some members of this sign can be real penny-pinchers, others are truly benevolent and open-handed. The typical water bearer considers himself a nonmaterialist. But financial security may occupy more of his thoughts than he cares to

admit. Although this practical idealist keeps one eye
on his visions for the future, the other is usually focused on his bank balance.

In *Hamlet*, when Polonius says, "Neither a bor-
rower nor a lender be; For loan oft loses both itself
and friend," he might have been quoting a basic
Aquarian creed. Aquarius can be extremely generous.
If you really need money, he will probably give it to
you as an outright gift rather than a loan because the
water bearer hates lending money. Aquarius usually
keeps his word and pays his bills on time, but for
some reason he isn't convinced that others will do
the same. Since he realizes that a broken promise or
an unpaid debt can ruin a friendship, he simply
would rather not take the chance. Water bearers also
hate to borrow money, and most would rather pay
cash than build debt and incur interest charges.

Aquarius deals best with problems on a distant
level, and is often more concerned with the welfare
of the world than with the welfare of individuals.
Although he derives a real sense of satisfaction from
helping humanity in general, on a one-to-one basis
the water bearer can be amazingly insensitive to the
pain and suffering of those closest to him. Even
Aquarians who are naturally sympathetic can have
great difficulty coping with common complaints from
friends, family members, or coworkers. Many water
bearers are uneasy in the face of physical illness, and
some will actually leave the house whenever someone is sick. Aquarius does not have a lot of patience
with anything he deems a weakness. He tends to
become distant and withdrawn when forced to deal

with anyone who demands more of his time and attention than he's willing to give.

Aquarius Romantic Dinner for Two

Aquarius the cook

In the kitchen, as elsewhere, no two members of this sign are exactly alike. Although virtually all water bearers love to eat, they are not all equally enthusiastic about cooking. While some members of this sign may be chefs of the highest order, others can't even boil water. Then there's Uranus-ruled Paul Newman, who is such a wonderful cook that he's started his own gourmet food corporation. However, in true Aquarian fashion, this altruistic actor does not see one penny of profit because at his request it all goes to charity.

Aquarians rarely enjoy spending a lot of precious time in food preparation. They are always on the lookout for viable shortcuts that will help get dinner on the table a bit faster. Strange and unusual dishes tend to appeal to Aquarius' quirky nature, and he's certainly not afraid to try new things. Aquarius' kitchen is his laboratory. He loves experimenting with new foods and creating dishes that are different and unusual. Although some of his creations are wonderful, others can be total failures. However, the water bearer is not easily discouraged in his ongoing quest to break new ground (culinary and otherwise). He will simply shrug off the failures, and try again.

The Aquarian native is friendly and social. He loves to chat and exchange ideas. If you ask to join him in the kitchen while he's fixing dinner, he's sure to say yes. But if you do, don't expect to eat on time. When it comes to doing two things at once, Aquarius enjoys multitasking almost as much as Gemini, but he's not nearly as good at it. When the easily distracted water bearer gets involved in a truly scintillating conversation, the house could burn down around him, and he might not even notice.

Aquarius the dinner guest

Aquarians are rarely picky about food. Most Uranus-ruled natives will eat whatever is put in front of them. The water bearer usually has a sweet tooth and may prefer a somewhat lighter meal followed by a rich and imaginative desert. If your Uranus-ruled lover suggests that you have your dessert first, don't lead him toward the bedroom. Get the Biscuit Tortoni out of the freezer. He's not talking in code, he means exactly what he says. Members of this sign tend to follow their own kind of logic, and they simply can't understand why the best part of the meal has to come last.

Just when you think you have him figured out, the water bearer does a complete turnaround. In spite of his partiality toward dishes that are unusual, foreign, and unfamiliar, Aquarius may surprise you by eating the same thing over and over again, especially if it is something he really likes. In line with their far-out ideas and beliefs, Aquarians are easy marks for food faddists. Although not as likely to be addicted to health food as Virgo, water bearers are often won over by unconventional or alternative ideas regarding health, food, and diet. Inevitably some Aquarians will choose to follow a specialized food regimen such as a macrobiotic or vegetarian diet.

When you invite an Aquarian to a romantic dinner for two, keep it subtle. If you overdo the candlelight and hearts and flowers, you may find that he is more than a little embarrassed by overt displays of sentiment and emotion. Typically the water bearer is not impressed by elaborate preparations. Too much fuss is more likely to turn him off than on. Remember, he has come to see *you*! He is probably more interested in what you have to say than in what you are serving for dinner. If your conversation is engaging enough, he may forget to eat altogether.

Foods commonly associated with Aquarius

Meat: none

Fowl: aquatic birds, duck, geese

Fish and Shellfish: shellfish, anchovies, squid, octopus

Dairy Products: yogurt, cheese

Vegetables and Beans: root vegetables, eggplant, dried beans, parsnips, sorrel, spinach, beets, olives, lentils, split peas

Nuts and Grains: rice, water chestnuts, chestnuts

Fruits: quinces, lemons, dried fruits

Beverages: coffee, tea

Herbs, Spices, and Miscellaneous: comfrey, water-cress, cumin, salt

AQUARIUS MENU

Antipasto Platter

Eggplant Parmesan

Garlic Bread

Biscuit Tortoni

Cappuccino

Aquarius Recipes

Antipasto Platter

Arrange any or all of the following on a large serving platter: Italian salami, pepperoni sausage, prosciutto (Italian ham), fresh mozzarella cheese, green olives, ripe olives, cherry tomatoes, marinated artichoke hearts, pickled beets, caponata (eggplant relish), pickled mushrooms, hot peppers. Serve the antipasto with breadsticks or crackers.

Eggplant Parmesan

1 medium eggplant
1 cup bread crumbs
1 teaspoon dried oregano, crumbled
1 large egg, beaten

salt

olive oil

6 to 8 ounces mozzarella cheese, sliced

2 cans (8 ounces each) tomato sauce

½ cup parmesan cheese, grated

Cut the eggplant into ½-inch thick slices. Sprinkle the eggplant slices with salt, and place on a paper towel to drain for 20 to 30 minutes. Mix the bread crumbs with the dried oregano. Dip each eggplant slice into beaten egg, and then into the bread crumb mixture. Sprinkle the slices lightly with salt to taste. Heat some olive oil in a skillet. Add the eggplant slices a few at a time and sauté to a medium brown (about 5 minutes on each side). Drain on paper towels.

Preheat oven to 350 degrees. Oil a baking pan and line the bottom with half of the eggplant. Place a slice of mozzarella cheese on each eggplant slice. Spoon one can of tomato sauce over all, and sprinkle with half of the grated parmesan cheese. Repeat above instructions to make a second layer. Cover the pan with tin foil, and bake for 45 minutes or until the sauce bubbles.

*Garlic Bread

½ cup butter or margarine, softened

2 to 4 garlic cloves, crushed

1 loaf Italian or French bread

In a small bowl combine butter and garlic. Cut the

bread lengthwise, and spread the garlic butter over the cut sides of the bread. Place bread halves, butter side up, on a cookie sheet, and bake in a 350 degree oven for about 15 minutes or until the tops are lightly browned. Put the two halves of the bread back together, and cut into two-inch serving slices. Serve warm. If you like, you can make this recipe ahead of time. Wrap the finished garlic bread in aluminum foil and refrigerate. Reheat the foil-wrapped bread in the oven just before serving.

Biscuit Tortoni

½ cup sugar
⅛ cup water
3 egg yolks
¼ pound macaroons, crushed
1 teaspoon vanilla
1½ cups heavy cream, whipped

Boil sugar with water until the syrup spins a thread when dropped from a spoon. Pour the sugar syrup slowly into lightly beaten egg yolks in the top of a double boiler. Cook, stirring constantly, until mixture coats the spoon. Add the vanilla, whipped cream, and all but 3 tablespoons of the crushed macaroons. Stir gently, pour into soufflé cups, sprinkle the tops with the remaining macaroon crumbs, and freeze until ready to serve.

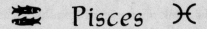

≋ Pisces ♓

February 19–March 20

Symbol: The Fish   Element: Water
Quality: Mutable   Planetary Ruler: Neptune
Polarity: Feminine

Life is a dream . . . we sleeping wake and waking
sleep.

—Montaigne
Essays, Book II

How to Identify Pisces

As the twelfth and final astrological sign, Pisces
brings together many of the characteristics of the
eleven signs that precede it in the zodiac. This sign's
reputation as one of the most perplexing and difficult
to pinpoint is well deserved. Its members are like
chameleons that change color to match their surroundings. Fish generally get along with all types of
people. Their combination of the water element with
the mutable quality gives them their special gift,
which is their ability to "fit in" no matter where they
happen to be. The aura of mystery that surrounds
the typical fish comes as much from Pisces' talent for
"shape shifting," changing his manner and appear-

ance in the blink of an eye, as from his inclination to keep his cherished dreams and secrets to himself.

Since Pisces is a water sign and mainly about feelings, its natives tend to relate to the world through emotion rather than physical action, practicality, or intellect. The Neptune-ruled are fascinated with dreams. Even when they are awake, they have a dreamy look in their eyes that gives them an air of otherworldliness. Pisceans are often shy and quiet. They tend to be elusive, refusing to show their real selves to the world at large. The pair of fish swimming in opposite directions that serve as the symbol for this sign emphasizes the basic duality of the Piscean nature. The two fish represent consciousness and unconsciousness, reality and illusion, sleeping and waking.

Frequently written off as an impractical dreamer, the fish's qualifications for worldly success are often grossly underestimated. Actually the Neptune-ruled have everything they need to make their dreams come true. Pisceans are quite capable of using these tools to help themselves and others. Pisces' prophetic vision goes way beyond mere intuition. He can tell when something important is about to happen. As a detector of trends with an innate understanding of patterns and cycles, Pisces is usually one step ahead of the rest of the crowd. He actually *knows* what is going to be in or out of fashion.

Since Pisces is mutable–water, it is the sign most closely connected to the collective unconscious. The Neptune-ruled feel everyone else's pain, and they absorb other people's moods like sponges. Fish are extremely idealistic. They don't always deal well with reality, especially when it intrudes on their dreams and illusions. Repeated disappointments can sap their vitality and make them feel lethargic and pessimistic about the future. Even those Pisceans who are totally devoted to their goals tend to become moody and discouraged when things go wrong. Depression can become a major problem for some fish.

Fish are charitable and self-sacrificing, but they can be too passive for their own good. Pisceans don't always have a strong personal agenda. Some are content to just go with the flow and see where life takes them. The Neptune-ruled are naturally artistic. Many fish have exceptional talent as actors, artists, dancers, and musicians, but they may be lacking in drive and persistence. Thin-skinned and easily hurt, Pisces sometimes tries to escape problems by abusing drugs or alcohol.

One of Pisces' greatest strengths is his sensitivity to the needs of other people. Fish are generally known for their ability to empathize with others and reach out to aid those who need assistance. Pisces truly enjoys helping people fulfill their dreams and potential. Just *doing* something in life is usually not enough for the helpful fish. His ultimate goal is to *contribute* something important and inspire others to do the same.

Don't expect to find order in a Pisces household. The Neptune-ruled have a personal sense of order that can't be explained, and doesn't follow any guidelines that might make sense to members of the other eleven zodiacal signs. Although his space may look like a mess, a typical Pisces probably knows exactly where to find each and every thing in it. And, if he can't find it, he probably won't care all that much. Fishes tend to live by faith and intuition. Practical considerations of everyday reality don't always correspond to their ideas about what is really important or even necessary in life.

Pisces' sexuality is inevitably wrapped up with his dreams. Most Neptune-ruled natives have an extremely romantic view of love and sex. In fact the fish is an incurable romantic who tends to imagine that people actually *are* whatever he fervently wishes they could be. Because Pisces lives in his imagination, when things do not go according to expectation he has great difficulty letting go of his illusions. The typical fish has wonderful dreams of his ideal lover, but tends to set such high standards that no real person is able to measure up. Then there are those Pisces natives who would much rather deceive themselves than admit to any fault whatsoever in their partners.

Although most fish make absolutely delightful friends, as mates or lovers they are extremely high-maintenance partners. In their quest to validate themselves, they require a great deal of devotion, attention, and encouragement. If you are an individual who prefers a solid, practical, down-to-earth companion, who can stand on his or her own two feet, perhaps you better stay away from Pisces. However, if you are looking for a partner who is truly idealistic, spontaneous, and sensitive to join you on a magical, mystical voyage filled with romance and enchantment, the imaginative fish may be *the one* for you.

Myths and Symbols Associated with Pisces

The astrological ruler of Pisces is Neptune. The parts of the body ruled by Pisces are the feet and the immune system. Its symbol, ♓, is thought to represent a pair of fish bound together and swimming in opposite directions. The sign is classified as mutable, water, feminine (negative, indirect, yin, and internal). Represented by the fish, Pisces' color is sea green, its metal is platinum, and its gemstone is aquamarine.

The Greek myth most often associated with Pisces is that of the goddess Aphrodite (Venus), her son Eros (Cupid), and the great beast Typhon. After the gods of Olympus, led by Zeus (Jupiter), defeated their predecessors, the Titans, they imprisoned the conquered giants in the lowest region of the underworld. Gaia (Earth) had a son, Typhon, who had been fathered by the incarcerated Titan Tartarus. Bent on revenge for the defeat of the Titans, Gaia sent Typhon, a terrible fire-breathing monster, to attack the gods on Mount Olympus.

In an attempt to escape from Typhon's wrath, the gods fled to Egypt where they hid themselves by assuming various animal forms. Zeus became a ram, Dionysius (Bacchus) a goat, Artemis (Diana) a cat, Hermes (Mercury) a bird, Hera (Juno) a cow. Aphrodite and Eros tied themselves together, and

jumped into the Nile. Once in the river, they transformed themselves into a pair of fish and swam
away. As a reward for their cleverness, the goddess
Athena (Minerva) placed the fish among the stars as
the constellation Pisces. She tied their tales together
so that they would never be separated.

The Greek legend of Odysseus' (Ulysses) return
from Troy is also associated with Pisces. Odysseus
was on his way home to Ithaca, where his faithful
wife Penelope awaited him. However, the god Poseidon (Neptune) was very angry with Odysseus, and
pitched him and his men into uncharted waters. For
twenty years the famous hero tried to make it back
home. Along the way he was cast onto many beaches
where he encountered various mythological creatures, both good and evil. His dreamlike journey was
one of amazing discovery, alternating with long periods of great confusion.

Although he was gone for twenty years, Penelope
never lost faith that one day her beloved husband
would return to her. She sent their son, Telemachus,
to seek news of Odysseus in the courts of the other
kings who had returned from the Trojan expedition.
While on the search, Telemachus received counsel
from the goddess Athena (Minerva), who told him
to go home. Then Athena presented herself to Odysseus, restored him to the vigorous manhood of his
lost youth, and helped him return home where he
was reunited with his son. Together father and son
outwitted a plot by one of Penelope's suitors to kill
Telemachus, marry his mother, and assume Odysseus' rightful position in Ithaca. In the end the tenac-

ity and perseverance of Penelope and Telemachus, who had never lost faith that Odysseus would return to them, was justly rewarded in a joyful family reunion.

Another legendary figure associated with Pisces is Dionysius (Bacchus). He was last of the gods to enter Olympus, and was worshipped in Greece as the god of wine. Dionysius traveled the world over teaching mankind about wine making and the culture of the vine.

The fish symbol is also very closely connected to the Christian era, which is sometimes referred to as the Age of Pisces. One especially interesting incident from the life of Jesus of Nazareth, that has definite Piscean connections, is the Miracle of the Loaves and the Fishes. Christ often used the fish as a metaphor for the coming of the messiah, and he promised to turn his disciples into "fishers of men."

The Pisces Man

As soon as you are certain you've got the Neptune-ruled man all figured out, he does something that takes you totally by surprise. As a member of the last sign on the astrological wheel, Pisces is especially difficult to pigeonhole or classify. His basic personality is actually a composite of traits gleaned from all eleven signs that precede his in the zodiac. Male fish are highly creative, artistic and intuitive. If you tend to regard them as wishy-washy, weak-willed, unworldly dreamers, think again. Some very successful individuals happen to be natives of this sign. Although not as up-front about his ambitions as Aries or Capricorn, Pisces aims extremely high. His lofty goal is to make his dreams come true, and he often succeeds in doing just that.

Typically Pisces is idealistic, and sometimes unrealistic, but when he becomes really excited by an idea or a pet project, he generally finds a way to make it work. The charming Neptune-ruled man has many influential friends who are more than willing to help him get where he wants to be in life. Above all, the fish is intuitive. He uses his imagination and insight, which sometimes verges on clairvoyance, to help him understand what new products and services people are going to want. He could be an artist, a gallery owner, an entertainer, a movie mogul, a teacher, a spiritual leader, or a businessman. His chosen profession isn't as important as the fact that he speaks directly to people's dreams. And it's lucky for him that he does. In today's market, dream fulfillment can command a very high price!

Sympathetic and impressionable, the Pisces man is a psychic sponge who absorbs the thoughts and feelings of the people around him. He actually feels their pain, sorrow, happiness, and joy. This sensitivity makes it easy for him to empathize with their problems and troubles. He is so suggestible that he often takes on another individual's moods just by standing next to that person. Although the Pisces man may not realize what's happening, his state of mind can change from happy and upbeat to down in the dumps in the blink of an eye. When people near him are sick, his very presence can help heal them, as he actually absorbs some of their pain and suffering. This is all very well for the other guy, but it can be hard on the Neptune-ruled individual unless he learns how to separate his own feelings from those of everyone else.

The two fish swimming in opposite directions symbolize Pisces' ambivalence and inability to make rapid decisions. His inner life is an ongoing tug-of-war in which his heart tells him one thing and his head tells him another. Of course in the end his heart always wins out. But before he decides, he must agonize over every tiny little detail. It doesn't really matter if the question is of major significance or only concerns what to eat for breakfast—he can't be rushed. And, like all mutable types, once he decides, he changes his mind a dozen times. As with most intuitive people, his first hunch is usually the right one. If you are involved with an indecisive fish, you might want to encourage him to have more faith in his initial impulse.

Compassionate Pisces is the proverbial white knight out to rescue the damsel in distress. Nothing turns him on like the chance to be someone's savior. Always a sucker for a good sob story, he feels compelled to help the underdog. However, his tendency to be totally self-sacrificing can lead to deep resentment. Philanthropic and caring, the typical fish can also be very demanding. When he helps you, he honestly believes he is doing it with no strings attached. But no matter what he says, his actions prove that he really wants the same consideration he gives others. If you are not sufficiently appreciative of his efforts on your behalf, he may not fuss or complain, but he'll probably be wounded to the core.

The Pisces man loves mystery, intrigue, and secrets. If he is a typical example of his sign, he can probably be seduced into an erotic affair. Even those fish that are totally loyal and refuse to stray from their partner's side usually spend a lot of time fantasizing about amorous extracurricular adventures. Passionately emotional, and somewhat unstable, Pisces is constantly being pulled by contrary impulses that cause him to say one thing and do another. He can promise you the moon and the stars, and he certainly means it when he says it. But when his excitement wears off, his attention may drift elsewhere.

Although not sexually aggressive, the Pisces man is among the most beguiling and seductive in the entire zodiac. When the fish falls in love, he falls hook, line, and sinker. His total immersion in his emotions often proves irresistible to the object of his affections. Just one look into his beautiful eyes, and you will be bewitched by this man's charms. Although his fear of rejection makes him skittish, and he's often reluctant when it comes to making the first move, the telepathic signals that he sends out are quite unmistakable. He telegraphs his feelings so completely that even the most psychically insensitive individual generally has little trouble getting the message.

Love is one of the few necessities in the life of this charming, romantic dreamer. Without love he feels empty and incomplete. If you are looking for an old-fashioned romance with someone who will write poetry for you, whisper sweet nothings in your ear, scatter rose petals on your coverlet, and make love to you by candlelight—then you are truly ready for a Pisces man.

The Pisces Woman

On the surface the enigmatic fish may seem fragile, but she's actually a lot tougher than she appears. The Pisces woman possesses a quiet inner strength that helps her cope in most situations. This intensely feminine lady has a strange haunting quality that attracts others like a magnet. Her beautiful, soulful gaze seems to speak volumes. Her bewitching, seductive glance holds the irresistible promise of both earthly and heavenly delights. Lady Pisces doesn't need to look for love. Love looks for her. Somehow the right person always seems to emerge at the most auspicious moment.

Don't try to put something over on the Neptune-ruled woman. She has seemingly magical abilities that allow her to see through deceit and deception. The fish generally shrinks from overt confrontation, and in a power struggle her style is subtle and indirect. The Pisces woman can be something of a tease, and she will employ her womanly wiles if she thinks they can help her get what she wants. She knows how to get around people. As a natural-born actress she easily adapts to any role. When she needs help or support, the female fish is not above appealing to your protective nature by convincing you that she is weak and totally defenseless.

All things spiritual, creative, mystical, and from the realm of dreams and imagination resonate with the Neptune-ruled woman. The world beyond her five senses is as much a part of her being as her down-to-earth reality. Pisces' intuition and her perception of the subtle messages that come from other planes of awareness help her forge her deep spirituality. Her unwavering faith and devotion to her ideals help her get through life's difficult twists and turns. However, she needs to develop her critical faculties. It is sometimes difficult for Neptune-ruled individuals to distinguish between true visionary insight and dangerous illusion.

The female fish is the very soul of caring and sensitivity. Her empathy comes through on many levels. She may choose to use her perceptive abilities as a healer, artist, psychic, entertainer, psychologist, or social worker. Typically Pisceans are not self-starters, and it often takes them awhile to find their direction in life. Although the unique combination of charm and talent that characterizes members of this sign often brings them fame and fortune, most fish don't actively seek celebrity.

What the Neptune-ruled woman craves most is the opportunity to put her creative talents to use where they will do the most good. Her artistic abilities may lead to a career in photography, advertising, or art. With her love of beauty and instinct for fashion, the Pisces gal often enjoys success as a hairstylist, makeup artist, or designer. Pisces' desire to help uplift the human spirit can take her into a religious ministry. And her profound love and understanding of animals may prompt her to seek work as a veterinarian.

No one is better at creating a calm, tranquil atmosphere for youngsters to grow up in than the female fish. Gentle, kind, sympathetic, and nurturing, she spends most of her life mothering others. She is a natural when it comes to caring for her own kids. No matter what her age, she retains many childlike qualities that help her relate to and understand all children. Fish are great storytellers. The Neptune-ruled lady is perfectly at home in that special atmosphere of fantasy and make-believe kids seem to inhabit. A hands-on parent, she plays with her children, reads to them, takes them places. She has no qualms about giving up her career in favor of staying home and raising a family.

In love, the Pisces female is a total romantic who views life through rose-colored glasses. She likes nothing better than retreating to her private world of fantasy and dreams. When things don't turn out as planned, she relies upon her active imagination to help her fill in the blanks. Given her ability to merge her identity with that of her partner, the Neptune-ruled woman's sense of self is not strongly developed. She often uses her close relationships as a measure of defining who she is. The Pisces woman needs to be extremely careful about the people she meets. She must choose her lovers and friends wisely. She's highly suggestible and easily led down paths she really should not travel.

Pisces is very much in demand as a romantic companion. She knows how to make her spouse or lover feel needed, wanted, and appreciated. The female fish generally prefers to stay in the background and let others take all the bows. Since she has no desire to dominate, she rarely tries to overshadow her partner. Even those Neptune-ruled who shine as major stars on the world's stage are usually willing to take a backseat to their mates in their personal lives. If the truth be told, the fish is perfectly able to take care of herself, but she'd much rather be cared for by someone else.

It is not unusual for Pisces to suffer in life. When she's hurt or upset, she often surrenders to feelings of self-pity. After all, she feels sorry for everyone else, why not for herself? Since the Neptune-ruled tend to wear their hearts on their sleeves, they are easily wounded by even the smallest of slights. Afflicted with overwhelming self-doubt, fish need to be constantly reassured of their worth and importance. Seeking her soul mate can lead Pisces through a series of disappointments. But she is not likely to give up on love and romance. She'll continue to search until she finds the right person.

The Shadow Side of Pisces

The Pisces shadow emerges most often when the Neptune-ruled individual carries a natural inclination toward self-sacrifice too far, and it turns into martyrdom. In this scenario the fish sacrifices everything for someone else, then resents that person for allowing him to do it. By putting everyone's needs ahead of his own, and then blaming those he's helped for his own misery, Pisces creates a situation in which there are no winners. When the object of his self-sacrifice does not reciprocate or respond as he'd hoped, Pisces becomes disillusioned and depressed and may try to escape his pain in bouts with alcohol or drugs.

Pisces natives are the most likely members of the zodiacal family to cling to abusive relationships or to participate in symbiotic associations. Since nobody has as much power as a martyr or a saint, when Pisces paints himself as the eternal victim he may take advantage of this form of empowerment by using it to gain sympathy and manipulate those around him. Typically the fish has a passive nature and a tendency to merge his own personality with that of the group or another person, thereby placing himself at the mercy of circumstances or other people. Too often he accepts negative situations as a matter of course. He usually prefers to adapt himself to them rather than work to change them. As a confirmed caretaker, Pisces often fits the pattern of the classic enabler who hurts others by trying too hard to help them.

The dark side of the Piscean nature is bolstered by a tendency toward escapism and the need to ignore or forget uncomfortable experiences. Some fish do not deal well with events and situations that do not fit their illusions. When things go wrong in the world around them, they turn their eyes inward and create a world that is always bright and rosy. People who react this way rarely learn from experience. They refuse to focus on the lessons that the real world has to offer them. Unfortunately talking to them about their problems doesn't usually help clarify their vision of reality.

The key phrase for this sign is, "I believe." Like the Red Queen in *Alice In Wonderland*, who says, "Why sometimes I've believed as many as six impossible things before breakfast," the Neptune-ruled definitely rank among the last of the true believers. Because of a particular combination of spirituality, mysticism, and the deep-seated need to believe in something *more*, Pisces can easily become the target of a religious cult. Moreover, if the leader is charismatic and his message attractive, his attempt to convert the gullible fish will probably meet with success.

Most fish abhor conflict. Like Libra, they tend to prefer peace at any price. However, unlike the scales, fish are rarely inclined to overlook a hurt or a slight. While it is true that Pisceans *forgive* easily enough, they are more like Cancer and Scorpio in that they tend to hold grudges and can continue to nurse their pain forever. The seemingly gentle fish often hides a great deal of pain and anger beneath a calm exterior, and these buried emotions sometimes erupt in a sudden burst of temper.

The Neptune-ruled are drawn to causes, and they're usually the first ones to volunteer to help those in need. However, the fish wants to help so much that he'll give away things that are not his to give. One Neptune-ruled hippie habitually invited at least one unfortunate soul each evening to come along with her for "a hot meal and a place to crash for the night." The problem was that this "Flower Child" had no home of her own and was staying with a friend, yet she had absolutely no compunction when it came to inviting others to share her friend's generosity.

Pisces Romantic Dinner for Two

Pisces the cook

Most members of this sign love to eat, and they also enjoy feeding others. Imagination plays a large role in their culinary skills. Pisces are inspired, creative cooks with a flair for dressing up even the simplest foods to become unusual and exotic dishes. Although fish may not be the best homemakers, they are generally among the very best hosts and hostesses. While they sometimes become bored with the tedium of preparing everyday meals, Pisceans always like cooking for special occasions. Pisces natives are skilled at giving large and small dinner parties for friends and family. The romantic fish absolutely shines when it comes to preparing intimate dinners for two.

The fish is extremely sensitive to the likes and dislikes of his guests. When he invites you to dinner, you can look forward to a meal you're sure to enjoy. However, don't be surprised if the menu remains a secret until the very last minute. The Neptune-ruled individual is fond of mysteries and surprises. Whatever you do, stay out of the fish's kitchen and don't ask your host for any of his recipes. Pisces is much too secretive to want to reveal what went into the pot. The fish cooks intuitively, tends to improvise, and rarely follows a recipe as written. He often does not even remember exactly what he did to cause a specific dish to turn out as it did.

After Leo, Pisces is probably the most flamboyant cook in the zodiac. And Pisces rivals all signs when it comes to the decoration and theatrical presentation of his culinary masterpieces. The nurturing, generous, fun-loving fish rarely worries about costs or health considerations. Unless he is a spiritually minded ascetic who has eschewed rich food and alcohol, the meals he serves will be tasty and abundant, and the wine will flow like water.

Pisces the dinner guest

Pisces natives tend to be fussy about their surroundings. The ambience surrounding a meal is as important to them as the food served. They appreciate nice table settings, romantic music, soft lighting, flowers, and a soothing atmosphere. When you invite a fish to dine with you in a restaurant, try to choose one that is on a body of water. At home, if your house has an outdoor pool, pond, fountain, or spa, your Pisces guest will probably prefer eating outside. When cooking for Pisces, it is best to prepare dishes that appeal to the aesthetic side of his nature. If you are making dinner on an outdoor grill, steer clear of traditional stuff like hot dogs, hamburgers, and ribs.

Choose instead foods that are lighter and have a subtle, delicate flavor.

Although the fish is naturally polite and will eat whatever you serve, if you really want to please him you will think in terms of foreign, exotic, and unusual dishes. All fish and shellfish, watery foods such as soups and aspics, anything cooked in a wine sauce, alcoholic beverages, and sweets appeal to Pisces. Fish also love things that create an illusion, such as dishes that appear to be something other than what they are. Any dish wrapped in paper or baked in a protective outer shell fulfills their poetic requirements. They adore surprising dishes such as baked Alaska, fried ice cream, or fried cheese.

Pisces is the ideal dinner companion, amenable and charming—unless he happens to be in one of his dark moods. He has a real knack for getting along with most people. The fish's natural inclination is to blend in, and he's adept at changing his colors in order to harmonize with his surroundings. In company he usually puts on his best face, which is warm and witty. When called upon, he can keep an entire dinner party amused with his comedic antics, fantastic stories, and amusing anecdotes.

Foods commonly associated with Pisces

Meat: lamb, pork, ham
Fowl: chicken, all water fowl
Fish and Shellfish: all fish, all shellfish
Dairy Products: none

Vegetables and Beans: artichokes, asparagus, brussels sprouts, cabbage, red cabbage, endive, seaweed, kale, parsnips, turnips, garbanzo beans

Nuts and Grains: almonds, pine nuts, chestnuts, wheat, barley, rice

Fruits: figs, dates, mangoes, currants, raisins

Beverages: all alcoholic beverages, tea

Herbs, Spices, and Miscellaneous: sesame seeds, cinnamon, cloves, nutmeg, thyme, chervil, sugarcane

PISCES MENU

Broiled Salmon Steaks

Rice Pilaf with Pine Nuts and Currants

Asparagus with Ham

Sesame Breadsticks

White Wine

Bananas Foster

Tea

Pisces Recipes

Broiled Salmon Steaks

2 fresh salmon steaks (totaling roughly ¾ to
   1 pound)
   salt and pepper to taste
2 tablespoons butter, melted

Season the salmon steaks on both sides with salt and pepper, and brush tops with melted butter. Heat the broiler. Place the salmon steaks on a broiling pan, and broil about 5 minutes or until golden on top. Turn and brush the other side with melted butter, and broil the steaks for another 5 minutes, or until the fish flakes.

*Rice Pilaf with Pine Nuts and Currants

- 3 tablespoons unsalted butter
- 1 small onion, finely chopped
- 4 teaspoons pine nuts
- 1 cup long grain white rice
- 2 cups boiling water
- 1 chicken bouillon cube (or 1 package bouillon powder)
- ¼ teaspoon cinnamon
- 2 tablespoons dried currants
  salt and pepper to taste
- 4 teaspoons fresh parsley, finely chopped

Melt the butter in a saucepan over medium heat. Add the onions and pine nuts, and sauté until pale golden brown, about 8 minutes. Add the rice and cook until opaque, about 5 minutes. Dissolve the bouillon cube in the boiling water. Add the bouillon, cinnamon, and currants to the saucepan. Season to taste with salt and pepper. Cover and cook over medium-low heat for about 15 minutes, or until all the liquid is absorbed. Sprinkle with parsley and serve.

Asparagus with Ham

¾ pound fresh asparagus
2 ounces prosciutto (Italian ham), thinly sliced
2 tablespoons unsalted butter
2 tablespoons grated parmesan cheese

Clean the asparagus and cut off the ends. In a vegetable steamer, steam the asparagus for 5 to 7 minutes or until tender. Remove them from the pot with tongs, and drain on paper towels. Divide the asparagus into bundles, and wrap each bundle in a slice of prosciutto, leaving the tips free. Place the asparagus–ham bundles on a greased cookie sheet, or baking dish. Dot with butter and sprinkle with parmesan cheese. Bake in an oven preheated to 375 degrees for 5 to 6 minutes.

Bananas Foster

2 ripe bananas
½ cup rum, light or dark
4 tablespoons unsalted butter
¼ cup light brown sugar, packed
vanilla ice cream

Peel the bananas, split lengthwise and halve crosswise. In a medium skillet, melt the butter over moderate heat. Stir in the brown sugar. Add the bananas and immediately turn to coat. Pour in rum, and swirl around in the pan to mix. Carefully ignite the alcohol in the pan. When the flame subsides, spoon the liquid over the bananas to baste. Remove the pan from the heat. Place a scoop of vanilla ice cream on each of two serving plates, and arrange the bananas around it. Spoon the sauce on top and serve immediately.

♈ ♉ ♊ ♋ ♌ ♍

Part Two

The Seventy-eight Romantic Combinations

♎ ♏ ♐ ♑ ♒ ♓

Aries with Aries

Initially this relationship can seem absolutely perfect. The chemistry is right, life together is never tedious or boring. Nights are filled with romance and passionate lovemaking, days with work, sports, hobbies, causes, and true companionship. However, fireworks can result when two dynamic, enthusiastic, impatient rams join forces. It usually doesn't take long before the blissful union is threatened by the twin Arien bugaboos of competition and domination. Rams are notoriously competitive. Instead of rooting for each other, they can become serious rivals in everything. Aries' natural inclination is to lead, so stormy quarrels and head butting will surely follow either partner's attempt to gain the upper hand. Two Aries natives may never enjoy a tranquil, harmonious union, which is just as well because they would both find it extremely dull. But they forgive and forget easily—and the making up is always wonderful.

Aries with Taurus

At first glance it would seem as if the ram and the bull have nothing in common. Aries needs freedom, Taurus tends to be possessive. Aries can be here today and gone tomorrow. Taurus is in for the long haul. Both love luxury and comfort. Taurus is cautious with money and fearful of debt. Aries prefers to fly now and pay, or worry, later. In spite of these differences, the sensuous, affectionate, romantic Venus-ruled Taurus represents an irresistible challenge to passionate, equally romantic Aries. Although Taurus may be slower to arouse, when Aries draws the bull out they both reach new heights of sexual pleasure. A lot of understanding is required when patient Taurus and fiery Aries decide to form a lifelong bond. With a little extra effort on both sides this unlikely partnership can be made to work.

Aries with Gemini

This combination usually results in a happy union. Although Aries is aggressive and will attempt to dominate the seemingly easygoing Gemini, the mentally adroit Mercury-ruled partner soon learns to avoid potential problems and arguments by outwitting or outmaneuvering the ram. Both are naturally active and restless, neither is overly domestic. Gemini tends to be something of a wanderer, Aries has the pioneer spirit. Together they can explore the world, or at least their small corner of it. Some difficulties may arise, though. When teamed with the intensely ardent Aries, Gemini can seem an emotional lightweight who doesn't take love and sex all that seriously. Yet both are passionate, curious, and more than willing to engage in sexual experimentation. Ultimately it is their shared love of freedom and the ability to grant each other separate space that keeps these two together.

Aries with Cancer

A strong physical attraction and a deep psychic bond often develops between the ram and the crab. Although fire and water don't mix well, intuitive Aries and sensitive Cancer can understand each other at a very deep level of consciousness. Both are passionate, sensuous, romantic, and sentimental. Sexually they can be very compatible. Problems may develop after the first glow of love has passed when Aries gets a taste of Cancer's pessimistic moodiness. Unlike straight-talking Aries, Cancer often refuses to verbalize problems. Aries hates playing guessing games. When the thin-skinned, secretive Moon-ruled native feels emotionally wounded and retreats into that Cancerian shell, the Aries lover may lose patience and walk away. If the relationship is to succeed, the ram needs to provide the crab with a certain amount of emotional support. In return Cancer must learn not to nag, mother, or cling too tightly to the freedom-loving Aries partner.

Aries with Leo

Aries wants to win, to be first in everything. Leo's aim is to rule, to be recognized as the best. Both are proud. The pride of the ram stems from the sense of accomplishment that comes from winning. The lion's pride derives from the divine right of royalty who believe they are born to rule. Initially each partner may try to dominate the other. Eventually Aries will recognize this is one contest he or she will not win because unless Leo can be boss the game is over. Once it has been decided that the Leo partner is the one in charge, or made to believe he or she is in charge, this can be one of the happiest pairings in the zodiac. Leo is loyal, affectionate, and generous. Aries is dynamic, exciting, and ambitious. As a couple they are temperamentally and sexually well matched. Problems, if they arise, will be minimal. As long as there is mutual consideration this fiery pair can remain lovers and friends for a lifetime.

Aries with Virgo

These two are about as unlike as two people can be. Each has a distinctly different approach to dealing with almost everything. Yet in spite of their differences there is a better than even chance they can create a happy life together—if each will learn to be tolerant of the other's foibles. The average ram is dictatorial, bossy, temperamental, and outspoken. Virgo is reserved, introverted, and totally unequipped to handle big emotional scenes. Virgos can be extremely critical, and most Ariens can't stand criticism of any kind. The virgin's tendency toward perfectionism, plus the meticulous analysis of everything and everyone, drives Aries crazy. Yet both are romantic idealists, albeit in different ways. The introverted, reserved Virgo is likely to be fascinated by the Aries boldness and zest for life. The truth is that there is a good deal of passion and desire smoldering beneath the cool Virgo façade. No one is better able to release it than the sexy, exciting Aries lover.

Aries with Libra

The best of times and the worst of times can result when these two opposites find themselves attracted to each other. Although an excellent combination on many levels, the Aries partner can be driven to distraction by Libra's procrastination and indecisiveness. Libra will inevitably feel rushed or pressured by Aries' faster-than-the-speed-of-light decision-making capabilities. Both signs are predisposed to falling in love with love. While Libra needs a partner to feel complete, Aries does not. Aries may sometimes feel hemmed in by Libra's consuming need for love, harmony, balance, and togetherness. The natural chemistry between cardinal–fire Aries and cardinal–air Libra is exceptionally strong. Their sex life together should be extremely pleasurable and mutually rewarding. However, faithfulness can become a major issue. Both the Mars-ruled and the Venus-ruled are consummate romantics who have an easier time falling in love than staying in love.

Aries with Scorpio

When complex, enigmatic Scorpio gets together with outspoken, up-front Aries, problems are sure to develop. Both like to dominate and control. The ram usually does it verbally through fussing and shouting. The scorpion controls mainly through mental manipulation. Scorpios are naturally jealous, Ariens are not. The scorpion's possessiveness can send the independent ram right up a wall. Flirtatious, free-spirited Aries will usually counter by providing mistrustful Scorpio with good reason for doubt and disbelief. Sexually they are well matched because both partners are ardent, energetic, imaginative, passionate, and sexy. Neither is bound by convention, each is adventurous and willing to experiment. While the Arien partner tends to view the act of love as exciting, pleasurable, and fun, the intense Scorpio lover is generally seeking a deeper connection, one that is spiritually and emotionally transforming.

Aries with Sagittarius

This combination is traditionally considered ideal. The free-spirited ram and the happy-go-lucky archer have a great deal in common. Natives of both of these fire signs are generally carefree, active, optimistic, athletic, idealistic, outgoing individualists with a life-affirming and healthy attitude toward love and sex. Physically and mentally they are well matched. The Arien tends to be more emotional, and may look upon the Sagittarian partner as somewhat unromantic, detached, or impersonal. These two will have frequent arguments because both can be combative, blunt, and outspoken. When their opinions differ, heated discussions are inevitable. Molehills become mountains because neither is prone to give ground or back down. One word leads to another—until a full-blown fight develops. However, both actually enjoy a good altercation. Once the air has cleared, they will return to their joyous, fun-filled existence as if nothing happened.

Aries with Capricorn

Rams are forever young. Most goats act as if they were born old and cantankerous. As romantic partners, impulsive Aries and conservative Capricorn will have some formidable obstacles to overcome. In company Capricorn can be quite reserved and restrained, while Aries is generally outgoing and vivacious. Nevertheless, with a lot of understanding on both sides, these two can forge a strong and lasting union. Ambitious Aries is drawn to Capricorn's success, steadiness, and strength of purpose. The uptight, seemingly prudish Capricorn, who actually possesses one of the stronger libidos in the zodiac, is intrigued by Aries' smoldering sex appeal. The main problem likely to arise relates to the goat's serious nature and predisposition toward pessimism and melancholy. The naturally cheerful and optimistic ram can become deeply resentful when confronted with too strong a dose of earthly reality.

Aries with Aquarius

When the Aries ram and the Aquarius water bearer decide to team up, there is never, ever, a dull moment. For the Mars-ruled "pioneer" and the Uranus-ruled "futurist" it's full steam ahead, with no looking back and few regrets or recriminations. True friendship and tolerance of each other's little idiosyncrasies form the basis of this relationship, even in its most passionate and intimate moments. Each of these freedom-loving partners respects the other's need for some downtime to be alone and recharge inner batteries. The Aries native tends to view Aquarius' reluctance to get too emotionally involved as a challenge rather than an obstacle. Fiery, demonstrative Aries may secretly wish that the airy lover were more ardent. However, Aquarius' lack of passionate displays of affection is more than compensated for by a freewheeling spirit, love of experimentation, and the willingness to try anything new—in bed or out.

Aries with Pisces

Temperamentally these too are quite different. Most Pisces individuals prefer art and music to sports. The fish's idea of a romantic date is likely to be a night at the opera. The typical Aries would rather go to a hockey game. Yet dreamy, ethereal Pisces appeals to the romantic side of Aries' nature. The ram is easily seduced by the dependent fish's need for love and protection. Aries takes pleasure in Pisces' erotic fantasies and intuitive sexual responses, though the ram's physical aggressiveness can scare away the timid fish. Like all water signs, the fish can be jealous and possessive. The ram wants to feel free and unfettered. Although it appears as if dynamic Aries might run roughshod over the sensitive fish, Pisces natives are adepts in the subtle art of getting their own way. There is great strength in water's ability to adapt to, and go with the flow of, a situation. Moreover, the Pisces partner genuinely admires and looks up to Aries. Few rams can resist that type of ego boost.

Taurus with Taurus

The pairing of two bulls usually results in an alliance that is romantic, steady, stable, emotionally comforting, and sexually satisfying. In all likelihood a Taurus–Taurus couple will be totally devoted to each other and in agreement on most issues regarding work, home, family, and finances. However, the union of two people of such similar temperaments may be somewhat lacking in excitement. Without impetus toward change and renewal, the relationship can stagnate and become frozen in time. With the thrill gone, one or both of the bored partners may begin to look elsewhere for stimulating companionship. Another major obstacle to happiness between two Taurus natives is their innate stubbornness. When two bullheaded people get together they are virtually guaranteed to lock horns. When bulls disagree, neither is likely to apologize or back down. It takes a lot of understanding and bovine patience to make this pairing work.

Taurus with Gemini

The biggest bone of contention here can usually be traced to Taurus' possessive nature and free-spirited Gemini's Peter Pan–like refusal to possess or be possessed. Still, there is rarely a dull moment when fast-talking Gemini decides to lead the placid bull on a merry chase. Taurus is invariably attracted to Gemini's devil-may-care attitude, artistic flair, intellect, and imagination. While together, this couple will never run out of things to do or talk about. Sexually and emotionally both partners should find the union stimulating, exciting, and satisfying. After a time, though, the bull may grow a little weary of hearing Gemini rattle on and on. And the swift-moving, Mercury-ruled twin may ultimately become annoyed by Taurus' stubborn and plodding nature, slow reactions, and perfectionist temperament.

Taurus with Cancer

Earth and water are complementary elements, and this combination often results in a near perfect match.

Taurus and Cancer are passionate, sentimental, affectionate romantic partners on the same sexual wavelength. Their shared feelings about comfort and security makes them natural allies. They tend to be interested in the same things: home, family, food, money, but not necessarily in the same order. Natives of both signs want very much to succeed and leave a mark in the world. The bull cares deeply about "making it," and may view Cancer's ambition and determination as valuable career assets. Together they can wine and dine the rich and famous, and also aspire to join their number. For this couple the obstacle to total bliss usually comes from Taurus' well-known bullheaded stubbornness and Cancer's frequent up-and-down mood swings.

Taurus with Leo

When these two fixed signs come together, get ready for a major battle of wills between the irresistible force (Leo) and the immovable object (Taurus). The bull wants to be loved and appreciated. The lion's desire is to be worshipped and admired. Leo is much too self-important to give Taurus the devotion he or she craves. The bull is too stubborn to pay homage to the imperious lion. Both are bossy. Each wants to take charge and control every aspect of their life together, especially the purse strings. Flexibility is in short supply in this relationship. Still, they can forge a surprisingly happy union if each partner is willing to give in just a little bit in an effort to work things out. Sexually they are well matched, both are enthusiastic and passionate, and neither is likely to have reason to complain about the other's lovemaking. Psychologically they are compatible because they enjoy so many of the same things including, but not limited to luxury, comfort, beautiful things and beautiful people, good food, music, and the arts.

Taurus with Virgo

Although these two earth signs should get along famously, there are several sticking points that may need to be addressed before they can ride off happily into the sunset. The typical Virgo is health-conscious and extremely fastidious with regard to food and drink. Taurus, on the other hand, prefers a rich diet and has been known to overindulge from time to time. When hypercritical Virgo suggests that Taurus modify personal eating habits and switch to a more wholesome regimen, fireworks usually ensue. The bull will not tolerate criticism or nagging of any kind. So a wise Virgo will learn to keep most of his or her opinions under wraps. Sexually the Taurus–Virgo pair is pretty well matched. Although the virgin may be slower to arouse, the bull has a lot of patience. With tenderness, warmth, and affection, Taurus easily melts the well-known Virgo reserve.

Taurus with Libra

Venus is the ruler of Taurus and of Libra. Romantically these two are often in perfect sync. Both partners are typically warm, loving, affectionate, sensual, and sexually responsive. They share an interest in everything that is artistic, beautiful, and luxurious. Libra loves to entertain and socialize. Taurus is happy to have a partner who is more than willing to help wine and dine the boss and prospective clients. Although it may appear as if the bull is the stronger of the two, remember that Libra is a cardinal sign— the one often characterized as "the iron hand in the velvet glove." Librans are the very essence of charm and diplomacy, knowing exactly the right thing to do or say to get their way. Most natives of these two signs are passive, and they will rarely fight or argue. However, the Venus-ruled are often guilty of Hamletlike procrastination. They put off making a decision for as long as they possibly can. This shared tendency toward inertia can cause them to lose out on many promising offers and opportunities.

Taurus with Scorpio

When the jealous scorpion and the possessive bull come together, their relationship often turns into one long battle. They have more in common than most zodiacal opposites, but there is little flexibility in this union of fixed signs. Both are passionate, but possessed of a tremendous amount of willpower, reserve, and fixed determination. Although they have tremendous admiration and respect for each other, each would rather die than admit it. Uncomplicated Taurus may be put off by Scorpio's devious behavior. The more serious scorpion tends to misinterpret the bull's playful sense of humor. In spite of their strong physical attraction, they achieve harmony only through the exercise of extreme tolerance and patience on both sides. If they can overcome their differences, they may forge a bond strong enough to last a lifetime.

Taurus with Sagittarius

The bull and the archer definitely march to the beat of a completely different drummer. Sagittarians need to feel free. Taureans, who prefer a more settled life, are always trying to pin archers down to long-term contracts. Taurus is slow, steady, and self-controlled. Sagittarius is active, adaptable, and impulsive. Archers think big and have little use for, or understanding of, the bull's persnickety attention to detail. But these two do have fun together. The passionate bull enjoys the archer's lusty sexuality. Yet Taurus is easily irked by the archer's ability to take love wherever he or she finds it. Fireworks erupt when happy-go-lucky Sagittarius refuses to be serious about Taurus' jealousy and possessiveness. To the typical Sagittarian a casual little romantic affair or one-night-stand has nothing at all to do with true love. Although a fiery sexual relationship helps soften their differences, this combination will not succeed unless at least one of them is willing and able to make considerable personality changes.

Taurus with Capricorn

Capricorn can be Taurus' ideal counterpart. Both of these earth signs are striving for emotional and material security. Each is serious, cautious, dependable, and willing to work for what he or she wants. Typically these natives tend to be conservative, not particularly interested in unconventional sexuality. Yet both have strong sexual needs and desires. Capricorn's passion often bubbles well beneath the surface, so it may be up to the Taurean partner to bring it out. Both desire status, money, and material possessions. Each is happiest when paired with someone ambitious and successful. If problems arise in the relationship, they are usually related to the goat's inclination to be autocratic or the bull's tendency toward stubbornness. The Venus-ruled Taurean may resent Saturn-ruled Capricorn's lack of poetry and romance. But with everything else going for them Taurus will usually overlook this minor detail.

Taurus with Aquarius

If the choice of a lover was ruled by the head instead of the heart, neither of these fixed signs would be the other's first pick because they are as different as any two people can be. The only traits they have in common are their legendary stubbornness and reluctance to change their ways. Uranus-ruled Aquarius is future-oriented and functions best on the mental plane; Venus-ruled Taurus is focused mainly on the present and the material plane. Taurus cares about physical beauty, but Aquarius is more interested in the beauty of ideas. Aquarians, with their minds tuned to universal love, are often less interested than other signs in the emotional aspects of lovemaking. Cool Aquarius may find the passionate and possessive Taurean partner too demanding. But the bull should be intrigued by the freewheeling water bearer's openness to sexual experimentation and willingness to explore new erotic techniques. Fixed Aquarius is sure to appreciate Taurus' loyalty and dependability.

Taurus with Pisces

This mix of earth and water generally results in a compatible combination. Neptune, Pisces' ruler, is the higher octave of Venus, Taurus' ruler. Both Pisces and Taurus are ultimate romantics, sharing a deep appreciation for beauty, art, and music. Although dreamy Pisces may sometimes try the earthbound bull's famous patience, these two have much to give each other. Realistic Taurus has what it takes to help the fish turn dreams into realities. Pisces' vision and imagination can aid the Taurean partner by encouraging the bull to follow a dream in order to reach a higher potential. Some problems are inevitable because Pisces has a casual attitude toward money and tends to be a careless spender. Taurus is shrewd in financial matters, so the fish's lack of thrift drives the bull up a wall. Still, as long as Pisces is warm, loving, caring, and attentive, the bull is usually willing to overlook most differences and concentrate on the positive aspects of their union.

Gemini with Gemini

Two twins equal four separate personalities, doubling the joys and challenges of the relationship. When twins get together, life can be great fun. At first each Gemini partner may think he or she has found a true soul mate. However, trust between them comes slowly, if at all, because both tend to resist confiding in anyone other than their twin selves. Eventually each partner may begin to wonder why the other talks so much and says so little. Although they may appear to the world as the ultimate fun-loving, interesting couple always ready to try anything new and different, their emotionally cool natures and tendency to overanalyze everything can open up a huge gulf between them. Ultimately a marriage between two Geminis is more likely to result in an alliance between two separate individuals than a merger of twin souls.

Gemini with Cancer

The basic temperaments of the members of these two signs are not at all alike. Gemini changes mind several times a day, Cancer changes mood just as often. Both are intuitive, albeit in different ways. The twins view the world through a mental window. Crabs see it through a cloud of emotion. Most Geminis are fun loving, flirtatious, and given to sexual experimentation. Typical crabs, though loving and passionate, tend to be sexually conservative and emotionally possessive. Still, union with a Cancer can provide footloose Gemini with a loving home and a feeling of stability. Both really love to travel, party, and socialize. Gemini can help the home-loving crab emerge from a shell. If Gemini learns how to respond to the Moon-ruled crab's sensitivity, and Cancer allows the Mercury-ruled twin some personal space, there is a good chance these two diverse personalities can forge a lasting bond.

Gemini with Leo

The fiery lion needs to be the center of attention. Airy Gemini wants to be the power behind the throne. Leo lives for compliments, praise, and recognition. Of all the signs Gemini is the most skilled at buttering up the regal lion. With Mercury-bestowed gifts of charm and glibness always at hand, Gemini knows the best ways to play on Leo's vanity. They both enjoy being caught up in a whirl of social activities. They also like money and the things that money can buy, albeit for different reasons. Lions seek wealth as a means of attaining the social status they believe to be theirs by right of birth. Twins view money as a way of gaining freedom and independence, and would much rather be respected for their mental abilities than for their material holdings. One thing Leo demands is loyalty and faithfulness. If these two are to be happy together, the Gemini partner needs to keep a lid on an openly flirtatious manner.

Gemini with Virgo

Communication or miscommunication is the key here. Gemini collects ideas and wants to know all there is to know. Virgo prefers to analyze facts and figures. Both of these Mercury-ruled signs love to talk, but neither is comfortable opening up and expressing true feelings. Either partner is capable of criticizing and harping on the other's mistakes, but Virgo tends to be the more critical of the two. Better able to dish it out then take it, virgins usually get upset when criticized by others. Twins also get upset, but prefer walking away to dealing with disapproval. Housekeeping can become a major issue between this pair. Many virgins are neatness freaks, most twins are messy (life is too interesting to spend it cleaning). Sexually they are on different wavelengths, but romantic Virgo can be swept away by fast-talking Gemini's seductive manner. Despite their differences, these two do share many interests in common. With a few sacrifices on each side the relationship can be made to work.

Gemini with Libra

Indecision reigns when these two dual signs get together. Libras can't make up their minds, Geminis are constantly changing theirs. Sometimes Libra wishes Gemini would just shut up! The scales need peace and quiet, the twins never stop analyzing and discussing. Libra is romantic and desirous of a permanent relationship, while Gemini may be something of a rolling stone yet willing to commit to the right person. Both are sociable and enjoy entertaining at home or going out on the town. Each likes to flirt. Because neither is especially jealous or possessive, flirting rarely presents a problem. Each is expert at masking the ability to get exactly what he or she wants. Sweet Libra covers steely determination with a layer of warmth and charm. Opportunistic Gemini uses wit and the gift of gab to convince others to do things the twin's way.

Gemini with Scorpio

Although there is often a strong physical attraction between the twin and the scorpion, this can be a difficult combination. Scorpio's burning intensity tends to overpower and frighten easygoing, unemotional Gemini. Scorpions have a jealous nature, twins can be fickle. If Scorpio holds the reins too tightly, Gemini will bolt. Romance, which is little more than a game to the Mercury-ruled twin, is serious business to the Pluto-ruled scorpion. Although Gemini may be both fascinated and captivated by Scorpio's smoldering sexuality, these two actually have little in common outside the bedroom. For two individuals with such basically incompatible temperaments, living together in harmony requires a tremendous effort with much give-and-take on both sides. Scorpio needs to be more flexible—and ease up considerably on the demands. Gemini must learn how to be more responsive to Scorpio's needs and desires.

Gemini with Sagittarius

Sagittarius is another of the double signs (half man, half horse), and also Gemini's zodiacal opposite. In relationships, opposite signs typically account for the best and the worst combinations. At first glance this one looks pretty good. Both fiery Sagittarius and airy Gemini are mutable signs, therefore quite adaptable. Natives of both signs are generally athletic, talkative, and intellectual. They love to travel, learn new things, meet new people. Both have a great love of personal freedom, a fairly casual attitude toward love and romance, and a tendency to shy away from permanent commitment. In spite of their mutual interests, they also have a number of disharmonious personality traits that can split them apart. Of the two, Sagittarius is the more self-righteous and temperamental. Archers can be extremely bossy, and twins hate being told what to do. For this pairing to succeed both partners must really want to be together, and they both must be willing to work at keeping the relationship fresh and interesting.

Gemini with Capricorn

This is definitely one of the more difficult combinations. Staid and stuffy Capricorn and ever-youthful Gemini haven't got very much in common. The twins are much too open-minded, unpredictable, and independent for the responsible, dependable, possessive, home-loving goat. Twins will pal around with anyone they consider interesting. Goats prefer to choose their friends from the "right" people. Gregarious Gemini loves to party and has many friends and acquaintances, though perhaps few really close relationships. Capricorn prefers to socialize with family members and a few proven friends. Goats are not romantic, but they do have strong physical desires. Capricorn finds Gemini's lack of reserve embarrassing, yet is fascinated by the twin's spirited behavior. To Capricorn, Gemini represents temptation. Deep down the goat admires the twin's freewheeling manner, and secretly wishes for the audacity to emulate it.

Gemini with Aquarius

When the Mercury-ruled twin and the Uranus-ruled water bearer meet, they may feel they have found a twin soul. This pairing often begins with a deep friendship that eventually grows into love. Even if the romantic relationship should end, Gemini and Aquarius are almost always able to salvage their friendship. Both are bright, sociable, and interesting. They enjoy the company of lively, intelligent, progressive people. Neither is particularly romantic or sentimental. They view love and sex as an extremely enjoyable part of life, but it is generally not uppermost in their minds. They take great pleasure in each other's company. A union here can be quite exciting because their sexual compatibility is virtually assured. They just need to stop talking long enough to discover that together they can be amorous, inventive, adventurous lovers.

Gemini with Pisces

Gemini and Pisces are both mutable signs and dual signs. Gemini is symbolized by the twins, Pisces by a pair of fish swimming in opposite directions. Any similarity between the two signs ends right there. Watery Pisces is the most emotional of the zodiacal signs, which puts an immediate crimp in any Gemini–Pisces union. Strong emotion is foreign to Gemini's airy nature. Natives of both signs have well deserved reputations for being evasive. Neither can stand confrontations of any kind. Both are more than willing to take liberties with the truth if it means keeping the peace. Fish are a lot tougher than they seem, not above using their vulnerability to gain sympathy from emotionally clueless Gemini. The Neptune-ruled are enigmatic and mysterious, and the Mercury-ruled just love solving mysteries. Sexually these two are matched, as Gemini quickly gets caught up in Pisces' fantasy. But when Pisces begins to get too possessive, or goes all weepy and clingy, frightened Gemini may take off in a blink.

Cancer with Cancer

Although differences may arise because crabs are sensitive, moody, and easily hurt, these two understand each other so completely that over the long haul this can be a truly happy union. It's not the most exciting pairing in the zodiac, but it can be one of the longest lasting, especially since neither partner likes letting go. Crabs tend to communicate in a roundabout way, so talking about problems can be extremely stressful. It's lucky that their ability to tune in to each other's thoughts and feelings makes it possible for them to communicate without words. This combo usually has an excellent relationship in the bedroom—and an even better one in the kitchen. Both are ambitious and shrewd with money. As long as they concentrate on building each other up, instead of tearing each other down, they can enjoy a comfortable, enduring alliance.

Cancer with Leo

This blending of fire and water presents obvious challenges, yet it can also yield rich rewards. Sun-ruled Leo likes to be the center of attention. The shyer, more retiring Moon-ruled Cancer seldom views this as a problem. The typical crab loves playing the role of power behind the throne, and is generally more than willing to stand in the lion's reflected light. Still, Cancerians need to feel that their efforts are noticed and appreciated by their partners. While most lions expect constant flattery, they are not always willing to give continual compliments in return. A sunny, self-confident Leo often serves as a stabilizer for moody, sensitive Cancer. Cancer appreciates Leo's support and encouragement, but usually resents being bossed around, told what to do. Sexually these two are almost always compatible, especially when the lion is able to demonstrate enough consideration, love, and devotion to reassure the insecure crab.

Cancer with Virgo

The relationship between this combination of earth and water often starts out as a friendship, then grows into a love match. Cancer and Virgo can develop a warm, loving, affectionate union. Their physical relationship can be extremely satisfying, in spite of the fact that the earth may not move for either of them. The crab is much more emotional than the shy, reserved virgin. Yet Virgo is an incurable romantic, and Cancer is an absolute sucker for romance. Both are practical and ambitious, and each considers home as a refuge, albeit for different reasons. Cancer usually knows just which buttons to push to motivate reticent Virgo to succeed in the world. The virgin usually knows the best way to help Cancer turn dreams into realities. The real question in this relationship is whether or not the hypercritical Virgo partner can manage to avoid hurting the feelings of the hypersensitive Cancer mate.

Cancer with Libra

On the surface it may seem that these two have similar characteristics, yet their basic temperaments are quite different. Both members of these cardinal signs are ambitious, both enjoy comfort and luxury.

Yet they are rarely able to give each other the extra push each needs in order to become really successful. Cancer is home oriented, often to the exclusion of everything else. Libra is a people person who likes going outside the home to socialize with friends and acquaintances. Libra tends to focus on humanity in general. Cancer is focused on self and family. Although Libra is the sign of partnership, it is also an air sign, more emotionally detached than the clinging crab. Major problems can arise if Cancer becomes excessively possessive. If Libra feels bored or suffocated and begins looking elsewhere, Cancer will try as hard as possible to hold on. The more Cancer tries, the harder Libra may struggle to break free.

Cancer with Scorpio

This is generally considered to be one of the best of all the possible zodiacal matches. The physical attraction between Cancer and Scorpio is usually strong and immediate. When the passionate, emotional crab and the highly sexed scorpion get together, sparks are sure to fly. Because they connect on many levels their chances of developing a lasting relationship are truly excellent. There are, though, some pitfalls along their road to happiness. Both of these water signs are imaginative, possessive, and jealous. They tend to see rivals even when none exist. The main issue here is likely to be one of trust. Above all, they should avoid the temptation to play games or to keep secrets from each other. As long as they maintain a sense of perspective, and keep the lines of communication open between them, they can expect to share a lifetime of passionate commitment.

Cancer with Sagittarius

Temperamentally the crab and the archer are about as different as two people can be. Watery Cancer wants a permanent union with a settled home life and all it entails. Fiery Sagittarius craves excitement, freedom, and adventure. Sagittarius is often referred to as the bachelor sign. This intensely independent Jupiter-ruled individual resents being tied down to anything and anyone. The crab's focus is on home and family. The archer's focus is on personal interests and career, sometimes at the expense of home and family. Given their different desires and opposite goals, Cancer and Sagittarius make an odd combination. When they find themselves attracted to each other, they really need to work extra hard to make a go of the relationship. If Sagittarius can learn to overlook the crab's possessiveness and shifting moods, and if Cancer can learn to tolerate the archer's roving eye, they can find happiness together.

Cancer with Capricorn

Cancer and Capricorn complement each other in many important ways. Both are passionate, and there is usually a strong sexual attraction between them. The crab and the goat have many of the same goals, including the need for a strong, stable home in which to raise their children. Money, status, and material success are important to this ambitious duo. They share the same respect for convention and tradition. Usually in agreement about most things, they should be in sync physically, mentally, and spiritually. The problems that arise between them are almost always emotional. Cancer is warm, caring, and demonstrative. Capricorn is a cool customer, not given to extensive shows of affection. The crab needs to understand that the goat really does care, but has a hard time dealing with emotions and feelings. Capricorn should reassure Cancer, so that the insecure crab can feel loved and protected.

Cancer with Aquarius

Cancer may feel that wants and needs must go unsatisfied because the Aquarius partner is emotionally absent. Free-spirited Aquarius, spooked by the crab's emotional neediness, may run for the nearest exit. The crab is fascinated by the past, preferring to conform to tradition. The quirky water bearer is a futurist, as unconventional as they come. The Moon-ruled crab is extremely intuitive and responsive to moods and feelings. The intellectual Uranus-ruled water bearer is mainly influenced by thoughts and ideas. However, both want to help others. Cancer likes to do it on a personal level, Aquarius favors aiding humanity as a whole. In spite of the fact that this isn't an easy match, these two should get along fine in the bedroom. With a concerted effort to understand each other's basic natures, they can overcome their differences and build a lasting union.

Cancer with Pisces

These two water signs have a natural affinity. Sexually and emotionally this can be a very good match. Both are ardent, affectionate lovers with an inclination toward romance and a desire to make the honeymoon last forever. Yet both are also extremely sensitive. When hurt, the crab has a tendency to hide in a shell. The fish breaks into tears or broods in silence. Each of them is always looking for someone to lean on. Cancer is generally the stronger of the two, and may end up assuming responsibilities for both of them. Cancer and Pisces love traveling together, sharing a fine meal and savoring an alcoholic drink or two. But they need to be vigilant, lest mutual enjoyment turn into mutual overindulgence. In the Neptune-ruled Pisces native, the Moon-ruled Cancer can find a spiritual counterpart and soul mate. Together they may reach the heights, or plumb the depths, of experience.

Leo with Leo

Many relationships between members of the same sign are quite happy and compatible. When two fiery lions get together the resulting union can be absolutely marvelous or a total disaster. For starters there is the burning question of which royal personage will rule. Sexually and romantically these two get along famously. Unless they agree to share the spotlight, their grand love affair may be short-lived. It is truly difficult for one Leo ego to make room for another, but that is exactly what each partner must do if they want the relationship to work. As a team they could rule the world, if only they can figure out how to agree instead of compete. Obviously compromise is the key to success in this relationship. But who has ever heard of a king or a queen who is willing to compromise their power?

Leo with Virgo

Leo lives for flattery. Virgo, who is naturally critical, has a tendency to puncture egos. Lions are domineering, virgins simply refuse to be dominated. Both are ambitious and both like money, but not for the same reasons. Virgo is looking for financial security. All the lion really wants is to be somebody. Leo regards both fame and fortune as the natural rewards of having made it big. The virgin is practical and careful with money and material goods. Leo tends to be extravagant and a spendthrift. Lions always look at the big picture, virgins concentrate on the details. Virgos thrive on routine, Leos crave change and excitement. It certainly doesn't sound as if this match is made in heaven. However, each one has the very qualities the other lacks. If the Sun-ruled lion and the Mercury-ruled virgin can minimize their differences by playing to each other's strengths, they will form a satisfying and lasting union.

Leo with Libra

On paper this blend of fire and air sounds like the ideal combination. There are pitfalls, though. Leo normally considers life in terms of *I* not *we*. Libra, born under the sign of partnership, has a tendency to think in twos. Like Leo, Libra thrives on flattery and compliments. Venus-ruled natives enjoy the spotlight as much as their Sun-ruled counterparts. Eventually Libra can become quite annoyed at Leo's insistence on monopolizing center stage. Leo–Libra couples make a marvelous addition to any social event. No pair is friendlier or more amusing, or has a better knowledge of how to work a room. Both love nice things, each desires wealth for the comfort and luxury wealth can bring. The big cat may be more interested in the physical side of love than airy Libra. But Leo usually knows just what to do to arouse the more languid Venusian mate. Typically Leo is the dominant partner in this union, which is generally fine with Libra whose specialty is cooperation.

Leo with Scorpio

The question here is not whether Leo and Scorpio will get along in the bedroom, it's whether or not they can stand to be together in the rest of the house. The natives of both of these fixed signs are loyal and passionate, but they can also be dictatorial and domineering. Sunny Leo is generally outgoing and open.

Pluto-ruled Scorpio is complex, secretive, and manipulative. The lion has a hard time putting up with the scorpion's jealousy and sensitivity. The scorpion may view Leo as a pretentious show-off. Although the Scorpio partner will always stick up for Leo when someone else hurts the leonine pride, if the scorpion is the one to inflict the blow, no power on earth can secure an apology. The immediate and intense sexual attraction between the lion and the scorpion gives rise to an all-or-nothing relationship that can only be made to work if both partners agree to pull in the same direction.

Leo with Sagittarius

Unless Leo insists on dominating, or Sagittarius demands total independence, this can be a wonderful blending of two fire signs. The extroverted archer's ability to make people laugh delights the fun-loving lion. Leo's sparkling personality and sunny, open manner are sure to draw a positive response from the easygoing, optimistic Sagittarian. Normally self-confident, the Sagittarius partner is not threatened by Leo's need to shine. The archer is perfectly willing to stand aside and allow the lion to strut his or her stuff. Their sexual relationship will be fiery and exciting, but the lion soon learns that the archer is less responsive emotionally than physically. The archer simply refuses to take love seriously. The Sagittarian tendency to avoid commitment definitely bothers the more settled lion. Over the short term these two will surely have a wonderful time together, but they may have to work at sustaining a lifelong union.

Leo with Capricorn

This combination involves two of the most ambitious signs in the zodiac. Both lions and goats are goal oriented, ever persevering in their efforts to gain their desires. However, the Sun-ruled Leo native cannot stand too large a dose of reality. Saturn-ruled Capricorn is all about dealing with reality. Leo loves to have a good time, but serious Capricorn generally disapproves of too much self-indulgence. Although both are highly sexed, Leo wants glamour and romance in lovemaking, but Capricorn may be too shy or uptight to supply it. Leo is warm and affectionate, Capricorn is reserved and undemonstrative. The goat usually can't give the lion the adoration that he or she expects from a loving partner. If neither one tries to dominate the other, they may find a way to forge a happy union that will last in spite of the great difference in their temperaments. Both want, and need, a secure and settled home life. Both aim to provide their children with the best possible advantages they can afford.

Leo with Aquarius

Members of these two fixed signs are extremely stubborn, but also up-front, loyal, and sincere. Between Leo and Aquarius there is no hidden agenda. What they see is what they get! Their initial attraction to each other may be nipped in the bud if Aquarius insists on analyzing and questioning all the lion's actions and decisions. Another possible sticking point is

Leo's need to dominate. No one tells the fiercely independent Aquarian what to do. The lion may resent the water bearer's airy emotional aloofness. Although intrigued by the water bearer's unconventional approach to lovemaking, the more conventional lion may become upset or turned off by too much sexual experimentation. Still, the lion and the water bearer actually have a lot more in common than most opposite signs. They generally get along quite well together despite the fact that Aquarius is much too proud to become Leo's devoted subject.

Leo with Pisces

Mysterious, mystical Neptune-ruled Pisces fascinates and intrigues the worldly Sun-ruled lion. Precisely because they are so different, Leo and Pisces find themselves attracted to each other. Yet the lion and the fish operate on totally different wavelengths. Their differences don't mesh. It probably won't take long for the actions of the flamboyant lion to grate on the nerves of the shy, introverted fish. And Pisces' moodiness and sensitivity will give the lion cause to bolt for the exit. Leo expects a lot of attention. Pisces has no problem flattering and fussing over the lion. But the insecure fish needs attention, too, and can be terribly hurt if it is not forthcoming. Leo thrives on public acclaim and the approval of an audience. Stay-at-home Pisces prefers a more sheltered life. Leo is a natural boss. Pisces has a tendency to lean on others. Any relationship between them usually works best when the fish allows the lion to assume the role of protector and adviser.

Virgo with Virgo

One possible problem when these two get together is that most members of this sign are somewhat shy about love and sex. Virgos possess an earthy sensuality, but are often inhibited or repressed sexually. However, the Virgo–Virgo combo may not consider sexual reserve a problem because they tend to view romantic alliances as something more than mere sexual encounters. The first question that usually arises between them concerns the dominant role in the relationship. Each is pretty much convinced that he or she knows what is best for both. Perfectionism times two can be difficult to live with. Two people with a tendency to criticize and complain may nitpick each other to distraction. Still, both are caring, responsible, and conscientious—and are quite capable of dedicating their lives to each other. For a long-term union this pairing can be a bit tense, yet ultimately fulfilling and enduring.

Virgo with Libra

Virgo is attracted to Libra's charm and intelligence. Airy Libra relates to the Mercury-ruled virgin's sharp, quick mind. But it's not easy for this pair to stay together for the long haul. Libra is the sign that represents love and partnership. Virgos are loners at heart. True, there are lots of closet romantics born under Virgo. But all that Libra love and affection out in the open is often more than the reserved virgin can handle. The main problem between them generally comes from Libra's love of fun and relaxation, which drives the ultraresponsible Virgo partner straight up a wall. Virgo regards Libra as indecisive and excessively easygoing. Libra can view Virgo as something of a stick-in-the-mud. This partnership works best if Libra can get Virgo to relax and indulge in an occasional luxury. Virgo can teach Libra the value of good health and the joy to be found in some of life's simpler pleasures.

Virgo with Scorpio

Earth and water get along well in most things. In the sexual sphere Virgo can be somewhat overwhelmed by Scorpio's lusty sensuality. With this combination, a lot depends on the Scorpio partner's approach to lovemaking. The virgin may be secretly thrilled by the scorpion's attempts to entice him or her into bolder sexual adventures. After awhile, Virgo may find Scorpio's passionate intensity more of a turnoff than a turn-on. Scorpio's possessiveness and fierce loyalty scare Virgo, while at the same time giving the virgin a strong sense of being loved and protected. Virgo's propensity for handing out unsolicited advice does not sit well with Scorpio. If these two are to get along, the virgin needs to realize that the scorpion won't put up with nagging, scolding, or criticizing. Both are practical and conscientious, and in everyday living they make a great team. A long-term relationship is possible if both partners are willing to compromise and work together to build a secure future.

Virgo with Sagittarius

In spite of some common interests, the energies of these two signs don't always mesh. Natives of both signs love animals and like to be close to nature. While the virgin enjoys bird watching, the archer prefers hunting and fishing. Both are mental types. Mercury, ruler of Virgo, represents the reasoning mind. Jupiter, ruler of Sagittarius, represents the abstract mind. Sagittarius looks for reasons and motives, Virgo appraises and analyzes. They make a great working team with Virgo's eye for small detail and Sagittarius' vision of the larger picture. Although the archer is a bit too chaotic and easygoing for the virgin's taste, Sagittarius just laughs off superorganized Virgo's nit-picking preciseness. Both are romantic, albeit in different ways. Their physical compatibility may depend upon the uninhibited Jupiter-ruled partner's ability to coax the shyer virgin out of propriety.

Virgo with Capricorn

Two earth signs are generally harmonious. There is often a strong attraction between Virgo and Capricorn right from the beginning. Although neither of these two practical, down-to-earth individuals will admit to frivolous thoughts or romantic ideals, both are probably a lot more interested in the physical and emotional side of life than they let on. The natives of both signs tend to be reserved, reluctant to express their deepest feelings. Both long for love and approval. If they can only learn to trust each other, they may forge a lifelong bond of intimacy. The virgin and the goat admire each other's practical, down-to-earth approach to life, and they are usually in sync regarding financial matters. Virgo is the sign of service to others, Capricorn the sign of duty and responsibility. These two absolutely thrive on the opportunity to aid family members in need, to perform community service, or to assist in philanthropic projects.

Virgo with Aquarius

According to *Linda Goodman's Love Signs*, this combination represents the ultimate challenge because "Virgo delights in bringing order out of chaos, and Aquarius delights in bringing chaos out of order." However, a match between this unusual duo can result in a happy union. In spite of obvious differences in temperament, both are rational and cerebral, and each loves to learn and teach new things. These two are often great friends, and under the right circumstances can be something more. Woefully absentminded Aquarius appreciates Virgo's elephantlike memory. Philanthropic Virgo validates Aquarius' altruistic instincts. Both signs have a somewhat distant quality. Pragmatic Virgo's apparent detachment stems from a reluctance to get too emotionally involved with anyone. Visionary Aquarius has many of the same reservations, but the water bearer's far-away look usually indicates that his or her thoughts are centered in the far-off clouds—or even on some distant galaxy.

Virgo with Pisces

There is often a strong attraction between these opposite signs. Each admires certain qualities in the other, and their differences tend to balance each other out quite nicely. Virgo grounds the dreamy fish, Pisces inspires the practical virgin. Virgos want to help everyone in their circle of acquaintances. Pisces natives also want to serve, but they yearn to help every individual in the universe. The Neptune-ruled Pisces is a warm and generous lover who is able to sense Virgo's moods and desires. The naturally reserved virgin is generally intrigued by Pisces' unrestrained sensuality. The major point of difference between them is that while Pisces is moody, insecure, and extremely emotional, Virgo, who can also be moody and insecure, keeps emotions under strict control. The fish's emotional nature is often difficult for Virgo to understand. In some cases Pisces' neediness will send the uptight virgin hastening to the nearest exit.

Libra with Libra

The initial attraction between these two can be unusually strong, with lots of laughter, fun, and socializing. At first they may seem perfectly compatible.

They have so much in common they often feel like soul mates. However, Libra–Libra combinations don't have very much staying power and often run into difficulty over the long haul. When the first blush of love is gone, harsh reality intrudes. The Venus-ruled are true romantics who hate to have to come down from the clouds long enough to deal with the practical details of everyday life. For two individuals who cannot reach any conclusion without extensive deliberation, decision making presents a serious problem. Although this relationship can work, it requires a strong dose of wisdom, pragmatism, and maturity to keep it going.

Libra with Scorpio

The question between them will surely be, "Who's the boss?" Scorpio appears to dominate, while Libra seems to cooperate. But when it comes to getting their own way, members of both signs are masters of manipulation. Call it clever or call it sneaky, remember that enticing Libra is an expert at using charm to persuade others to do his or her bidding. Scorpions are more secretive yet equally resourceful. Moreover, they know how to work behind the scenes in order to get people to go along with their plans and ideas. There is a lot of physical magnetism between these two, but their relationship can run into major difficulties. Scorpio is ardent and down to earth, but also extremely jealous. Libra tends to be easygoing, otherworldly, romantic, and flirtatious. A short passionate affair is probably a better bet than a long-term union. Still, the alliance can be successful if each partner is willing to make the effort to understand the other.

Libra with Sagittarius

This combination of fire and air shares a wonderful chemistry. Libra and Sagittarius are supposed to get along very well together. Problems quickly arise, though, because Libra is partnership minded and looking for a committed relationship with a fixed home base. The fiercely independent Sagittarian is in no hurry to settle down. The spontaneous Sagittarius partner is ready to jump into a new adventure at a moment's notice. The scales' indecisiveness and vacillation can drive the archer crazy. Sexually they are well matched, in spite of the fact that the Venus-ruled partner prefers a more romantic approach than the enthusiastic, frank, broad-minded Jupiter-ruled lover is capable of providing. Both are flirtatious. Neither is especially jealous unless one of them actually professes interest in someone else—then sparks fly. They are good friends as well as lovers. If they are willing to work out their differences, the scales and the archer may enjoy a long and happy union together.

Libra with Capricorn

Members of these two cardinal signs are more likely to be drawn together as business partners than as marriage partners. However, there is often a strong physical attraction between them, so the possibility of a more intimate relationship cannot be discounted. Despite their personality conflicts they have some complementary traits. Both consider money extremely useful, although not for the same reasons. Libra regards a healthy bank account as assurance of a comfortable life. Capricorn views money as a means to security and power. The hardworking Saturn-ruled goat may be offended by the Venus-ruled native's inclination toward self-indulgence. Libra can be put off by Capricorn's frugal practicality. The goat is almost sure to dislike Libra's constant socializing. Libra may resent Capricorn's solitary ways. Although not a match made in heaven, it is one that can succeed if worked at by both partners.

Libra with Aquarius

Relationship-minded Libra may view quirky Aquarius as a bit too independent. The fixed water bearer can find the scales' hesitancy and indecision rather annoying. Yet these two air signs have a natural affinity. If nothing else, they will surely hit it off as friends. Libra and Aquarius have many things in common including a strong artistic sense and an ingrained love of literature and learning that requires constant intellectual stimulation. Both are extremely friendly and sociable, yet tend to remain somewhat detached emotionally. At times freedom-loving Aquarius can resent Libra's need for togetherness. The romantic Libran may be turned off by Aquarius' matter-of-fact approach to love and sex. Although

Libra may be more money-conscious and interested in luxury than Aquarius, they both enjoy many of the things that money can buy, especially with regard to study, travel, books, and art objects.

Libra with Pisces

In Pisces, Libra finds a partner who truly understands the scales' need for love and romance. Although air and water don't mix well, this combination sometimes works out beautifully. Both are basically kind, considerate, and sympathetic, although Pisces is generally more sympathetic than Libra. The devoted fish fulfills Libra's need to be adored and admired. Sexually they are compatible, emotionally they are on different wavelengths. The main sticking point here is Libra's emotional aloofness. Pisces feels things very deeply, is emotionally needy, easily hurt, and inclined to cling and cry. Libra's attempts at consolation may appear insincere or patronizing to the overly sensitive fish. Eventually Libra starts to resent Pisces' dependency. And the fish begins to think of the scales as cold and inconsiderate. This combination works best if Libra is willing to give Pisces the reassurance necessary to feel loved and secure and if Pisces allows airy Libra some breathing space.

Scorpio with Scorpio

Scorpions generally get along famously with other members of their own sign. Two Scorpios will understand each other about as well as any two people can. Because of their ability to read each other's minds, they easily become each other's best friend. By and large they have the same interests and the same likes and dislikes. The friendship between them may last a lifetime, even if the love affair should burn itself out. The powerful combination of Scorpio–Scorpio generally works extremely well in the bedroom because both partners are likely to be strongly sexed: The Pluto-ruled are intensely passionate, also jealous and possessive. Problems will arise if either of them decides to try and run the show. If one offends or hurts the other, the resulting battle will not be very pretty. However, if they work at learning to share power and responsibility, this loyal and devoted pair may spend many wonderful years together.

Scorpio with Sagittarius

It's sexual attraction at first sight when the archer meets and flirts with the scorpion. However, Scorpio can cool down pretty quickly if he or she realizes that the lighthearted Sagittarian is just out for some fun and games. Scorpio's intense sensuality immediately attracts Sagittarius. But when the jovial, open archer tries to get close to the secretive, brooding scorpion, the archer may quickly become disenchanted and skip gaily off to the next party. By and large the only attraction between these two is sexual—even that may not last more than a few nights. Although no combination is impossible, this one often fizzles before it can get off the ground. Two things that Sagittarius cannot stand are jealousy and possessiveness, and Scorpio has oodles of both. For this pairing to work the archer would have to be willing to accept Scorpio without changes, and the scorpion would have to try to lighten up—a tall order on both counts.

Scorpio with Capricorn

These two have a great deal in common and understand each other better than most. Both the scorpion and the goat are serious and responsible. Neither one is inclined to skip out when the going gets rough. Each is materialistic, ambitious, hard-working, and desperately searching for security and acceptance. Sexually they are well matched as far as physical passion is concerned. While Scorpio feels things deeply, Capricorn is typically cool and unemotional. Saturn-ruled Capricorn likes to be in charge and will attempt to take control in most situations. Not unlike Scorpio, Capricorn tends to play the cards close to the chest. Compared to Scorpio, though, the goat is more up-front about the desire for power. The Pluto-ruled Scorpio native is a control freak who secretly attempts to pull the strings from behind the scenes. While this combination may not work on a superficial level, if they can get past the inevitable power struggle, the scorpion and the goat can forge a bond that will endure for a lifetime.

Scorpio with Aquarius

Absentminded, freedom-loving Aquarius and possessive Scorpio (who never forgets anything) make an odd couple. Both are determined, to the point of obstinacy, in their opinions and beliefs. The scorpion generally finds it impossible to control or dominate the water bearer. Aquarius is more or less oblivious to Scorpio's power games, schemes, and manipulations. In order to gain the literal-minded water bearer's attention, Scorpio needs to be forthright about feelings, desires, needs, and intentions—something the scorpion finds extremely difficult to do. In spite of all their differences, or perhaps because of them, Scorpio and Aquarius often find each other fascinating. A love affair between them can be very exciting. A lasting relationship can't be ruled out either. If these two fixed sign natives decide they want each other, nothing will deter them from their chosen course.

Scorpio with Pisces

These two share the kind of deep psychic link that typifies true soul mates. Because they are so extraordinarily in tune with each other, it is easy to overlook the fact that both the scorpion and the fish are extremely sensitive and capable of some pretty wild mood swings. Members of these two water signs often experience black periods. If both partners should become depressed at the same time, there would be no one to help bring them back from the brink. The other negative in their relationship is the possibility that a gentle fish may feel somewhat overwhelmed by the scorpion's strength and power. Because Pisces typically looks for someone to lean on, he or she may not regard this as a bad thing. Sexually they are a good match. Pisces is sensual and imaginative, Scorpio passionate and persevering. Although this pair may go through many emotional ups and downs, their intimate moments together will be filled with so much ecstasy that the angry spats and pouting silences may be soon forgotten.

Sagittarius with Sagittarius

Initially these two freedom-loving, independent souls seem perfectly suited to each other. Over the long-term they could find that they actually have too much in common for a successful union. While this combination generally makes for a superexciting, exhilarating roller-coaster ride, once the fun stops they often drift apart. Although they were probably attracted to each other through their similar tastes and mutual interests, their easy camaraderie can turn sour if one or both of them thinks personal freedom is being threatened. Ideally the archer will find a mate who willingly takes care of all the petty details of domestic life. In other words, Sagittarius plus Sagittarius can equal chaos—unless at least one of them is equipped to keep the home fires burning and the family together while the other goes out to play.

Sagittarius with Capricorn

The big question here is whether or not the Capricorn partner can deal with Sagittarius' lighthearted approach to life, and whether or not the archer can put up with the goat's dour outlook and controlling ways. The archer's frankness is sure to rile the sensitive goat. Capricorn's cautious approach to finances certainly won't sit well with the free-spending archer. Still, this union can work over the long term. Capricorn grounds the somewhat flighty Sagittarius native, the archer injects excitement and adventure into the goat's otherwise humdrum existence. Sagittarius and Capricorn can have a satisfactory, if not totally blissful, physical relationship. Sexually the archer is warm-blooded and desirous. The goat, while not overly demonstrative, can be passionate and responsive. Everything considered, this is a difficult but not totally impossible combination that usually works best when each partner is willing to accept the other without trying to change him or her.

Sagittarius with Aquarius

Aquarius is the least possessive of the zodiacal types. The water bearer's willingness to live and let live is guaranteed to please the freedom-loving archer. These two usually fall in "like" at first sight, and can be great buddies as well as lovers. Their shared curiosity and adventurous spirits extend to the bedroom where the lovemaking is sure to be imaginative, uninhibited, and full of fun. The warm archer may be a bit put off by Aquarius' remoteness, but will eventually find that the intense mental connection between them more than makes up for any lack of emotional intimacy. Problems may arise when this duo realizes that the Jupiter-ruled archer is basically more traditional than the modern, unconventional, and somewhat eccentric Uranus-ruled water bearer. Both have oodles of friends. Yet Sagittarius finds it difficult to accept the idea that Aquarius will pal around with anyone and everyone, and has no interest whatsoever in meeting the "right people" or going to the "best places."

Sagittarius with Pisces

Sagittarius is easily captivated by ethereal Pisces' well-known aura of mystery. Archers love to get to the bottom of things. They tend to regard the dreamy fish as a puzzle that needs solving. However, these Neptune-ruled natives often prove to be quite inscrutable. Although Pisces is attracted to Sagittarius' vitality, the archer's buoyant spirit can be dampened by the fish's tendency toward dependency and timidity. Sagittarius has a magnetic personality and is self-assured, outgoing, charming. Archers love meeting people and generally enjoy an active social life. Pisces is pleasant, but apt to be moody and likely to want to stay at home an evening or two. Archers are usually big sports fans; fish generally prefer art and music. Any long-term relationship between them could present problems because Pisces is needy and inclined to be overly possessive while Sagittarius typically resents restrictions.

Capricorn with Capricorn

Although there is a natural rapport between these two, this same sign match may turn out to be too much of a good thing. If both are responsible workaholics, when will they find time to be together? More to the point, when will they have any fun? Sexually they should be a good match because goats have well-developed sexual appetites. Even though Capricorn is passionate, he or she can be rather reserved in the bedroom. Without a more carefree partner who is willing to experiment and try new moves, the Capricorn–Capricorn combo's sex life may eventually end up somewhere between dull and nonexistent. Still, no one will ever understand Capricorn as well as another Capricorn. If each one can just curb the impulse to boss the other, these two may spend many happy years together planning and building a marriage, a home, a family, a fortune—even a dynasty.

Capricorn with Aquarius

The goat is conventional. Aquarius was born to rebel. The water bearer requires freedom to come and go without questions or restrictions. This trait doesn't sit well with the possessive goat. Status-conscious Capricorn's inability to understand why Aquarius insists on hanging around with an assorted group of oddballs drives the bohemian water bearer absolutely crazy. Still, there is a curious fascination that can arise between these two. Although the fixed Aquarian probably doesn't even realize it, he or she likes Capricorn's constancy and stability. Both tend to be physically responsive, yet each is somewhat cooler emotionally. Aquarians cherish their independence and often prefer friendship to marriage. But Capricorns can be very persuasive. If they do enter into a long-term union, the goat and the water bearer can be faithful companions who ultimately discover they complement each other very well.

Capricorn with Pisces

In astrological tradition the best chance for a lasting marriage is thought to occur between individuals whose natal suns are sextile to each other (two signs apart). Although at first glance it may seem as if the goat and the fish don't have very much in common, they actually have a great deal to offer each other. A loving, kind, caring Pisces will look up to Capricorn in a way that makes the goat feel secure and appreciated. Pisces is drawn to Capricorn's determination, strength, and efficiency. The fish is usually more than happy to have someone else take charge, get things organized, and keep them running smoothly. Sexually their relationship should be close and satisfying, even if the Pisces partner may sometimes wish the goat were more romantic and emotionally accessible. Both of these signs are prone to depression. Their black moods can put an enormous strain on the relationship, especially if the two of them are feeling blue at the same time.

Aquarius with Aquarius

The initial attraction between two Aquarians is often purely mental. They may be great friends before they ever become lovers. Although these two quirky individualists each have their own interests, they'll soon discover they also have many interests in common. Both tend to be stubborn and somewhat bossy. But they respect each other's individuality so much that neither one will try to tell the other what to do. Sexually they are very well matched. Although not as passionate as some signs, these two make inventive lovers who are open-minded and generally willing to try anything, at least once. They know how to stimulate each other mentally and physically. While their combined emotional temperature may be a few degrees cooler than that of other couples, the bond of loyalty between them is sure to be a lot stronger than most.

Aquarius with Pisces

At first glance these two appear to have common interests. After all, Aquarius is a humanitarian who wants to help people, and so is Pisces. However, Aquarius is basically logical, rational, and unemotional, while Pisces is intuitive, emotional, and often irrational. The water bearer prefers to remain aloof from those who are helped, but the fish jumps right in and gives comfort along with aid. Ultimately Aquarius may be turned off by the fish's sensitive nature, and Pisces can come to resent the water bearer's cool, detached manner. It can be difficult for this pair to ever satisfy each other's needs, especially if Pisces demands constant attention and proof of love when all Aquarius wants is to be left alone. Sexually the sensuous fish projects an air of mystery that fascinates the water bearer. But the spell is broken if their intimate moments turn into an emotional tug-of-war. For this combination to work, each partner must be willing to compromise and able to set aside some expectations.

Pisces with Pisces

When two Pisces natives come together, their deep emotional ties provide them with an almost spiritual understanding of each other. Both are likely to be sensitive and caring—they share a love of peace and beauty unparalleled in the zodiac. Sexually they are well matched, their lovemaking blissfully romantic and physically satisfying. The passivity of their basic natures makes this an easy coupling, so they can live and work together without much conflict. The drawback to this union is that neither one is likely to care very much about the practical realities of day-to-day living. Too much alike to avoid chaos and confusion, these two may need to hire a housekeeper and a financial manager to help keep their lives in order. Moodiness and a tendency to overreact emotionally can also put a damper on their relationship. They must be careful not to feed each other's negativity, or to bring each other down.